SCHOOL-LINKED SERVICES

School-Linked Services

PROMOTING EQUITY FOR CHILDREN, FAMILIES, AND COMMUNITIES

Laura R. Bronstein
and Susan E. Mason

COLUMBIA UNIVERSITY PRESS NEW YORK

COLUMBIA UNIVERSITY PRESS
Publishers Since 1893
New York, Chichester, West Sussex

cup.columbia.edu

Library of Congress Cataloging-in-Publication Data

Names: Bronstein, Laura R., author. | Mason, Susan Elizabeth, author.
Title: School-linked services : promoting equity for children, families, and communities / Laura R. Bronstein and Susan E. Mason.
Description: New York : Columbia University Press, [2016] | Includes bibliographical references and index.
Identifiers: LCCN 2015041676| ISBN 9780231160940 (cloth) | ISBN 9780231160957 (pbk.)
Subjects: LCSH: Community and school. | Children with social disabilities—Services for.
Classification: LCC LC215 .B7 2016 | DDC 372.42/5—dc23
LC record available at http://lccn.loc.gov/2015041676

Columbia University Press books are printed on permanent and durable acid-free paper.
This book is printed on paper with recycled content.
Printed in the United States of America

c 10 9 8 7 6 5 4 3 2 1
p 10 9 8 7 6 5 4 3 2 1

Cover design: Rebecca Lown

References to websites (URLs) were accurate at the time of writing.
Neither the author nor Columbia University Press is responsible for URLs that may have expired or changed since the manuscript was prepared.

FROM LAURA: FOR ARIA, ALEXANDER, AND EVAN, LIGHTS OF MY LIFE; AND FOR CHUCK, FOR YOUR LOVE AND SUPPORT.

FROM SUSAN: TO MY PARENTS WHO WOULD HAVE UNDERSTOOD MY REASON FOR WRITING THIS BOOK; AND TO VICTOR, FOR UNDERSTANDING ME, AND FOR YOUR LOVE.

AND FROM US BOTH: FOR THOSE EVERYWHERE WORKING TO BREAK THE CYCLE OF POVERTY AND PROMOTE EQUITY: OUR STUDENTS, COLLEAGUES, AND COMMUNITY MEMBERS IN ALL CORNERS OF THE GLOBE

CONTENTS

FOREWORD

▸ JANE QUINN

Vice President for Community Schools, and Director, National Center for Community Schools, The Children's Aid Society, New York City

SCHOOL-LINKED SERVICES: *Promoting Equity for Children, Families, and Communities* is the right book at the right time. It is the right book because it does such a masterful job of marrying theory with practice. As seasoned university professors, the co-authors are well versed in both historical and current research, which they use to undergird their many cogent arguments about the why and how of schools' partnerships with families and communities. On the practice side, Bronstein and Mason highlight a wide array of partnership exemplars, and allow the voices of their initiative leaders to take center stage—providing authenticity and passion for the work.

Now, on to why it is the right time for this book. For many decades, the idea of school, family, and community partnerships fell into the "nice but not necessary" category of education reform strategies. Researchers rarely deemed the topic worthy of serious study, and philanthropists virtually ignored its potential. Likewise, schools of education hardly mentioned the subject, and working educators mistakenly thought family and community partnerships would distract them from the "laser-like focus on instruction" they were encouraged to pursue.

But recent research has converged with contemporary practitioner experience to create a new understanding. Perhaps by sheer coincidence, 2010 was a landmark year during which two critical studies hit the educational radar and substantially bolstered the case for intentional, well-designed partnerships between schools and their families and communities. The first study, conducted by the Consortium for Chicago School Research, analyzed seven years of data collected by two hundred Chicago public schools and proved definitively that schools' partnerships with families and community were an essential ingredient of school improvement (Bryk et al. 2010). In the second important study published in 2010, Teachers College professor Charles Basch documented the causal links between seven common health issues and student success, arguing not only that "healthier students are better learners" but also that schools ignore this issue at their peril and that they need to partner regularly with health providers who can remove barriers to student achievement (Basch 2010).

Increasingly we find this and other research converging with the experience of classroom teachers and their school leaders. "School cannot do it alone" has become a frequent cry for help in this new educational landscape punctuated by higher education standards and needier students.

School-Linked Services recognizes and complements this landscape by providing a new paradigm in which professionals from multiple disciplines come together in a collaborative setting and combine their knowledge and skills on behalf of America's children. This book can be a powerful resource for pre-service programs in education, social work, nursing, and public policy as well as a guide for working professionals—practitioners, policy-setters, and grant-makers. By weaving rigor with compassion, Bronstein and Mason have made a significant contribution to our nation's schools and, ultimately, to our nation's children.

INTRODUCTION

SCHOOL-LINKED SERVICES: *Promoting Equity for Children, Families, and Communities* consolidates a wide array of literature and presents conversations with a diverse range of key informants to illustrate that partnerships between schools and communities are as important to educational success as classroom practices. We proceed with the premise that integrating services and expanding family and community partnerships with schools are ways to enhance both academic achievement and social and physical well-being for children and their families. We use the overarching term *school-linked services* to discuss these partnerships that are based both at schools and in the community. We address a range of types of school-linked services and the myriad ways they can contribute to breaking the cycle of poverty, with a focus on full-service community schools as the "gold standard" of integrated strategies in family-school-community partnerships. The book's focus is on children from low-income families and their schools since, for the most part, middle-class families are able to send their children to school "ready to learn" and to provide enrichment activities and services that support and maximize learning; children from low-income families often do not have this benefit. Therefore, in the interest of addressing the cycle of poverty, our emphasis (and those of the providers of school-linked services) is largely on partnerships located in economically impoverished communities throughout the United States.

Throughout this book, we draw from literature and profiles with leaders of exemplary initiatives to illustrate methods used to close the achievement gap among students from different socioeconomic backgrounds by implementing strategies and providing services, programs, and relationships critical for children's success in school and in life. Driven and individualized according to local needs assessments, these strategies include afterschool and summer programs, early childhood education, health and mental health services based at and/or linked with schools, family engagement, youth leadership, etc. In addition to showcasing successful strategies, we also address the policy and funding context within which these partnerships function, including those that enable them to be put in practice and to thrive. Using voices of leaders in the nation—both through an extensive review of literature and through our conversations with them, this book illustrates the variety of ways these partnerships can be actualized to promote equity and help individuals, families, and communities to partner and to advance. Also included in this book are arguments from some who challenge the view that school-linked services are critical to educational success. By including these challenges, we offer the reader an understanding of some of the obstacles faced by proponents of school-linked services, who see them as a means to educational success.

While many excellent books highlight particular programs and strategies, along with the funding mechanisms and policies that impact them, this book is distinctive in that it consolidates and presents an array of practice and programmatic strategies used across the United States, in rural and urban areas alike, and throughout grade levels, as well as including a chapter on what school-community partnerships look like around the world. The book aims to be useful to students and professionals from a wide range of disciplinary and professional backgrounds and to those engaged in a variety of studies such as social work, education, psychology, public health, counseling, nursing, public policy, etc., because the book's premise is based on collaboration across professions and organizations.

The following outlines the main emphases of the chapters in the book, while the chapters themselves are enriched by information drawn largely from literature and conversations with key leaders in the field presented in their own words and are supplemented by the authors' years of experience and own research.

Chapter 1: "Making the Case for School-Linked Services": This chapter introduces the key points that frame the book: the links among health, education, and income; the need for complementary external and internal school reform strategies; progressive universalism—doing for everyone with a focus on those most in need; and the range of school-linked services and strategies for implementation of them. This chapter also describes services for children and families over time, addressing the history of service provision in homes, in communities, and in schools.

Chapter 2: "The School": This chapter considers the array of professionals who work in and with schools and their current and potential roles in school-linked services, including the importance of constituent voices of students and families in educational success.

Chapter 3: "School-Linked Services Today": This chapter focuses on current school-linked services (predominantly in the United States) and features partnerships with businesses, expanded school mental health services, school-based health centers, family resource centers, and full-service community schools. Drawn from profiles from leaders in the field, exemplary strategies are outlined so that readers have an opportunity to understand their similarities and differences and make their own assessments of the strengths and challenges of each model. Since full-service community schools are the "gold standard" integrated model of school-linked services, exemplary community schools are represented through the voices of those who develop, implement, and evaluate them around the nation. The following critical foci of school-linked services are addressed: extended hours, family engagement, attendance, dropout prevention and intervention, and nutrition.

Chapter 4: "Working Effectively Across Systems": This chapter addresses the ways that service integration, collaboration, and collective impact across systems enable school-linked services to function well. Exemplars of specific partnerships are outlined, as well as challenges faced in the areas of confidentiality and information sharing.

Chapter 5: "Settings": This chapter addresses the various settings where school-linked services are implemented, such as disenfranchised communities and urban and rural settings, considers their roles in these settings, and looks at the range of age and grade-level considerations in their success.

Chapter 6: "International Initiatives": This chapter outlines international school-community partnership initiatives in Europe, Africa, Canada, Asia, New Zealand, and Latin America.

Chapter 7: "Public Education, School-Linked Services, and Relevant Policies": This chapter outlines policies guiding the work of schools with an emphasis on their implications for school-linked services. Highlighted are compensatory programs, outcome-based policies, policies at the federal, state, and local levels, and organizations' policies that support school-linked services.

Chapter 8: "Funding": This chapter addresses funding to support students' educational success, including public funding at the federal, state, and local level. It also focuses on the 2013 U.S. Commission on Equity and Excellence, business, foundation, and university support, the politics of funding, and the role of the courts in funding formulas and decisions.

Chapter 9: "Assessing Outcomes": This chapter provides an overview of evaluation methods and outcomes for education, including the role of standardized testing and alternative assessment tools useful in assessing the benefits of school-linked services.

Epilogue: This section provides a practical starting point for developing school-linked services in the readers' own communities.

SCHOOL-LINKED SERVICES

1

Making the Case for School-Linked Services

EDUCATORS INCREASINGLY LAMENT THAT THEIR ABILITY to do their job of teaching students is hampered by issues outside of their professional purview. One principal from England states, "I was finding, because of the nature of the community, when I looked at my role as a head teacher which is about leading the learning and the teaching, so much of my time was being taken up dealing with the social work issues. . . . I did a review over a four week period of my time and 60 percent of that time was social work related and that's not where my strengths are. My strengths are in teaching and learning" (Cummings, Dyson, & Todd 2011:57). In response to this need, educational reform efforts, both in the United States and other parts of the world, examine ways to support teachers through community partnerships so that teachers are able to focus on what they do best—teach—while other professionals focus on supporting students overcome barriers to their ability to learn.

These partnering approaches have a number of names, including *school-linked services*, *school-based services*, *full-service community schools*, *school-community partnerships*, and *extended schools*, among others. They have been around for over a hundred years and are increasingly needed as social problems become more prevalent and complex. In 1998, McKenzie and Richmond argued that when schools don't address children's health by design, they are forced to do so by default. In 1945, Carr referred to the need to "throw bridges across the deep moat which typically separates the school from its community. Each bridge will be a two-lane highway so that the community can utilize the resources of the school and the school can use the community" (vii). Even further back, in 1910, Richman noted that "the school is the legitimate social centre of a community, and that from the school or through the school there should radiate all those influences that make at least for child betterment, if not for complete social betterment" (161). Today, in the United States, we continue to try to build these bridges for child and social betterment, and unfortunately, in most cases the structuring is the result not of systemic priorities but of individual school-by-school efforts.

This book aims to address the gross inequalities that characterize the educational system in the United States and make learning too often a function of socioeconomic status as opposed to one of effort and skill. In large part the country's public schools are dependent upon the income level of their community. A solution to this inequity is needed so that all children have resources needed to succeed. That solution is to attend not just to what happens inside the classroom, but also to the critical environmental variables that impact students' abilities to take advantage of their classroom experiences, especially those that disproportionately impact children living in poverty. Because schools focus primarily on the academic needs of children, in order to level the playing field for children of all economic backgrounds, partnerships between schools and communities are critical, and have been shown to be the most likely solution to building equal opportunities for all.

Hare defines school-linked services as an "innovative system of delivering services in which community agencies and schools collaborate to provide a variety of health and social services to children and their families at or near school sites" (1995:r34520). Alongside those advocating educational reform, many health and social service professionals see these approaches as a logical and effective means of delivering health and social services for all children and families (Dryfoos 1994). Since most children are at school most days, accessing supports outside the structure of the school requires greater means and time than accessing services connected with and at school.

In this book we advocate the idea that the *school-linked services paradigm* (an overarching term we use to describe all methods of student support that link and/or integrate community services and organizations with schools) should be embraced and developed by an array of professionals whose roles are to deliver services to children, families, and communities.

This includes educators, social workers, nurses, public health workers, physicians, counselors, psychologists, etc. Linking services with schools has been shown to improve academic outcomes as well as access to services to which children and families are entitled. These linkages support early detection for physical and mental health issues, treatment, and often prevention, and therefore in addition to being effective at promoting quality of life, they are also cost-saving in that they keep problems from exacerbating. As Steen and Noguera state, "Viewing students' academic struggles in isolation from external factors (e.g., issues occurring outside of school) has proven to be short-sighted and often unsuccessful" (2010:44). An integrated, holistic approach that adds health and social services to public schooling's role makes sense for children in *all* settings: home, school, and community.

While many in both the education and the health and social service realms regard the need for school-community partnerships as vital, there is currently no federal initiative in the United States "to reduce educationally relevant health disparities as part of a national strategy to close the achievement gap" (Basch 2010:5). There are however, individuals and organizations that argue for linkage on the national level. In 1994, the U.S. Department of Education (DOE) and Department of Health and Human Services (HHS) joined together to declare the need for partnership and integration across the health and education sectors (Ferro 1998). One of the eight DOE goals for 2000 included the proposition that "every school will promote partnerships that will increase parental involvement and participation in promoting the social, emotional, and academic growth of children" (McKenzie & Richmond 1998:7). In 2013, the Equity and Excellence Commission chartered by Congress to advise the secretary of the DOE stated, "Communities, tribes, states and the federal government working together must create a policy infrastructure for providing services to underserved children by crafting standards to support at-risk children, encourage family engagement, and provide health care and health education and expanded learning time" (U.S. Department of Education 2013:30). While government rhetoric and recommendations have supported a partnership approach to education, and while there are several exemplary programs, there still exists no systematic way to ensure that school-community partnerships benefit all children regardless of the socioeconomic characteristics of their neighborhoods.

So it seems that despite the fact that partnerships are espoused, and despite the availability of a number of model school-linked service and community school exemplars in the United States and abroad, the school-community partnership movement needs a great deal more advocates, including both researchers to increase, shore up, and consolidate evidence and policymakers to provide funding. The advocacy, research, policies, and funding need to come from all sectors: those currently associated with schools, those that provide community services, local businesses that employ community residents, and area colleges and universities. In other words, what is needed are integrated community initiatives with support at the national and state level, and, because of the varying needs of different communities, design input at the local level.

While these partnerships have the potential to support *all* students, the greatest need is in communities with the most vulnerable children. Longitudinal studies have shown the link between academic achievement and communities' levels of crime and child abuse and neglect (Bryk et al. 2010). A critical barrier to academic achievement is income. Almost a quarter of the children in the United States now live below the poverty line, and researchers have found a direct correlation between that circumstance and the academic achievement of these children as compared with more affluent children (Fuhrman et al. 2011). While it is true that distracted, hungry, worried, and ill children have a more difficult time focusing in the classroom, the impact of poverty stretches beyond the classroom itself. Steen and Noguera make the case that "poor and minority students acquire knowledge in school just like more advantaged students; however, their lack of participation in learning activities before and after school as well as during summer breaks limits their carryover and sustainability of this information" (2010:48). In addition, school readiness is a critical factor impacted by income, which can also be accelerated by high quality early childhood programs.

MAXIMIZING SCHOOLS' POTENTIAL: INTERNAL AND EXTERNAL REFORM

In 1997, the World Health Organization stated, "Schools could do more than any other single institution to improve the well-being and competence of children and youth" (1). Clearly educators are not solely responsible for children's well-being, and providing supports that extend beyond academic guidance and assistance in the classroom is not something that educators can do on their own. Epstein states that without partnerships, educators segment students into the school child and the home child, ignoring the whole child. This parceling "reduces or eliminates guidance, support, and encouragement for children's learning from parents, relatives, neighbors, peers, business partners, religious leaders, and other adults in the community" (2011:5). All community partners need to come together to address unmet needs of children and families, and the school is the perfect place for this assembly to occur.

The Children's Aid Society (CAS) continues to be a leader in the community schools effort in the United States (see details of the CAS, chapter 3). Regarding the current challenges facing educators in their efforts to serve students, the CAS observes: "While strengthening instruction, aligning assessments and improving teacher effectiveness are all critical elements of school reform, these approaches fall into the 'necessary but not sufficient' category" (2011:vii). Communities in Schools (CIS), another leading organization linking schools and communities, serves over one million children throughout the United States. The CIS model positions site coordinators inside schools to assess students' needs and provide resources to help them succeed in the classroom and in life. These coordinators help schools partner with local businesses, social service agencies, health care providers, and volunteers to provide resources including food, school supplies, health care, counseling, academic assistance and positive role models—whatever is needed to help children succeed in school (http://www.communitiesinschools.org/about/our-story/) (see chapter 3 for more on CIS).

Well-respected educators, including those at some of the United States' most prestigious universities, argue that in order for schools to educate all students according to democratic ideals of equity, the public education system requires both internal and external reform. Rothstein, for example, delineates three tracks that need to be simultaneously and "vigorously" pursued in order to make significant progress in narrowing the achievement gap. The first involves "school improvement efforts that raise the quality of instruction in elementary and secondary schools. Second is expanding the definition of schooling to include crucial out-of-school hours in which families and communities now are the sole influences. This means implementing comprehensive early childhood, after-school, and summer programs. And third are social and economic policies that enable children to attend school more equally ready to learn. These policies include health services for lower-class children and their families, stable housing for working families with children, and the narrowing of growing income inequalities in American society" (2004:8).

Steen and Noguera (2010) also cite evidence that focusing solely on school improvement is not enough to ensure learning outcomes, especially for poor and minority students. Adelman provides a useful model for the reform of children's services using the school as an anchor. This model incorporates reform efforts that address school improvement and instruction, on the one hand, and variables often external to the school, on the other, in order to develop a "comprehensive, coordinated, and increasingly integrated set of interventions for students and their families" (1996:434). As Dryfoos observes, "The marriage between the school and 'everything else' is taking place. It is not a marriage of convenience; it is one of dire necessity" (1991:135).

PROGRESSIVE UNIVERSALISM

Cummings, Dyson, and Todd describe the *progressive universalism* model of delivering school-linked services in England. The authors cite former Deputy Prime Minister John Prescott, who defines progressive universalism as "universal because we aim to help everyone; . . . and progressive because we aim to do more for those who need it most" (2011:14–15). This approach fits with the need for promoting, developing, and implementing school-linked services in the United States. It is an approach from which all communities can gain, especially those that are low-income. For example, Lawson and Alameda-Lawson's research with low-income Latino children in Sacramento finds that unless high levels of family stress, unsafe social and physical environments, elevated likelihood of illness and school absence, residential transience, and school mobility are addressed, "low-income Latino children may be destined to fall short of their desired goals and potential" (2011:2). A longitudinal study in Chicago conducted by Bryk et al. produced similar findings, and while the authors argue that sometimes simple solutions (i.e., eyeglasses) can be the difference between academic success and failure, often there are many more complex needs requiring attention, where "one-fourth or more of the elementary-school students might be living under an extraordinary set of circumstances, such as homelessness, foster care, domestic violence, abuse, or neglect" (2010:59).

Because of the strong connections between health disparities and school performance, low-income children, who often have a more difficult time accessing services, are at greater risk for academic failure. Basch notes five areas impacted by health disparities, including sensory perception, cognition, connectedness/engagement with school, absenteeism, and dropping out (2010:4). School-linked services, and especially full-service community schools, have been shown to have a positive impact on attendance and school drop-out rates in low-income communities where summer learning loss is but one of the factors that accelerates academic challenges for these students (Steen & Noguera 2010:48).

CONTINUUM OF SCHOOL-LINKED SERVICES AND NEED FOR INTEGRATION

School-linked services look different in different schools. And they should look different depending upon the community, residents, and their needs. The development and adoption of school-linked services emerge from a wide array of variables. Dryfoos and Quinn (2005) describe the continuum of school-linked services that we see in schools:

1. one or two components, such as after-school programs or school-based clinics, offered by outside agencies but not integrated with school;
2. three or four components, such as after-school, before-school, clinic, and family resource center, not integrated with school; and
3. three or four components, such as after-school, before-school, clinic, and family resource center, integrated with one another and with the school curriculum, with a full-time coordinator from a lead agency.

A number of organizations/researchers give different names to this third option. The most common name is *community school*. Such a school implements "a strategy for organizing the resources of the community around student success" and functions as "a coherent, learner-centered institution, rather than as a regular school with add-on programs" (Children's Aid Society 2011:1, 21).

The Centers for Disease Control and Prevention (CDC) refer to schools with integrated means for delivering health and social services as employing a model of coordinated school health (CSH). They describe CSH as a systematic approach to improving the health and well-being of all students so they can fully participate and be successful in school. "CSH brings together school administrators, teachers, other staff, students, families, and community members to assess health needs; set priorities; and plan, implement, and evaluate school health activities. CSH integrates health promotion efforts across nine interrelated components that already exist to some extent in most schools. These components include: health education, physical education, health services, nutrition services, counseling, psychological and social services, healthy and safe school environments, staff wellness, and family and community involvement" (2010:3).

Adelman describes an approach for integrated school-linked services wherein educational supports move away from "(a) fragmented, categorical, and specialist-oriented approaches toward a comprehensive and cohesive programmatic approach, and (b) viewing activity in this arena as supplementary toward a policy that establishes the component as primary and essential" (1996:435).

While having a single community partner linked with schools has potential to provide needed assistance that can impact children's well-being and their academic performance, it is the coordination and integration that provide the opportunity for systems change and reform in children's services. In order to be most successful, such integration needs to occur at *all* levels: policy, program, and practice. In the United States, advocates of community schools see a need for a supportive national policy. However, a supportive national policy, while crucial for far-reaching change, is not sufficient. For example, in Scotland, despite an integrated national policy for children's services, including education, "it is scarcely impacting on teachers' practice" (Smith 2012:134). Some advocates suggest that communities develop a "children's board" that parallels a school board to "integrate children's services" (Marx, Wooley, & Northrop 1998:xii). In their longitudinal study of Chicago schools, Bryk et al. (2010) cite partnerships with community health, recreation, and social service agencies, as well as the police department, as being vital to ensuring students' academic success. However, these partnerships cannot "stand alone." As Pappano states, "It is tempting for schools to partner with whoever offers help, but schools must be somewhat picky. Partnerships need to be meaningful and fruitful, because schools cannot afford to spend so much energy and time just for the sake of having a partner" (2010:126). It seems clear that to be most effective, school-linked services need to be thoughtfully integrated into a movement that will reform services for children and youth, transforming systems and promoting success in *all* realms: physical and mental health, academics and communities. Government policies that support these partnerships can go far to ensure that this occurs in ways that are relevant and sustainable.

HISTORICAL CONTEXT: SERVICES FOR CHILDREN AND FAMILIES

Since the 1800s, services for children and families have been based out of three settings critical to their lives: home, neighborhood, and school. Prior to that time, childhood was not viewed as a unique stage of development; children were instead viewed as miniature adults, and so early community programs focused on helping children confronting challenges in finding work and remaining employed. Educators and psychologists helped to alter this view, and apprenticeships and almshouses were replaced by services dedicated to nurturing children.

Home and Community-Based Services

In the 1800s, "friendly visiting" involved home visits to poor families by wealthy women who belonged to charity organization societies and who provided "a mixture of support, scrutiny, and advice" (Weiss & Halpern 1991:12). However, friendly visiting and its goal of reforming people in poverty did not lead to the moral improvement it was intended to address. Growing largely out of the Progressive Era of the early 1900s, the development and establishment of settlement houses began to replace charity organization societies' efforts at social reform. A focus on home-based services was supplemented by community-based efforts, including settlement houses and efforts by voluntary youth-serving organizations, and reflected a belief in the importance of neighborhood-based supports (Cahill 1997). These programs did not see themselves as competing with formal institutions like schools, but rather as complementing what other formal institutions were already providing (Connell 1992). Then, in the 1920s, there was a move away from meeting and serving people in their own homes and communities as public health nurses came under physicians' supervision and community-based social work gave way to psychiatric social work.

In the early 1960s, Mobilization for Youth took the lead in noting the many barriers that made community-based services challenging, including the lack of opportunities for positive youth development. It linked issues like inequality in schooling with youth outcomes and advocated for a comprehensive approach (Cahill 1997; White & Radin 1969). This period also saw the rise of Head Start, spearheaded by pediatricians and developmental psychologists who believed that children born into poverty were unable to escape a life of hardship without assistance. Head Start, operating as a partnership among schools, homes, and communities, became a model school-linked service. It was also during this time that some began to consider the possibility that "low-income families, especially minority families, reflect inequality rather than produce it" (Weiss & Halpern 1991:19).

As community-based services continued to proliferate and some began to think about poverty in a larger way, a 1989 evaluation of the Boys and Girls Clubs of America's Smart Moves program shed light on the role of the service delivery location and access to services as a precondition of positive outcomes for children. This evaluation revealed that the location of a Boys and Girls Club in a public housing site had a much more positive impact on lowering risk-taking behavior than the particular intervention itself (Cahill 1997).

As the variables that perpetuate poverty and their impact on educational attainment have become clearer, and as the components that provide support have come to be understood, there have been more indicators that school-linked services are an optimum approach to serving children and families, especially those without means. As Rebell and Wolff state, "While vital school improvement efforts must continue, the nation's ambitious educational goals can't be met unless we understand and confront the core problem underlying the achievement gap: the extensive pattern of childhood poverty that inhibits educational opportunity and educational achievement" (2012:62). Although school-linked services do not necessarily or immediately move children out of poverty, they can serve to ameliorate many *impacts* of poverty.

Historically, children's services were conceptualized as part of a holistic notion of child welfare, but the demand for assistance, coupled with the spread of urbanization and industrialization and the development of professionalization, led to service and regulatory divisions among the institutions and professions of education, juvenile justice, child welfare, and others serving children (Jonson-Reid 2000). Today community-based services for youths are most successful when they are rooted in a youth development model. Youth development efforts address needs of all young people, assuming that the transition from childhood to adulthood is fraught with challenges and requires support. This approach grows out of a public health model with a focus on strengths and competence, and is rooted in the philosophy that in order to improve the lives of youth, we need to improve the communities in which they live. It also involves youth in planning, delivering and evaluating services (U.S. Department of Health and Human Services 2007).

School-Linked Services

Because the vast majority of children in the United States attend public schools, school-based collaboration has the potential to address both the fragmentation of children's services as well as the need to maximize limited funds (Jonson-Reid 2000). Student test scores are affected by a range of student-specific, out-of-school factors that have a larger impact on test scores than all within-school effects combined (Weiss 2015), which is another major argument for linking services and schools. Weiss identifies some of these out-of-school variables as home environment, health and nutrition, residential mobility, peers, trips to museums, libraries and parks, help with homework, and summertime support for learning. Because these healthy activities are often more accessible to middle-class children, it is children in low-income communities that benefit the most by linking such programs with schools. While knowledge of school-linked services has not yet reached the mainstream population in the United States, they have existed in an array of forms for over a century. This section outlines the development of school-linked services in the United States from the 1890s to the present time.

The 1890s Through 1920

Dedication to maximizing coordinated partnerships between educational institutions and other institutions of a child's life has ebbed and flowed for over a century. Historians of school-linked services (Tyack 1992) and

(Dryfoos 1994) date the origin of this movement back to the 1890s and the Progressive Era. Tyack and Dryfoos note that the United States was then experiencing (for the first time) many of the same powerful influences that make school-linked services so critical today: industrialization, urbanization, and immigration. Schools that had formerly been accommodating wealthy children suddenly found their classrooms filled with lower-class children. Teachers were ill equipped to teach these children who brought so many other needs into the classroom (Dryfoos 1994). These conditions sparked writers Jacob Riis, Robert Hunter, and John Spargo and settlement workers Jane Addams and Lillian Wald to demand that government pay attention to the health and social impediments to children's educational attainment (Dryfoos 1994; Tyack 1992).

Initial reform efforts during the Progressive Era came mostly from outside of the schools, and included physicians, dentists, women's clubs, city park and recreation staff, settlement house workers, foundations, and the federal government (Tyack 1992). Jane Addams, credited with bringing the settlement house movement from the United Kingdom to the United States, helped establish these houses with programs that included college extension classes, social clubs, literary offerings, ethnic festivals, art exhibits, recreation, kindergarten, visiting nurses, legal services, labor union meetings, public forums, research, and gatherings for social change (Benson et al. 2009). Many settlement houses originated in people's homes. As the movement expanded, schools became the obvious location for programming (Campbell-Allen et al. 2009).

In 1894, physicians in Boston schools led the country's first citywide system of "medical inspection," geared toward examining immigrant children for contagious diseases (Dryfoos 1994; Tyack 1992). Here, doctors visited the schools on a daily basis, and the rates of communicable disease decreased subsequent to this program (Dryfoos 1994). As a result of these "inspections" children were often sent home from school for rest and further treatment. Settlement workers began sending workers to these homes in efforts to assist families in securing treatment for their children. This was the impetus for the creation and implementation of the country's first school nursing service in New York City in 1902, with Los Angeles following in 1907. In 1906, physicians went so far as to perform tonsillectomies in schools (Dryfoos 1994). The American Medical Association (AMA) supported these efforts throughout the Progressive Era, but in the 1920s it succumbed to negative pressure from private physicians who had been opposing these services for some time. Ultimately, the AMA officially denounced free medical services in the schools as "socialized medicine" (Dryfoos 1994; Tyack 1992).

Dental services also found their way into the schools during this period. Unlike physicians, however, private dentists supported free clinics for children, including clinics linked with schools. This has been attributed to dentists' feelings that children were difficult patients, as well as to their experience that parents frequently refused to pay the dentist's bill for children's care (Tyack 1992).

In addition to health services introduced by physicians and dentists, (Tyack 1992) notes that lay volunteers guided the introduction of social services into the schools. Women's clubs provided free meals and extended day care for poor children. Settlement house reformers developed the roles of visiting teachers and vocational guidance counselors. Visiting teachers (as precursors to school social workers) served as links between immigrant families and schools. They helped ease adjustment to a new country through educating teachers and assisting with families' concrete needs. Vocational guidance counselors took on finding jobs for students. Unfortunately, although their intentions were good, these "elite reformers" often assumed they knew what was best for the immigrants, and clients were rarely asked to identify the services they felt they needed. By and large, families appreciated free meals, English classes, and "vacation schools" (extended care programs), yet many immigrant parents fought against the more intrusive activities of those who sought to "improve" them and their children (Freeman 1995; Tyack 1992).

The 1920s Through the 1940s

The early stages of innovations in school-linked services were met by the advent of World War I, the conservative Harding and Coolidge administrations, restrictive immigration policies of the 1920s, early fears of communism, and the Great Depression. During this time, the American Medical Association and the National Education Association officially shifted their earlier support for actual medical treatment within the schools in favor of health education, assessment, counseling, and emergency care (Dryfoos 1994). Despite this, some form of public health service involving physicians and dentists did manage to continue in large urban schools (Tyack 1992).

Social services, too, suffered an erratic fate during these years. The free lunch program had to overcome many arguments and was not institutionalized during this period. In addition, summer school programs, commonplace in the 1920s, decreased by half during the 1930s. While the numbers of social workers increased during this time, there were forces that kept these workers from providing services for needy families. One was a push from school districts for social workers to take on the role of "attendance monitors" whose primary function was following up with children with excessive absences. Another was a drive from within the social work profession to adapt a "mental health model" focusing on individual psychopathology and middle-class clients, as opposed to delinquency prevention and those living in poverty. Workers were encouraged by their own colleagues to work in "good, average, or superior school districts in many cities before attempting work in less privileged ones, in order to avoid any stigma" (Tyack 1992:26). Similar "goal displacement," as Tyack calls it (1992:26), occurred in vocational education and in vacation schools, where services became generalized to the whole population, rather than being focused on people in poverty and minorities. Funded by local property taxes, wealthier neighborhoods had more resources for these "ancillary" programs. An example is the affluent Chicago suburb of Evanston, which kept its health and social services intact throughout the Great Depression, while neighboring inner-city Chicago drastically cut back its own (Sedlak & Church 1982).

One program that grew out of the Progressive Era and gained more widespread attention during the Depression years was the community school. Characteristics of an urban community school included the year-round use of the school building as a center for leisure and intellectually oriented activities, as well as a space for health clinics, counseling services, employment and legal aid services, opportunities for residents to address community issues, and the "facilitation of open communication between the school and the community" (Dryfoos 1994:30). The Benjamin Franklin High School in East Harlem, developed during this period, is credited as the first school to use school-community committees to address social problems such as inter-group relations, sanitation, and poor housing. "This was the first model that made the school 'the coordinator' of social services" (Campbell-Allen et al. 2009:4).

In the 1930s, Charles Manley and Charles Stewart Mott, founders of the Mott Foundation, developed recreation, health, and social service programs to serve the children and working parents of Flint, Michigan, in vacant school buildings in the evenings in what turned out to be a "pivotal" factor in the development of community schools (Campbell-Allen et al. 2009:4). Under the name "Community Education," and with support from First Lady Eleanor Roosevelt, similarly focused "lighted schoolhouses" drew interest from around the country (web.utk.edu/~fss/minutes /history.doc).

The 1950s and 1960s

After the Second World War, renewed attention was focused on school-linked services. The impetus for this came from the high rejection rate among Selective Service registrants for conditions that could have been treatable with earlier detection and intervention. This led to the introduction of a variety of legislative bills and an expansion in health-related school personnel. A large demonstration project, the Astoria Plan, was launched and subsequently adopted by the entire New York City school system and a number of other cities. In this project, students (with a parent in attendance) were given a medical exam at the beginning of the school year, followed by one or more conferences between teachers and school nurses over the course of the year. One set of evaluations revealed the system to be highly effective in improving services, follow-up, coordination, parent involvement, and record-keeping. Another series of evaluations questioned the efficiency of a system that relied heavily on an expensive resource (the physician), when only a small number of illnesses were detected. These disparate findings remain reflective of our present system, where the federal role in the delivery of children's health resources is well established; yet there remains a range of opinions and policies about how these programs should be administered, run, and funded and at whom they should be targeted (Dryfoos 1994).

Two significant programs initiated by the federal government in the mid-1960s are the Head Start program and the Individuals with Disabilities Education Act (IDEA). This high quality early intervention program and system for educating children with disabilities hold many of the key ingredients, including services collaboration and parental involvement, central to comprehensive school-linked services programs today (Dryfoos 1994; Kelley & Kahne 1995).

The 1970s and 1980s

The early 1970s saw the development of four model school-based health programs, all funded at one point by the Robert Wood Johnson Foundation, an early supporter of school-linked services. The Carter administration's arrival in Washington raised hopes that these programs would flourish. The secretary of Health, Education and Welfare at the time, Joseph Califano, is quoted as having told participants at a National School Health Conference that Carter was interested in exploring "possibilities for using schools to provide a full range of services to children and families, including health and social services as well as education" (Dryfoos 1994:40).

School-linked services were also supported during the 1970s, when community school advocates became politically active under two new national organizations founded by Mott: the National Association for Community Education (NACE) and the National Center for Community Education (NCCE). Together, advocates from these organizations successfully supported federal legislation designed to help develop infrastructure for community schools. Despite the passage of this legislation in 1974, neither the AMA nor the subsequent Reagan administration allowed it to come to fruition. Reagan's budget cuts to human services and pressure from private physicians to keep health services out of the schools pointed to a dim future for school-linked services (Dryfoos 1994). Momentum was lost once again, and federal funding for the community schools program ended in 1981 (web.utk.edu/~fss/minutes/history.doc.).

Despite the failure of federal support during this time, a number of effective state initiatives emerged, with two of the largest and most innovative developing in New Jersey and California. In 1987, the New Jersey Department of Human Services (DHS) added $6 million to its budget for school-linked services. New Jersey's School-Based Youth Services Program was geared to establish "one-stop shopping," where an array of services is located in a single, accessible location to promote collaboration between the school and at least one other public or nonprofit organization (Melaville & Blank 1992). Shortly thereafter, in 1991, the California legislature passed the Healthy Start Support Services for Children Act, with an appropriation of $20 million and a requirement that all grants be matched by a consortium with a local contribution of one dollar for every three dollars awarded by the state (Wagner 1993). The Foundation Consortium for School-

Linked Services, composed of thirteen grant-making foundations in California, was a major partner in the Healthy Start initiative (White 1993).

The 1990s

The last decade of the twentieth century saw a large resurgence of the school-linked services/full-service community school movement. The Children's Aid Society's (CAS) commitment to community schools began in 1992, and their technical assistance center was launched in 1994 (http://nationalcenterforcommunityschools.childrensaidsociety.org/faqs/on-the-center). Under the umbrella of the Institute for Educational Leadership, the Coalition for Community Schools (CCS), initiated by Pete Moses from CAS alongside Joy Dryfoos and Ira Harkavy, emerged in 1997 as a national voice for this effort (web.utk.edu/~fss/minutes/history.doc.).

The Twenty-First Century

It is easy to see that over time, the movement for school-linked services has shifted significantly with the changing political climate. While the history highlights the vulnerability that has characterized these efforts over more than a century, there is hope: throughout the changing times, school-linked services programs have endured, and they are not going away. In a paper presented to the 2013 Equity and Excellence Commission, American Federation of Teachers (AFT) president Randi Weingarten states: "No community can flourish unless its children are safe, healthy, well-nourished, and well-educated; and no school can be a strong pillar of a thriving community without deep community responsibility for and ownership of the school's academic success. Thus, recognizing that the fate of communities and their schools are inextricably linked, we must make schools stronger by educators embracing community resources, expertise, and activities; and we must make communities stronger by anchoring them around highly effective schools" (2013:4).

• • •

In this first chapter we address the links among health, education, and income; the need for complementary external and internal school reform strategies; and the notion of progressive universalism—doing for everyone with a focus on those most in need. Looking at the continuum of school-linked services, we argue for the importance of a strategic, thoughtful, and integrated approach to partnerships. We also summarize the history of services for children and families, and their varying settings over time, including homes, communities and schools, with a focus on the history of services linked with and/or based at schools.

The next chapter takes a look at the school as an organization and ways the varying professionals whom schools employ and/or with whom they interface can join with children and families to support successful school-linked strategies.

2

The School

ALL ORGANIZATIONS HAVE THEIR OWN SETS of norms and mission statements. As an entity, the American public school system's mission is to educate children. Most school districts today are large bureaucracies—complex, multilevel social organizations run by full-time professionals (DeMarrais & LeCompte 1999). Schools are among the largest buildings in most communities, and in many communities the educational system is the largest industry and employer. The school bus system that is intricately tied with schools is a related institution with employees possessing a great deal of information about a community's students by virtue of the time they spend with them. Despite their size and contact with children and families, most school buildings lie vacant after mid-afternoon and on weekends, and many employees including bus drivers and cafeteria workers are unfortunately overlooked as strategic resources for students, beyond their basic functions. Thoughtful, meaningful partnerships of school staff with community members and organizations maximize the contributions of school employees and property to benefit students, families, residents, and neighborhoods.

Unlike education systems in most parts of the world, the U.S. system of education is highly decentralized (DeMarrais & LeCompte 1999). Because of the critical role of local property taxes, there is a strong correlation between funds for schools and the wealth of a community, making it often impossible for schools in poorer communities to provide the resources of those with a wealthier tax base. While there are state dollars available for these districts, they do not make up the income gap, leaving schools in poorer communities nowhere near as well-resourced as those in wealthier ones. Because state dollars are tied to attendance, schools where students miss school due to illness, familial responsibilities, crime, etc., are also financially hampered. These schools tend to be in poor communities.

While the primary instructional mission of schools has not changed, the traditional means by which to educate students to be successful citizens no longer works in the current context, characterized by an increasingly diverse society confronted with an expanding array of psychosocial problems. To deal with these changes the traditional model of education that occurs completely within a school building and is provided solely by school employees needs reviewing. As Bryk et al. point out, "Instruction matters and it matters a lot; but so does the social context in which it is embedded" (2010:209). Others agree. Gardner argues that schools "act as if they could effectively address the problems of students who are physically in school during only 9 percent of their lives from birth to adulthood" (1993:189). Pappano wisely states, "Flooding schools with innovative ideas will yield little if the deepest problems are outside the building" (2010:23). In other words, schools must address their mission in concert with families and communities, since students' lives accompany them into their classrooms, and their classroom behavior, attention, and learning are impacted by their families, communities, strengths, and worries outside of school. Bryk et al.'s longitudinal study of low-performing Chicago schools found five organizational subsystems that *all* need to be addressed for education to improve: a school's instructional guidance subsystem; its professional capacity—the human resource subsystem; parent-community-school ties; a student-centered learning climate; and leadership.

Perhaps most importantly, their study revealed that even with four of these components in place, "a sustained, material weakness in any one of these subsystems undermined virtually all attempts at improving student learning" (2010:96). While many educational reformers focus primarily on what happens inside schools, this book focuses on parent-community-school ties, including what they look like in different communities and how to develop and sustain them.

SCHOOL PROFESSIONALS AS COLLABORATORS

Schools that invest in partnerships require collaboration to be effective. Despite recognition of the need for interprofessional education and collaboration in the workplace, the vast majority of professional training, practice, and funding—be it in education, health care, or other arenas—continues to occur in silos. Health and social service professionals, business people, and others who serve children in schools, are socialized and educated differently from traditional teachers and school administrators. Recent research by Phillippo (2013) reveals that neither the education profession nor schools help teachers fulfill expanded roles beyond teaching, leaving teachers dependent upon others to address physical and psychosocial impediments to their students' learning. Phillippo also found that teacher education programs "emphasize a narrow teacher role, in spite of many educators' and programs' independent efforts to promote teachers' broad understanding of their students and their learning needs" (2013:147). Other professionals who work in the school or partner with teachers from community agencies must understand as much as they can about educators' socialization and role requirements so that they can support them in their job as the "central" professional in the school. Likewise, teachers need to understand the socialization, roles, skills, and knowledge of their interprofessional collaborators so as to use them most effectively and efficiently in ways they can support the educational mission and teachers' efforts in the classroom. The sections that follow address the roles of different professionals, families and youth in the educational process, making the case for the voice of each in children's success. We delineate where these groups find support for this collaborative approach to success, in addition to addressing the challenges each may experience in these efforts. We begin with teachers—the central professionals in the schools.

Teachers

It seems obvious that as stated in the U.S. Department of Education's Equity and Excellence Commission report, "Teachers, together with principals, are the single most important *in-school factor* affecting student achievement" (2013:21). Everyone would agree that the central task of a teacher is instruction, but what truly matters is how this task is accomplished. In past decades, when all children were not expected to graduate, teachers did not have to attend to the unique psychosocial and learning needs of every single student in order to fulfill the requirements of their jobs. However, the nature of educators' work has changed, particularly in the past decade. There is a fundamental dissonance between how many teachers are attempting to respond to the multiple needs of their children and the expectations that some school administrators, teacher education programs, and communities have of teachers as purely performing teaching tasks (Phillippo 2013). Forbes and Watson argue, "While educational work in our contemporary society requires creativity, ingenuity and complexity, the way educators are being prepared and the images of what is involved in teaching have turned more toward technical competence" (2009:92). Certainly policies like No Child Left Behind and Race to the Top, as well as the prevalence of "teaching to a test" methods, reinforce this technical focus.

Even when teachers are told that they are responsible "only" for instruction, inside many classrooms, teachers go above and beyond that role, acknowledging that instruction cannot occur without attention to the "whole" child as well as the community and family settings where children spend most of their time. Many teachers frequently address children's needs beyond academic ones even though they are not "required" or trained to do this. Yet this attention is variable, depending on a range of factors. Mooney, Kline, and Davoren state, "Like children, teachers are different too; they do not all possess the same degree of skill in recognizing and accommodating the range of academic and psychosocial diversity in the classroom. Even teachers who are highly skilled and intuitive in responding to children's needs cannot be totally successful when the number of children with serious needs is skewed" (1999:111). Chang and Lawyer cite a recent survey where 50 percent of first-year teachers agreed that "many children come to school with so many problems that it's difficult for them to be good students" (2012:3). This is an astounding percentage requiring a serious look at support for instruction. Chang and Lawyer go on to point out that a majority of educators believe that student access to integrated social, health, and educational services is central to academic achievement today.

As stated above, despite being formally unprepared for this work, teachers often provide mental health and other psychosocial support to students as best they can when impediments to learning arise. Like unused school buildings and support personnel whose knowledge is also left untapped, teachers, too, are an "underutilized resource" (Berzin et al. 2011:494). A recent study found that while the most intensive mental health supports continue to be provided by mental health personnel in schools, response to intervention (RTI), as instituted in many schools, has seen the provision of universal in-classroom supports involving teachers to a large extent. Teachers are also collaborating with mental health professionals in providing targeted interventions (Franklin et al. 2012). Therefore, we are beyond the debate about *whether* teachers should have support to attend to the circumstances and conditions that interfere with children's learning; the question instead is how to structure and provide these supports to maximize impact and, in so doing, provide an environment where teachers can do what they do best: teach.

Educational reform efforts like No Child Left Behind and Race to the Top (elaborated on in later chapters) advocate evaluating teachers' performance according to their students' test scores. This has proven to be a highly unreliable model. A 2010 report by the Economic Policy Institute noted that one study found that "across five large urban districts, among teachers who were ranked in the top 20 percent of effectiveness in the first year, fewer than a third were in that top group the next year, and another third moved all the way down to the bottom 40 percent. Another found that teachers' effectiveness one year could only predict from 4 percent to 16 percent of the variation in such ratings in the following year" (Weiss 2011:20). Weiss goes on to argue that better methods of assessing teachers do exist. Such methods are characterized by performance standards with descriptive examples of observable teaching behaviors, peer assistance, and other qualitative approaches, and they are being implemented in communities of different sizes in Maryland, New York, Minnesota, Ohio, California, and other states and individual districts.

What we do know about teacher competence is that schools serving low-income and minority students tend to have disproportionately high numbers of teachers who are "inexperienced, untrained and teaching in subjects for which they have little or no training" (U.S. Department of Education 2013:21). Lower teacher salaries in poor communities compound this, which in turn leads to high teacher turnover in many of the schools with the largest teaching challenges. American Federation of Teachers (AFT) national president Randi Weingarten states, "We must be prepared to get the best teachers and principals to the highest-need students (including low-income students, minority students, English learners, and students with disabilities)" (2013: 4). What do structures that promote the best teachers look like? Countries with the highest quality teaching forces are characterized by competitive teacher salaries, free higher education, and common instructional materials aligned with rigorous national curriculum frameworks; because of these conditions, these teachers also have more professional development, collaboration, time, teaching resources, and supportive "teaching teams" (U.S. Department of Education 2013:22).

Administrators

School leaders, especially principals, are critical in shaping strong relationships among parents, communities, and educators. They play important roles in decisions that determine whether and how parents and community members are part of the daily lives of teachers, classrooms, and schools (Ishimaru 2013). Van Voorhis and Sheldon (2004) suggest that principals are central in initiating programs and processes in school-community relationships.

Though most principals express an interest in working with the community and with parents, those working in low-income areas and communities of color are often not adequately trained or prepared for authentic engagement. Leadership preparation programs can exacerbate this when such programs support learning and practicum environments using traditional hierarchical models where parents and neighbors are not considered part of the school community (Ishimaru 2013).

Principals who are most successful in relationships with their communities value partnerships with teachers and parents, liken their school communities to families, and describe a sense of community as vital to student success (Ishimaru 2013; Khalifa 2012). Khalifa applies lessons learned from early black school leaders in segregated communities about the importance of building home-school relationships and of having strong school principals who were as highly regarded as other black community leaders, including pastors, and seen as authorities on educational, social, and economic issues.

Today, two major national associations of principals are working to expand service linkages and community partnerships. Both the National Association of Elementary School Principals (NAESP) and the National Association of Secondary School Principals (NASSP) promote community engagement as a core component of their leadership development and reform agendas. Leaders of both organizations are active partners in the Coalition for Community Schools. Specifically, NAESP "encourages principals to build greater ownership for the work of the school, to share leadership and decision making, to encourage meaningful family involvement, and to connect families with the health and support services students need for successful learning" (Berg, Melaville, & Blank 2006:1). NASSP recommends that schools institute structural leadership changes that support meaningful communication and involvement in decision-making by students, teachers, family members, and the community. They also recommend that high schools build partnerships with community organizations, businesses, and universities, to create authentic avenues for community engagement (Berg, Melaville, & Blank 2006).

Social Workers

The history of school social workers dates back to the early twentieth century when the Rochester (New York) Board of Education initiated and financed in-house social work services (Oppenheimer 1925). Prior to that, lay advocates from community agencies provided social work–related services in schools (Tyack 1992). The role of the visiting teacher, which predated school social workers, was developed to enforce compulsory attendance laws (Huxtable & Blythe 2002). Visiting teachers supported immigrant families by easing adjustment to a new country, educating teachers about immigrant families, and helping families access needed services (Bronstein et al. 2011; Hernandez Jozefowicz et al. 2002; Oppenheimer 1925). In the 1930s, school social workers began to take on the role of social caseworker, which became their primary role between the 1940s and the 1960s (Peckover et al. 2012).

In the 1970s, social workers' roles in the school began to expand, and Alderson (1972) identified the following four models of school social work practice operating during that time:

1. The traditional clinical model of social casework;
2. The school change model that addresses school climate;
3. The community-school model emphasizing building relationships between the community and the school; and
4. The social interaction model that focuses on facilitating communication among students, the school, and community.

The Education for All Handicapped Children Act (EAHCA) of 1975 provided a new stream of funding for social workers functioning as social caseworkers with children with disabilities, thus prioritizing the traditional clinical role (Peckover et al. 2012).

Since the 1980s, No Child Left Behind (NCLB) and the Individuals with Disabilities Education Act (IDEA) have influenced and changed the roles of school social workers (Peckover et al. 2012). In addition to the impact of federal education reform policies, and with the advent of the ecological perspective (Tourse & Sulick 1999), and varying state policies (e.g., as described by Anderson-Butcher et al. 2008), the role of school-based social workers has become extremely diverse from one district to another. While most school social workers continue to focus largely on clinical work (Kelly et al. 2010), in some districts they still function as attendance counselors, and in others they mobilize community resources, engage families, and/or take on other boundary-crossing and/or multilevel systems interventions. Testa (2012) outlines the following roles of school social workers that go well beyond the provision of clinical services and which are in line with an integrated model of school-linked services:

1. Forging schools and community linkages, especially in the context of educational and social disadvantage;
2. Delivering and coordinating seamless services through full service community schools; and
3. Promoting social capital, health, and well-being through health promotion activities.

In addition to the different roles social workers play, schools also have different arrangements for utilizing them. Some schools employ school social workers; others contract with community-based agencies to provide social work services on school grounds or in partnership with schools; and some schools employ school social workers *and* have relationships with community-employed social workers.

When there are both school-employed and agency-employed social workers in a community, concerns are often raised about whether school systems under intense budget constraints will lay off school-employed social workers. This is considered to be a huge mistake, as school-employed and agency-employed social workers have complementary perspectives and play complementary roles supporting youth in the schools (Weist, Ambrose, & Lewis 2006). While agency-employed social workers based in schools provide access to psychosocial and mental health services that students would otherwise have to travel for when there is not enough in-school capacity to serve all these needs, it is school-employed social workers who have the knowledge and relationships critical for coordinating school-linked services. School social workers are also best able to educate agency-employed social workers about framing their work around the academic mission of the school and in assisting agency-employed workers in forming relationships with, and understanding the culture of, the school.

Nurses

Nursing in the United States can be traced back to multiple beginnings—to the late eighteenth century and a series of lectures organized by Valentine Seaman, a New York physician for nurses who cared for maternity patients, and to the mid-nineteenth century and the work of Florence Nightingale in Britain and advent of the Civil War in the United States. Public health nursing, which guides the work of school-based health centers (SBHCs), has its roots a few decades later, in the late 1890s, when Lillian Wald founded the Henry Street Settlement House. The settlement house provided nursing and other social services to families and children living in poverty on the Lower East Side of New York City (http://www.nursing.upenn.edu/nhhc/Welcome%20Page%20Content/American%20Nursing.pdf) and laid the groundwork for collaborations between social workers and nurses to serve children and families. Wald's work was replicated in other parts of the country and led to the growth of the field of public health nursing, expanding the type of services provided by nurses.

In 1902 the country's first school nursing service was established in New York City, with a second one established in Los Angeles five years later. In 1968, the National Education Association established the Department of School Nurses (DSN), an association dedicated to the advancement of school nursing practice and the health of school-aged children. Eleven years later, in 1979, the National Association of School Nurses (NASN) was incorporated and continues today as the largest association of school nurses and the hub for state affiliate associations (http://www.nasn.org/AboutNASN/OurHistory).

Just as social work services in schools today can include a combination of school-employed social workers and agency-employed social workers who are based at schools, nurses in schools can also be a combination of school nurses (employed by schools and represented by the NASN) and agency-employed nurses, who are often part of school-based health centers and work out of the public health model of nursing implemented by Lillian Wald. The School-Based Health Alliance (recently renamed from the National Assembly of School Based Health Care) and NASN have clarified the distinct roles of these groups of nurses. For one thing, funding comes from different sources; the majority of school nurses are paid through the education system, whereas school-based health center staff are usually funded by state health departments and/or local hospitals/community health centers and health insurance reimbursements. Roles are also different, but complementary: school nurses are charged with day-to-day management of students' health, whereas nurses who are part of school-based health centers address health promotion and prevention through screening and daily health services; they also include nurse practitioners who prescribe and dispense medications (http://www.nasbhc.org/atf/cf/{B241D183-DA6F-443F-9588–3230D027D8DB}/SBHCS%20AND%20NURSES%20FINAL.PDF).

School-based health center nurses and school nurses collaborate to educate students and families about healthy behaviors and nutrition; enroll students and families in public insurance programs; and provide immunizations (Allison et al. 2007). NASN has been a critical partner with the School-Based Health Alliance in their work in school-based health centers (SBHCs). Recently, they have worked collaboratively to address high rates of human immunodeficiency virus (HIV) and sexually transmitted disease (STD) infection among African American and Latino males ages thirteen to nineteen, specifically young men who have sex with men (YMSM). With support from the Centers for Disease Control, school nurses and nurses in SBHCs work together to build strategic partnerships among school districts, youth-serving organizations, community-based organizations (including those serving gay, lesbian, and bisexual youth), parent organizations, adolescent health care, mental health, and social service providers (http://www.sbh4all.org/site/c.ckLQKbOVLkK6E/b.7697107/apps/s/content.asp?ct=11675171).

School Counselors

Every six years, the Centers for Disease Control and Prevention (CDC) conduct the School Health Policies and Programs Study (SHPPS). In this process, they gather data from state education agency personnel in all fifty states and the District of Columbia, as well as a nationally representative sample of school districts and personnel in elementary, middle, and high schools. In a recent SHPPS survey, although states and districts generally had not adopted policies stating that schools will have mental health and social services staff, 77.9 percent of schools had at least a part-time counselor. Fewer schools had school psychologists or social workers. Consequently, counseling services were more common in schools than were psychological or social services, making school counselors the primary in-school support for mental health (Brener et al. 2007).

The American School Counselor Association (www.schoolcounselor.org) delineates direct and indirect services engaged in by school counselors. Direct services include interactions between school counselors and students, including implementing the School Counseling Core Curriculum in collaboration with educators using classroom and group activities; coordinating ongoing activities that assist students in establishing goals and developing plans; and implementing responsive services that address students' immediate needs and concerns. Indirect services include referrals for assistance, as well as consultation and collaboration with parents, teachers, other educators, and community organizations.

The American School Counselor Association affirms the importance of school counselors' roles in school-family-community partnerships like school-linked services and identifies these roles as advocate, facilitator, leader, liaison and initiator. Despite this endorsement, only 40 percent of school counselors say they are involved in partnerships, and only 37 percent report having received training in developing and implementing these relationships (Bryan & Henry 2012).

Psychologists

In 1896, Lightner Witmer established the first psychological clinic addressing students' school-related difficulties at University of Pennsylvania (Perfect & Morris 2011). Although this clinic was not school-based but rather housed at the university, in 1907, Witmer stated in a speech to the American Psychological Association (APA) that there was a need to train students for a new profession of psychological expert in schools. Supporting the expansion of school mental health services, one of the priority outcomes of the 2002 Conference on the Future of School Psychology was "promoting health and mental health and increasing child and family services in schools, while simultaneously finding linkages with community services" (Cummings et al. 2004:337).

School psychologists (e.g., Weist, Adelman, and Taylor) have been prominent in the interdisciplinary school mental health movement. Despite this and the fact that school psychologists claim to be interested in an expanded role in providing a range of services that support mental health, the majority of their time continues to be devoted to psychological assessment, including special education eligibility determinations (Splett et al. 2013). Splett et al. point out that school psychologists are educated to provide school mental health services across the range of tiers—universal, selective, and indicated—and should be utilized to do so. They state that school psychologists bring the following areas of knowledge and skills to their work: an understanding of child development, psycho-educational assessment, special education law, consultation methodology, program evaluation, and interventions at the individual and systems levels. A barrier to psychologists utilizing these areas of expertise emerges when other school professionals view their role as solely conducting assessments and thus do not utilize them in the provision of various prevention and intervention services that can expand school-linked efforts for students. Additionally, psychologists report inadequate preparation in working with diverse, multicultural students (Splett et al. 2013), who often live in low-income communities without access to mental health resources when such resources are not linked with the school. One remedy to these barriers includes partnerships among schools, communities, and professional education programs in universities.

CONSTITUENTS AS COLLABORATORS

Bryan & Henry describe the kind of partnership that should characterize relationships with constituents as a democratic collaboration, where "school personnel share power with students, families, and community members and view them as equal and valuable experts in the children's education and the partnership process" (2012:410). Such partnerships are based in empowerment and involve the following principles:

1. Intentional engagement of culturally diverse and low-income parents and community members;
2. Purposeful diminishing of professionals' roles as experts;
3. Respecting families and community members' knowledge and insights;
4. Focusing on each person's assets and resources;
5. Involving constituents in mutual and equitable definitions of issues and decisions regarding goals, activities and outcomes; and
6. Avoiding blame.

The literature on collaboration defines partnership with constituents as a marker of quality collaborative practice (Bronstein 2003). In schools this means full partnership with students and their families.

Students/Children

Full partnerships with students means involving their voices in the critical life of the school, including defining, implementing, and evaluating goals. Beacon Schools (see chapter 3), define youth engagement as "involving youth in responsible, challenging action that meets genuine needs, with opportunities for planning and/or decision-making affecting others in an activity whose impact or consequence is extended to others." As a result, "adults and young people jointly decide on the issue/problem/action they want to work towards, share responsibilities for the process, and collectively work towards change" (Youth Development Institute 2009:7–8). Reflective practice, power sharing, planning, transparency, and training are all strategies that maximize effective youth engagement. There are varying models of meaningful student engagement in decision-making, an area where full-service community schools have demonstrated commitment and the development of high-quality practices. Cummings, Dyson, and Todd found that many "extended" schools in England require "the participation of students in decision-making, and the development of leadership capacity amongst students as future leaders of their communities" (2011:127). In the United States, Ruglis and Freudenberg emphasize the importance of leadership roles for young people, moving them to advocate to be heard in the policy process and to conduct research needed "to make their case" (2012:380).

Carlyon, Carlyon, and McCarthy discuss the importance of viewing those whom we educate in classrooms as children as opposed to "just" students, stating that "if educators view students as children, they are likely to see both the family and the community as partners with the school in children's education and development" (1998:67). Educators are also more likely to view children as having goals and challenges beyond academics, as well as lives outside the classroom that naturally impact (and are impacted by) their classroom experiences and behaviors.

Dallago et al. (2013) implemented the Adolescents, Life Context, and School Project in Padova, Italy, with twelve-year-olds to engage their voices. The researchers invited youth participation, giving them opportunities for genuine voice in decisions ordinarily reserved for educators and community providers. Using a quasi-experimental design, in just three months' time they found a statistically significant difference among the participating youth in their sense of civic responsibility to their neighborhood. Such initiatives highlight the reciprocal nature of school-family-community relationships where all benefit by these partnerships. As Noddings (2005) asserts, a better community member makes a better student.

An exemplar in youth-driven programs that uses "authentic" youth participation to support schools and communities is Youth Engaged in Leadership and Learning (YELL), developed in 2000 at the John W. Gardner Center for Youth and Their Communities at Stanford University. In its first endeavor, middle school youth conducted research on community needs and strengths and used what they learned to leverage needed resources. "Through this process, youth learned about their communities and tapped into their own strengths and ideas to lead a change effort. In addition, adult leaders came to solicit the perspectives of young people and apply those perspectives to local policy" (Youth Engaged in Leadership and Learning 2007:xiv). Most exemplary school-linked services programs maximize the involvement of youth and engage them as full collaborative partners.

The Children's Aid Society stresses the importance of involving children in school-community partnerships. As part of their policy, they call for student input in school decisions. "Because they will be the individuals most impacted by changes in their school, students must have input into the effort. Including children and youth in the planning and implementation of the strategy will build a sense of ownership. Older students can be given real opportunities to develop leadership skills and a sense of responsibility for the welfare of their community" (2011:37).

The School-Based Health Alliance, the "national voice for school-based health centers" (SBHCs) (http://www.sbh4all.org/site/c.ckLQKbOVLkK6E/b.7505827/k.2960/About_SchoolBased_Health_Alliance.htm) has developed a "toolkit" to support youth engagement in SBHCs. This includes ways to maximize youth voice in efforts and decisions, including community asset mapping and needs assessments; input on types of services; outreach and promotion of services; peer-to-peer health education; and policy and advocacy mobilization (http://www.sbh4all.org/site/c.ckLQKbOVLkK6E/b.7796473/k.C203/Youth_ToolkitSec_1.htm). Such efforts reinforce youth voice in supporting school success beyond traditional classroom instruction.

Families

Because of the central government's mandate for integrated services for children in England, English policy regarding family involvement provides a roadmap for those looking for policy that supports family participation in schools. In describing extended schools and the roles of families, Cummings, Dyson, and Todd propose a strategic and thoughtful approach to family engagement: "Families and communities are as present in classrooms as are the students themselves. The choice is not whether to allow the outside world into the school. It is whether to do so openly and thoughtfully, embracing the challenges and opportunities this presents, or to pretend, against all the evidence, that the outside world does not exist" (2011:131).

Many school leaders and teachers in the United States agree with this position, but feel they lack the time and skill for family engagement efforts. Educators often enter schools without adequate understanding of the backgrounds, cultures, languages, races, and other critical characteristics of their students' families, making it impossible for them to work in partnership with the people that mean the most to their students (Epstein 2011). Building the case for the family's importance, as well as researching and sharing methods for family engagement, are critical. The Children's Aid Society (2011) has found that family engagement not only is good for children but also supports teacher retention. Some districts reveal a correlation between schools with the highest number of community and parent volunteers and the highest test scores (Berg, Melaville, & Blank 2006). Many community school efforts target family engagement as a priority and provide a range of services to support this endeavor, including medical, social, and emotional support services offered to families on school grounds or through formal relationships with service providers linked with schools. Every Children's Aid Society community school has a parent coordinator and a family resource room, in addition to a variety of other family engagement such as leadership training. Communities in Schools, with a focus on dropout prevention, believes that the effort to support students in schools "starts with the family" (http://www.communitiesinschools.org/blog/category/families/page/2/).

A major block to family engagement efforts is the negative view school professionals sometimes hold about families, especially in low-income communities. Racial and class differences between parents and school professionals often lead to a lack of trust (Berg, Melaville, & Blank 2006; Noguera 2011). We ourselves have heard this in our own work with families and schools. And despite the more supportive government mandates in some European countries, the same has been heard there: "We have found in our work, an overwhelming emphasis on the inadequacies and shortcomings of local people, with much less acknowledgement either of the adversities facing those people, or of their resourcefulness" (Cummings, Dyson, and Todd 2011:124).

Such views are often held by school professionals because of the lack of involvement by families in schools, but many families do not know they are welcome to be involved in their children's schools. Involvement in a school-linked services project with Haitian immigrants in Miami revealed these families thought they were insulting teachers by addressing the educational process (Bronstein & Kelly 1998). It took intensive outreach to help these family members learn that teachers welcomed their input and involvement. Pappano (2010) also found the value of targeted outreach to maximize family engagement in Hartford, Connecticut. She reported on a school for which the typical audience size on a back-to-school night was about ten to fifteen families; when a staff person called every sixth-grade family to personally invite them to the event, two hundred attended. Bryk et al. (2010) found that safety and family involvement were the factors best predictive of student attendance, a prerequisite for learning and a requirement for school funding.

Head Start and other early childhood education programs often are models for substantive involvement of families. In 2010, the Affordable

Care Act included the Maternal, Infant, and Early Childhood Home Visiting program (MIECHV), which supports efforts that pair at-risk mothers of children up to age three with trained professionals through home visits. While a Pew Foundation study in 2011 found that this program was not being well-utilized, the situation is being remedied, and this legislation is now seen as making "home visiting one of the bright spots of progress in early education" (Guernsey et al. 2014:7).

James Comer's Yale Child Study Center School Development Program (SDP), begun in the 1960s, shows some of the earliest and most robust outcomes of efforts to involve families in meaningful ways in their children's schooling. SDP is based on the philosophy that development and academic learning are inextricably linked, that development occurs in well-functioning environments, and that organizations are most effective when there is participatory rather than authoritarian governance. Leadership and participation must be both respectful and synchronous. The SDP model is based on a team model of school governance called the *school planning and management team* (SPMT). The SPMT is made up of representatives from school staff, parents, and other adult stakeholders. Its mission includes: "a.) the development and monitoring of a comprehensive school plan with specific goals in the social climate and academic areas; b.) staff development activities based on building-level goals in these areas; and c.) assessment and modification—periodic assessment that allows the staff to modify the program to meet identified needs and opportunities" (Comer & Emmons 2006:359). Other successful models of family engagement are discussed in more detail later, when we outline critical foci of full-service community schools.

• • •

Even without identifying partners who function largely outside of the school, most schools have an array of professionals alongside their constituent children and families, all with critical parts to play in successful collaborations. Understanding, respecting, and maximizing the roles of each is essential in fostering school-community partnerships with the best odds of success for all students. The next chapter looks at the wide range of ways that professionals and constituents are involved in school-linked services and the diverse ways these strategies and models look as they are implemented in communities across the United States.

3

School-Linked Services Today

AS THE LATE LEADER OF THE full-service community school movement, Joy Dryfoos, stated, "Somewhere in the United States, it is possible to find an example of almost every category of human services located in a school" (1994:47). The range of programs serves not only students, but their family members from infants to grandparents, and some serve community members who reside in the school community but who do not have relatives in the school system. The services span what is offered in the health and human services, including: medical, dental, mental health, psychosocial services and counseling; social competency training, mentoring, family resource centers, recreation and cultural enrichment, afterschool centers, day care, transportation, school remediation, and dropout prevention; and consultation with teachers, administrators, and parents regarding school reorganization. In addition, new partnerships between schools and businesses are on the rise, where businesses support internships and provide services in schools as role models, mentors, and engaged community members.

The continuum of school-linked services goes from individual schools partnering with a single community agency for a single service (e.g., afterschool recreation, mental health counseling, health care, etc.) for a single population (e.g., immigrants, elementary school students, etc.) to full-service community schools that integrate a range of services at and/or near schools for all community members and according to community needs. Below we highlight some of these services to illustrate their range, including school-based health centers (SBHCs), family resource centers (FRCs), partnerships with businesses, and (expanded) school mental health. Following that, we provide more details on an exemplary model of promoting mental health in schools known as *expanded school mental health*. A large section of this chapter is devoted to the different models and manifestations of exemplary community schools across the United States, presented by those who develop and implement them.

SCHOOL-BASED HEALTH CENTERS

School-based health centers have a unique identity. SBHCs provide "comprehensive preventive and primary health care services to students on or near a school campus" (Holmes 2012:433). In some schools, these centers are the sole community-provided program, and in others they are part of a larger system of coordinated children's services linked with and/or based in schools. The primary mission of SBHCs is to contribute to the health of young people and thus to their education, as children are less likely to miss school because of ill health when they are in proximity of a health care provider for potential monitoring or interventions, as in the case of asthma.

The SBHC phenomenon expanded rapidly in the 1990s, increasing from fewer than one hundred at the beginning of the decade to close to two thousand by the end. Unfortunately, their growth has virtually ground to a halt since the beginning of the twenty-first century (Wright & Richardson 2012). While SBHCs were originally developed to increase access to physical health care for underserved youth, it was quickly apparent that mental health and psychosocial concerns needed to be addressed as well; subsequently, these became core components of the service delivery system of the vast majority of SBHCs (McNall, Lichty, & Mavis 2012). In addition to interventions in physical and mental health, prevention is a primary focus of SBHCs, which offer "a natural site" where healthcare professionals can develop positive relationships with healthy youth through modeling and education. Prevention activities address such issues as drug, alcohol, and tobacco use; depression and suicide; teen pregnancy and sexually transmitted diseases (STDs); and accidents and interpersonal violence (Armbruster et al. 1999:225).

Today, SBHCs are among the most common school-based services, with almost two thousand such centers in schools throughout the United States and over 40 percent located in Title I schools (Wright & Richardson 2012).

Although the primary focus of these clinics is often viewed as physical health care, many students come to the clinics with concerns about contraception, drug and alcohol use, physical and sexual abuse, and relationship issues (Adelman 1998; Soleimanpour et al. 2012). According to a national survey by the Substance Abuse and Mental Health Services Administration (2007), approximately three million youths received school-based services for behavioral or emotional problems during the 2005–2006 academic year (Franklin et al. 2012).

A central value of SBHCs is their accessibility, including ease of case management and follow-up (Clayton et al. 2012). While most SBHCs are located on school grounds, others follow the school-linked model where schools have formal relationships with community-based health centers, some of which offer transportation between schools and community health center appointments. Whether school-based or school-linked and off school grounds, these centers offer care "in an accessible, youth-friendly environment" (Soleimanpour et al. 2012:27).

Even though SBHCs are located in a range of communities, they are most often found in urban and rural low-income areas where families may have difficulties helping their children access medical appointments due to their own health constraints, lack of insurance, work obligations, and/or limited available transportation. Currently, about four million school-age youth are receiving care through SBHCs, with more than 70 percent of these being children of color (Christopher 2012). These SBHCs take a team-based approach to engage those relevant to a youth's life, including teachers, peers, parents, school staff, and clinicians, in the effort to provide preventive care and treatment to underserved children and adolescents (Clayton et al. 2012).

Specific services provided in each SBHC differ among communities and are determined collaboratively by service providers, the schools in which they are located, and the communities served. Because of their link with educational outcomes, the extent of health disparities negatively impacting urban minority youth, and the feasibility of implementing evidence-based school-based programs, the following are often strategic priorities of SBHCs: vision, asthma, teen pregnancy, aggression and violence, physical activity, breakfast, and inattention and hyperactivity (Basch 2010). SBHC staff are in a position not only to address these issues when they emerge, but also to implement prevention activities to minimize them and implement follow-up when they are diagnosed.

One reason an expansion of SBHCs has not occurred since 2000 is due to the unevenness of funding. Strong support for SBHCs has come from the W. K. Kellogg Foundation, which has "an intentional and sustained focus on multicultural and racial equity" (Christopher 2012:xvi). Other private foundations as well as some public monies (e.g., local health departments, state funding such as full-service school support in Florida; Maternal and Child Health block grants; and Medicaid) have been used for support, however most SBHCs operate without the security of ongoing funding (Armbruster et al. 1999). Under the Affordable Care Act ("Obamacare"), SBHCs received for the first time authorization as a federal program with vehicles for their expansion (Christopher 2012).

The SBHC movement benefits from a national organization committed to its growth through a multipronged approach. The School-Based Health Alliance (formerly the National Assembly of School Based Health Centers [NASBHC]), based in Washington, D.C., is funded primarily through grants and foundations. In 2011, NASBHC developed four teams that emphasize its priorities and whose leaders report to the organization's president. These include: the program and professional services team, policy and advocacy team, outreach and engagement team, and organizational performance team (National Assembly of School Based Health Centers 2011).

Rebell advocates for the government to support a series of SBHCs as pilots and then to phase them in over a larger geographic expanse if/once they prove successful. His plan includes the following as core services:

1 An annual early periodic screening, diagnostic, and treatment health checkup and necessary follow-up;
2 Treatment of minor, acute, and chronic medical conditions, with referrals to, and follow up for, specialty care;
3 Mental health assessments, crisis intervention, counseling, treatment and referral to a continuum of services, including emergency psychiatric care, community support programs, inpatient care, and outpatient programs;
4 Dental services;
5 Vision services (including eyeglasses prescriptions); and
6 Health education services (2013:2).

While more research is necessary, particularly related to cost-effectiveness and return on investment, there are initial results about the value of SBHCs in a range of areas. Not surprisingly, positive results have included a reduction in parents' time off work (Children's Aid Society National Center for Community Schools 2011), health concerns identified earlier (Green 2005), reductions in emergency room visits (Webber et al. 2003), and reduced hospitalizations (Clark & Grimaldi 2005). Guo et al. (2012) estimated that the "social benefits" of SBHC usage in Cincinnati translated to $3.35 for every $2.00 spent, and Van Cura (2010) found that SBHCs led to a significant reduction in class time lost to health needs. In addition, cost analysis of SBHCs shows they provide savings to Medicaid, mostly as a result of fewer prescriptions and asthma-related hospitalizations (Guo et al. 2012). Studies such as these are critical to the cause of securing additional, more stable funding for these centers.

FAMILY RESOURCE CENTERS

Another model for linking schools and community resources is the family resource center. FRCs often exist in schools, but also operate in community centers, hospitals, churches, or free-standing centers throughout the country and offer a range of services depending on need. FRCs provide "multiple services under a single roof; placing the services in a familiar, accessible, and user-friendly site; and focusing solutions on the family rather than on individuals or specific problems" (Plant & King 1995:290). The U.S. Department of Health and Human Services' Administration for Children and Families provides the following description of FRCs and list of sample services:

> Family Resource Centers are sometimes called family support centers, family centers, parent-child resource centers, family resource schools, or parent education centers. Family resource centers serve diverse populations and are located in a variety of community settings, including churches, school buildings, hospitals, housing projects, restored buildings, or new structures. Family resource centers promote both the strengthening of families through formal and informal support and the restoration of a strong sense of community. Services may include: parent skill training; drop-in centers, home visiting, job training, substance abuse prevention, violence

prevention, services for children with special needs, mental health or family counseling, childcare, literacy, respite and crisis care services, assistance with basic economic needs, and housing (https://www.childwelfare.gov/preventing/programs/types/familyresource.cfm).

A number of states have strong systems of FRCs. New York, for example, has several, with the specific location of each being determined by the presence of a high-need population and the lack of existing services in that area. A priority is placed on access and outreach to hard-to-reach families, including those in rural areas (http://ocfs.ny.gov/main/publications/Pub5071.pdf).

Kentucky may have the most robust system of FRCs, with over five hundred across the state (Kalafat 2004). FRCs in Kentucky have an interesting history. In 1989, the Kentucky Supreme Court responded to *Rose v. Council for Better Education, Inc.* by striking down the existing system for funding public schools as a violation of a state constitutional mandate that all students be provided with adequate education. This unprecedented "opportunity—or calamity, as some in Kentucky would say" (Carter 1992:42), led to a series of needed changes in the system of public education, including the governor's signing into law "the most comprehensive structural reform in the last decade," the Kentucky Education Reform Act (KERA) (Russo & Lindle 1993:179). KERA enacted sweeping changes in finance, governance, and curriculum and in attention to the physical and emotional needs of students. Its precepts include: all children should begin school ready to learn, parental and family involvement is critical for educational success, and the community should provide services to increase the educational capacities of families and schools. KERA encompasses a number of innovative reforms: the creation of FRCs for elementary schools and youth services centers for schools serving children over twelve years of age and the provision of funding to link schools and social service systems were among KERA's most comprehensive strategies. Today, Kentucky FRCs are staffed by a coordinator, an assistant, and volunteers. School districts begin the process of developing an FRC with a community needs assessment. In order to be eligible for funding, initially at least 20 percent of the children or youth enrolled in the school are required to be eligible for free and reduced lunch. However, all children, youth, and families in a funded school are eligible for services.

PARTNERSHIPS WITH BUSINESSES

While health and social services are the primary partners in school-linked services, businesses are increasingly partnering with schools in service provision and support in order to benefit the citizens and communities where they operate. Today's relationships between schools and businesses differ from those in the past, which often provided add-on programs with little positive impact on children, as opposed to operating in full partnership (Waddock 1999). In contrast, since the 1990s there has been a shift in focus on the interrelationships among schools, families, and businesses, leading to deeper partnerships positively affecting outcomes for children. The Hartford, Connecticut, schools, for example, are models for these partnerships. One Hartford principal stated, "'For awhile I had this perception that when you formed a partnership with a corporate powerhouse that they would be writing you large checks,' . . . [but] they also 'want good press and they want to get their people involved in doing things in the community'" (Pappano 2010:134). Partnering with Hartford businesses has not been a smooth process, but it has developed as schools and businesses have continued to expand their ideas of what each has to offer. Big business partnerships are not always about giving money, but instead sometimes about giving resources. They are involved in efforts such as planning and implementing fund-raisers and developing systems that enable company employees to tutor students—activities that build long-lasting depth and breadth into community-school partnerships.

Cincinnati schools have also built strong partnerships with local business. The CEO of Cincinnati Bell says, "At the end of the day, the shareholders don't care about my benevolent side. They care about profit and loss. . . . The best way to impact these factors . . . is by improving schools, and in turn, job opportunities and earning prospects for students and the people in the community this company serves" (quoted in Pappano 2010:128–129).

In New York City, the PENCIL model (pencil.org) links schools and business leaders in partnerships based on five focus areas including school leadership, family engagement, college and career readiness, student engagement, and school infrastructure. As of 2014, the program has served more than three hundred schools in New York City and has generated the Pencil Fellows program, which arranges summer internships with businesses for over one hundred students each year. The organization's data show that through matching business leaders with specific schools, they are making a difference in each of their focus areas (www.pencil.org).

EXPANDED SCHOOL MENTAL HEALTH

One of the more popular school-linked initiatives with a focus on mental health is the expanded school mental health (ESMH) model (see ESMH exemplar). While focusing on mental health, this model supports the implementation of a broad range of services designed to support the unique needs of the local school and community. According to Flaherty, Weist, and Warner (1996), achieving this often requires "going outside of the box" and the school building and engaging professionals in mental health care agencies as well as parents. The partnership between schools and community agencies is mutually advantageous, because schools receive increased support to address mental health issues through additional staff and added financial support while benefiting from the reduced stress and liability associated with being the sole provider of mental health care, and community agencies benefit from a new point of contact with otherwise inaccessible youth (Weist, Evans, & Lever 2003).

A description of expanded school mental health follows; it includes how the program began, what it looks like in practice, and its challenges and future directions, based on conversations with its founder, Mark Weist, PhD.

EXPANDED SCHOOL MENTAL HEALTH (ESMH/SMH) (Information provided by Mark Weist, Professor, Department of Psychology, University of South Carolina)

BRIEF OVERVIEW

The University of Maryland Center for School Mental Health (CSMH) was established in 1995 through federal funding from the Maternal and Child Health Bureau to advance school mental health programs in the United States. From the beginning, the center has focused on a "shared agenda" of schools, families, and community systems working together to promote a full continuum of mental health promotion, prevention, early intervention, and treatment in schools for youth in general and special education (see Weist 1997 for this definition of expanded school mental health). Mark Weist directed the center for fifteen years through 2010 and three rounds of federal funding. Funding for the center has since been renewed, and Nancy Lever and Sharon Stephan are now directors of the center.

ORIGINAL OBJECTIVE

The original objective was to advance training, practice, research, and policy in school mental health (SMH) and the interconnections among these realms.

PROCESS OF DEVELOPMENT

In 1995, Mark Weist initiated the program through the federal grant mechanism to establish one of two national centers for SMH with colleagues from the university and local stakeholders in education, child and adolescent mental health, family advocacy, and other systems.

COLLABORATIVE ACTIVITIES/STRUCTURES

Embracing a community of practice framework (see Wenger, McDermott, & Snyder 2002), the development, growth, and improvement of the center has been based on the foundation of strong and inclusive (of all relevant stakeholders) collaborative relationships, which set the stage for systematic work (e.g., advancing evidence-based practices in schools).

TARGET POPULATION

(E)SMH works with students from pre-kindergarten through high school.

FEATURED PROGRAM

Patapsco Elementary and Middle Schools joined the University of Maryland School Mental Health Program (SMHP) in 1995; this partnership is still ongoing. The SMHP was established in 1989 in four schools (two middle and two high schools) connected to school-based health centers in which mental health concerns quickly became the number one reason for referral. The SMHP grew to include around ten schools in the early 1990s, around fifteen by 1995, and at present serves students in twenty-six Baltimore schools. Since 1995, it has worked collaboratively with the CSMH in delivering the most promising evidence-based practices in schools and in deeply exploring issues related to the effective delivery of these practices within a framework emphasizing high quality and ongoing youth, family, and other stakeholder involvement. Related to leadership of the principal, enthusiasm for SMH services, and location in a neighborhood characterized by very high need, Patapsco became a key partner school with the CSMH in demonstrating the promise of SMH and strategies to overcome barriers. For example, this school was a part of the Excellence in School Mental Health initiative funded by four local foundations (Abell,

Blaustein, Krieger, and Strauss Foundations) and focused on consistent and coordinated implementation of evidence-based practices in the areas of broad school health and wellness promotion (tier 1, universal), prevention and early intervention (tier 2, targeted), and treatment (tier 3, intensive). Most notably, as part of this initiative and under the guidance of SMHP clinicians, the school dramatically increased family involvement from just a few families consistently participating in efforts to improve school environment and support students, to more than fifty families doing the same, garnering the attention of city leaders including the superintendent of schools and the mayor. In addition, Patapsco was one of about thirty schools piloting and implementing the PATHS to PAX intervention, an integrated intervention reflecting training of students in social and emotional learning skills and participating in the Good Behavior Game. These initiatives led to documented student improvements, including increased attendance, reduced behavioral problems, and, for some students, stronger academic achievement.

LOCATION OF SERVICES

Programs/services are school-based and located in neighborhoods characterized by high levels of violence and socioeconomic challenges.

SERVICE PROVIDERS/PARTNERS

University of Maryland faculty, postdoctoral fellows, and staff (typically clinical social workers) provide the services. Throughout the nation, the full array of mental health providers, including social workers, psychologists (school, clinical, counseling), professional counselors, child and adolescent psychiatrists, and other staff (e.g., nurses with mental health training, marriage and family therapists) are involved in the provision of expanded SMH services.

TYPES OF SERVICES DELIVERED

Services include: school climate enhancement, participation on teams, organizing and bringing resources into the school, prevention groups, working collaboratively with educators to improve classroom behavior, focused and brief individual, group, and family therapies, more intensive therapy services, case management, and helping link students/families to other programs and services in the community.

FUNDING

Child and adolescent mental health systems can very readily outstation staff into schools and use existing funding mechanisms, including Medicaid. Some communities (e.g., Minneapolis) have made strong connections with private insurers, but this is an area in need of significant enhancement. Other mechanisms of funding include: school reallocation of resources to enable an expanded SMH approach, allocations from local health departments and other youth-serving systems, and federal grant mechanisms (e.g., the Safe Schools–Healthy Students initiative).

IMPLEMENTATION CHALLENGES

SMH is a new construct, and schools are often not used to providing this range of mental health services. Consequently, SMH clinicians may feel unwelcome and not become integrated; in turn, they often have gaps in knowledge and training to work effectively within the culture of schools.

EVALUATION

The center was, and is, evaluated based on usage of its resources by a range of stakeholders, in addition to qualitative research on perceived impact. SMH programs are evaluated in relation to their role in assisting students to meet goals associated with school success, such as improved attendance, assignment completion, behavior, and academic performance.

FUTURE DIRECTIONS

SMH programs are not reliably administered within communities and states, so moving toward more consistent implementation is crucial. Bridging the gap between research and practice is critical, including moving towards strategies and supports to make evidence-based practices achievable. Another central theme is working collaboratively with positive behavioral interventions and supports (PBIS) to build multiple tiers of high-quality behavioral and mental health services and supports. There is a need for greater family and stakeholder involvement in programs, as well as social marketing to integrate SMH into the fabric of society as a needed and effective approach to reducing barriers to student learning and assuring their school and life success.

FULL-SERVICE COMMUNITY SCHOOLS

The U.S. Department of Education defines a full-service community school as an "elementary or secondary school that works with its local educational agency and community-based organizations, nonprofit organizations, and other public or private entities to provide a coordinated and integrated set of comprehensive academic, social, and health services that respond to the needs of its students, students' family members, and community members" (*Federal Register* 5/6/2014). Social worker Jane Addams and educator John Dewey are two of the primary reformers credited with laying the foundation for the community school movement at the turn of the twentieth century. They came from different disciplinary backgrounds and both valued the idea of schools as community hubs. Throughout the United States and in other parts of the world, everything from pilot programs to full-scale community school efforts are gaining increasing support in the twenty-first century. In his prior role as CEO of the Chicago Public Schools, U.S. Secretary of Education Arne Duncan developed and expanded an impressive network of community schools in that city. In his more recent role as Secretary of Education in Washington, he continued to articulate his support for community schools. In a speech to the U.S. Chamber of Commerce in 2009, he stated, "I'm a big believer in community schools—keeping school buildings open for 12 hours a day and opening up the computer lab, the library and the gym on weekends for our children and their families" (Duncan 2009). At Harvard University in 2012, Secretary Duncan again touted this effort, announcing his support for "high-quality out-of-school programs, including full-service community schools" (Duncan 2012). Similar efforts and sentiments to those expressed by Secretary Duncan at the federal level are also occurring in at the state level. In 2012, New York Governor Andrew Cuomo created an Education Reform Commission to recommend reforms in education. The second of the commission's 2013 eight initial reforms is to "create statewide models for 'Community Schools' that use schools as a community hub to improve access to public, non-profit, and private services/resources, like health and social services, for students and their families" (New York, Education Reform Commission 2013).

The primary drive for full-service community schools is an interest in equity, particularly in low-income communities. The community schools concept reflects John Dewey's theory that "the neighborhood school can function as the core neighborhood institution that provides comprehensive services, galvanizes other community institutions and groups, and helps solve the myriad problems schools and communities confront in a rapidly changing world" (Harkavy et al. 2013:525). The Children's Aid Society (2011) delineates the realities that make community schools much needed: persistent poverty; educational inequity, where poor children have diminished access to educational resources and opportunities than their peers; a growing achievement gap between minority and white students; changing family patterns, leaving many families too overwhelmed to participate fully in their children's learning and development; inadequate community supports, leaving children unsupervised and unsafe in their neighborhoods; increasing immigration linked with an increasing proportion of children who are English language learners; and worries about school violence. Cummings, Dyson, and Todd (2011) deduce that unlike typical schools that interact with their students' parents solely in relation to their children, full-service community schools are less "school-centric," seeing parents as "customers" and community members.

The Coalition for Community Schools (CCS) defines a community school as both a place and a set of partnerships between the school and other community resources. A community school holds an "integrated focus on academics, health and social services, youth and community development, and community engagement leads to improved student learning, stronger families, and healthier communities. Schools become centers of the community and are open to everyone—all day, every day, evenings, and weekends." (Shah et al. 2009:5). The hallmark of community schools is that they function as centers and social hubs of community life (Adams 2010; Benson, Harkavy, & Puckett 2007; Harkavy et al. 2013).

Community schools develop out of needs not only for educational reform, but also for community development and equity. While the interest in educational reform through community schools is based on a belief that in order to maximize students' learning, their well-being, families, and neighborhoods need strengthening (Children's Aid Society 2011), such schools offer many other benefits beyond educational ones. Green (2005) cites how community schools support economic development strategies through hiring community residents; providing entrepreneurial education, adult basic education and ESL, and college courses; and partnering with financial institutions and boosting community businesses. In addition, community schools are defined not by their distinct components, but by how their components work together to reduce the fragmentation that characterizes our human service system. As the Children's Aid Society says, "The real hallmark of a community school is the transformational effect of all the ingredients as they interact with one another, everyday" (2011:5). In England, the development of extended schools involved similar reciprocal relationships such that "services and activities were not simply bolted on to an otherwise unchanged school, but were seen as central to the way the school tackled inequalities in educational achievement, and to a wider social role through which the school contributed to the well-being of the communities it served" (Cummings, Dyson, & Todd 2011:53).

Developing Community Schools

A healthy full-service community school is one that grows out of a collaborative community effort. Thus, it involves a model of "cross-boundary leadership," whereby leaders from all groups associated with the community school "share responsibility for student and school performance and . . . work collectivity toward common outcomes" (Adams 2010:13). As Cummings, Dyson, and Todd state, the transition to a full-service school "demands a willingness to learn, to take risks, and to question fundamental assumptions. It means rethinking how the school is managed, funded and staffed. . . . The extent to which schools are successful in this transition is likely to depend to a significant degree on the support they receive from national and local policy frameworks" (2011:71). These schools are flexible enough to make adjustments as their residents, service systems, and communities change. Because they see community residents as customers with choices and rights, these schools focus not only on solving problems for children and families, "but also [on] getting students involved in community projects so that they build a sense of pride in the locality, and develop their skills as entrepreneurs so that they can develop new kinds of employment in the area" (Cummings Dyson, & Todd 2011:34). That is why no two full-service/community/extended schools look the same: they develop in response to a specific community's needs and resources.

Neighborhood Services in Community Schools

Critical to the success of a community school is the surrounding neighborhood's ability to drive the school's agenda. This suggests that programs should be distinctive and vary from one another while also remaining open to change as they adapt to best meet local community needs. Despite their differences, most community schools benefit by a community school director who functions as the right hand of the principal (Children's Aid Society 2011). In addition, most also include some or all of the following components:

1 Additional learning opportunities: afterschool and summer programs, longer school days, and early childhood programs.
2 Health services: primary health care, dental care, mental health services, nutrition counseling, and referrals to community providers.
3 Family support and engagement: family literacy, adult education, job skills training, and English as a Second Language classes.
4 Coordination of services: a dedicated coordinator or support teams to handle logistics and match services with student needs.
5 Data systems: tracking student needs and progress, measuring academic success, and capturing early warning signs of academic failure (Chang & Lawyer 2012:4–5).

Exemplary Full-Service Community Schools

As detailed in chapter 8, full-service community schools almost always grow out of a diverse composite of funding streams. Their development is sometimes initiated by a nonprofit organization and at other times by a city, county, or other entity. This chapter includes exemplary full-service community schools that have grown out of three different sectors: nonprofit, school district/city, and county. Within these sectors, all initiatives involve a combination of support in their development and ongoing programming from multiple sectors. We feature details of three nonprofit initiatives, including Beacons, Children's Aid Society, and Elev8; three school district/city-led initiatives in Hartford, Connecticut, Tulsa, Oklahoma, and in and around Sandy, Utah; and the county-wide initiative in Multnomah County, Oregon, called SUN Service Systems. Reviewing the details of these exemplary efforts profiled from conversations with program leaders provides opportunities for readers to understand the wide range of ways these initiatives are developed and sustained.

The three nonprofit-led initiatives described below have many similarities, but also areas where one may place more emphasis than another. For example, sometimes the initiator is the primary nonprofit partner, as is the case with Children's Aid Society, whereas with others, like the Beacons and Elev8 Chicago, a community-based organization (CBO) participates as prime partner. Both the Beacons and Elev8 currently focus on middle schools, although Beacons have historically worked across school levels, while Children's Aid Society seeks to support a mix of elementary, middle, and high schools. Elev8 is the newest of the initiatives, beginning less than ten years ago, while both the Beacons and Children's Aid Society were established in the 1990s. All initiatives emphasize community voice and needs assessments to drive programming. The Beacons are known for their strong youth-led programs. The Children's Aid Society has made a name for itself with its technical assistance, helping schools and communities in the United States and in other parts of the world to develop community schools. Elev8 has developed a particularly strong and successful model of parent mentoring. Hence the examples below show a range of ways that nonprofits develop, mount, implement, evaluate, and fund community schools.

BEACON COMMUNITY SCHOOLS (Information provided by Sarah Zeller-Berkman, Director, Beacons National Strategy)

BRIEF OVERVIEW

Beacon community schools function as school-based community centers. Currently, over 180,000 young people are served by Beacons across the country in locations that include New York City, San Francisco, Denver, and Minneapolis. While Beacons serve young people in school, they also have a commitment to opening up the infrastructure of the school to the broader community to serve people from six to sixty years old. The core program areas vary by city, but usually include those that support education both for youth and for adult learners, such as athletic programs, arts-based offerings, English as a Second Language (ESL), etc. Ideally, Beacons meet the needs of their own community. When they began in the 1990s, community needs assessments were conducted to determine what offerings community members wanted to supplement (e.g., child care). Presently, the Beacons in New York City (where the largest number of Beacons are located) have a middle school focus, addressing critical transitions and issues confronting young people in these middle school years and supporting them in the transition to high school.

ORIGINAL OBJECTIVE

Beacons were originally developed to provide a space for families to come together and organize, access services, and attempt to ameliorate some of the variations in privilege by introducing quality afterschool programming for young people. Sixteen of the Beacons in New York City have preventive programs that involve funding from the Administration for Children's Services (ACS) and support young people who are in jeopardy of being brought into the ACS system by providing them with services in their school with minimum stigma.

Some Beacons have physical health components within the school, including clinics for prevention and treatment. Those without their own health services refer people to the services they need.

When the Beacon Trust started in 1991, community activism and outreach were instilled as core components of the Beacon model, focusing on soliciting needs from community members and youth-led efforts. Today, a variety of leadership programs exist in many different Beacons. For example, a program focused on elementary school students creates potential for a model where high school students work with middle school students, and middle school students work with elementary school students. Central to the Beacons movement is involving young people in community development work through advocacy.

PROCESS OF DEVELOPMENT

In 1991, ten Beacons were funded in the most disadvantaged areas of New York City. In San Francisco in 1994, children's advocates demanded that the Office of Family and Children's Service start Beacons there. In 1998, the Wallace Foundation funded another national replication, which then expanded to other cities. By the turn of the century, there were eighty Beacons in New York. Currently, Beacons operate in New York City, Denver, Minneapolis, and San Francisco. Cities were selected based on a high population of incarcerated individuals, which was attributed to the 1980s crack epidemic that ravaged New York City in particular. Many Beacon community schools have had longstanding partnerships among communities, schools, and organizations. Even though principals have come and gone, the Beacons have remained, meaning that many children of alumni currently attend a Beacon school. Beacons operate as hubs for organizations to collaborate and offer needed services.

COLLABORATIVE ACTIVITIES/STRUCTURES

To initiate the process, a lead CBO applies to be a Beacon with a particular school. Ideally, the school and the director of the Beacon (an employee of a CBO) conduct collaborative planning and implementation. There are also partnerships with the lead CBO running the Beacon and other CBOs in the neighborhood to co-locate services and supports. They work with the Beacon director, assistant director, and office staff employed by the CBO to determine space assignments. In best-case scenarios, Beacon initiatives have collaborative structures on the systems level (i.e., between their departments of education and their youth services and health departments). In San Francisco, people come to the table from private foundations and public city agencies to serve together on a steering committee that guides the work of the Beacons alongside Beacon providers. In Minneapolis, youth-adult partnerships guide the work of Beacons at both the site and the systems level. The level and depth of these collaborations vary based on the Beacon or a specific initiative. In all cases, partnerships are a cornerstone of the model.

TARGET POPULATION

In New York City, the eighty Beacon schools offer services to people six years of age and older. Many Beacon programs have offerings for seniors, but the focus is on youth. Beacons have a historical commitment to serving elementary, middle and high school youth. Beacons also employ youth as staff, giving young people opportunities to work or volunteer at their Beacon while in college. Beacons serve other community members, young and old, who may not be connected to the school. The Beacon model opens up the public school infrastructure to the community, effectively making it a community hub.

FEATURED PROGRAM

The New York City Center for Family Life has a Beacon program in Sunset Park that has been functioning for thirty years using a social group work model. It provides services from 6 to 9 p.m. for all ages, with a wide array of programming, including intergenerational knitting and cooking classes. It also has a strong counselor-in-training (CIT) program, through which young people develop leadership skills and acquire roles and responsibilities in their Beacon communities. And it provides training on working with youths and offers them their own space to reflect on various issues. After years of advocacy efforts, the Sunset Park Beacon successfully acquired the space and funds to open a local high school.

LOCATION OF SERVICES

Beacon programs are largely school-based. When needed services are unavailable on site, schools coordinate referrals to off-site community programs. There is a new initiative in New York City called Cornerstones that uses a Beacon model in public housing facilities. This initiative is expanding rapidly—there are seventy-five Cornerstones across New York City.

SERVICE PROVIDERS/PARTNERS

All Beacons are led by a CBO; this can vary from a small local organization to a large one, like Good Shepherd, which has services across New York City. While there are variations, all Beacons partner with organizations in the community and have co-locators as part of the model and mandate.

TYPES OF SERVICES

There is a strong focus on developing individuals, but there is also a critical focus on developing the community, including family engagement. Beacons also provide a wide array of afterschool programming, including academic support, exercise classes, fitness centers, free gym space, karate classes, crafts, etc., in addition to youth and adult partnerships for community improvement work.

The Beacon leadership program often employs college students who have been part of the Beacon program of leadership for a number of years. Even though they are eighteen years old, these young people often have five to seven years of experience as part of the Beacon social group work methodology. Many Beacons around the city have "ladders to leadership" programs (scaffolded youth leadership and employment programs that support young people through critical transitions between middle and high school and high school and college). While the extent of intentional leadership training varies across the Beacons, the commitment to youth leadership development has been a core program component from the beginning.

While some Beacons are connected to school-based health centers, there is opportunity for greater intentionality about using the Beacon as a health service hub or referral center. San Francisco has used their Beacon infrastructure to implement health initiatives around the city. There are some ACS health programs funded at sixteen New York City sites, which offer preventive services and mental health support for families in addition to other Beacon services. This is an area the national network hopes to expand.

All Beacon programs are open six days and evenings per week. Intergenerational programming is generally open to the community from 6 to 9 p.m. Programming from 3 to 6 p.m. focuses services mainly on elementary, middle, and high school students. There is a reciprocal relationship between what the community can offer to the school and what the school offers by becoming a hub of the community. Beacon staff engage in local outreach to increase involvement, and as part of this work, there is attention to cultural competency. For example, a Beacon in Minneapolis is located in a school serving a predominantly Native American population. In a San Francisco school, the programming reflects the needs of a large Pacific Islander population. Beacons have incredibly rich cultural programming, though some better attend to cultural differences than others. Beacons often hire from within the community, and Beacon youth often become Beacon staff.

FUNDING

For cities with a dedicated funding stream, financial resources for individual Beacons come through a request-for-proposal (RFP) process from the cities. Cities that do not receive city money for their Beacon initiatives raise money through private foundations and/or apply for federal grants, such as 21st Century Community Learning Centers.

IMPLEMENTATION CHALLENGES

In New York City, there was a period of time when Beacons were widely accessible. Presently, however, the city does not fund the basic model requirements for running a Beacon. Sites augmenting city funds with other monetary resources have more comprehensive, higher-quality programs accessible by the entire community. Meanwhile, sites that are not well funded are unable to fund extra staff time for meetings, where there is potential for discussing challenges and proposing potential solutions. If Beacons exceed a certain number of hours, they are required to offer paid health benefits, which many of them cannot afford. Cities with fewer Beacons to manage have an easier time supporting program structure and operate at a higher quality. In New York City, there is great variability in quality among the eighty Beacons depending on the lead agency, available funding, and the program manager. In addition, these Beacon community schools have wait lists for the Beacon services a family can access.

EVALUATION

Beacon initiatives in each city collect evaluation data. The national network seeks to measure certain constructs across cities, including data at the student level and data from community index surveys and surveys measuring the quality of the partnerships between schools and the CBOs. This data collection began in spring 2014.

FUTURE DIRECTIONS

Future goals include: better systems level integration in all Beacon cities, cross city evaluation, ladders to leadership program models in more Beacons, using the Beacon infrastructure to support larger community school initiatives, expansion of the Beacon model into public housing community centers, and the use of the Beacon infrastructure across the country to initiate large scale community-youth development initiatives.

Because Beacons exist as part of a national network, there are always opportunities for individual schools to learn from one another. For example, a youth leadership retreat in Minneapolis enabled young people to spearhead conversations about issues and structures that empower and expand their own voices. When retreat participants went back to their own cities, they were able to apply what they had learned about youth organization to their communities.

THE CHILDREN'S AID SOCIETY'S (CAS) COMMUNITY SCHOOLS & NATIONAL CENTER FOR COMMUNITY SCHOOLS (Information provided by Jane Quinn, Vice President for Community Schools, and Director, National Center for Community Schools)

BRIEF OVERVIEW

The Children's Aid Society partners with the New York City Department of Education in sixteen public schools located in four low-income NYC neighborhoods (East Harlem, South Bronx, Washington Heights, Staten Island). This partnership is now in its twenty-second year. Since 1994, the CAS has operated the National Center for Community Schools, a practice-based technical assistance center that assists educators and community organizations that want to learn how to work together in a more comprehensive and integrated way.

ORIGINAL OBJECTIVE

The CAS's community schools seek to promote children's learning and healthy development in ways that prepare them for productive adulthood. This objective is aligned with the overall mission of the CAS, which is "to help children in poverty succeed and thrive." (Note: the CAS is New York City's oldest and largest youth-serving organization, having been founded in 1853; it currently serves seventy thousand New York City children and their families each year and has an annual operating budget of $110 million.)

PROCESS OF DEVELOPMENT

The CAS developed the community schools strategy in a strong partnership with the (then) New York City Board of Education and the City of New York through a series of strategic planning meetings and discussions that started in 1987. At that time, city planners had identified the northern Manhattan neighborhood of Washington Heights as the most underserved area of New York City, as a result of significant demographic changes.

After five years of joint planning with the city government and board of education, Children's Aid opened Intermediate School 218 in Washington Heights as its first community school in 1992. Since that time, CAS has added schools to its portfolio on a regular basis, with a view toward responding to unmet need while also managing growth. It seeks to maintain a mix of elementary, middle, and high schools.

COLLABORATIVE ACTIVITIES/STRUCTURES

The CAS community schools follow a lead agency model, with Children's Aid serving as both a provider and broker of supports, services and opportunities. The CAS is fully integrated into each school's governance and decision-making structure, such as the school leadership team, pupil personnel team, school safety committee, and principal's cabinet.

TARGET POPULATION

The primary target population is students at the school and their families. Some schools offer teen programs for graduates of the school and other neighborhood adolescents; and some schools offer adult education classes and community events that are open to area residents.

FEATURED PROGRAM

Children's Aid has become nationally recognized for its extensive and highly successful parent and family engagement programs, which are an integral part of its community schools. The basic model has four key components: parent resource centers; parent coordinators; adult education and training; and leadership development. Building on the success of this basic approach, Children's Aid subsequently created a comprehensive parent leadership program that serves the Washington Heights neighborhood and annually graduates over five hundred parents, who are recognized for taking a sequence of courses that include educational, vocational, recreational, and public service components as part of the Ercilia Pepin Parent Leadership Institute.

LOCATION OF SERVICES

Most of the services are school-based, but Children's Aid also developed a school-linked model in the South Bronx, which involves providing medical and dental services for community school students at the CAS's Bronx Family Center, which is located within walking distance of several CAS community schools.

SERVICE PROVIDERS/PARTNERS

The New York City Department of Education and the Children's Aid Society are the lead providers/partners in these community schools. Additional partners are recruited and managed by Children's Aid in its role as the lead agency, and these partners vary from school to school. An example of a long-term partnership recruited and managed by Children's Aid is a fifteen-year relationship with the Alvin Ailey Dance Theatre, which results in a six-week summer camp for middle school students conducted at the Mirabal Sisters Campus, a community school in Washington Heights. Another vibrant partnership involves Helen Keller International, which provides vision screening and services to all CAS community schools. In this partnership, Children's Aid manages the scheduling and other coordination, while Helen Keller staff provides the optical services (vision screening, prescribing and making glasses, referral for ophthalmology services).

TYPES OF SERVICES DELIVERED

Services offered at CAS community schools include: out-of-school time (afterschool, summer, and holiday) programs; early childhood (Early Head Start and Head Start) programs; parent engagement and family support programs; medical, dental, mental health, and social services; and community and economic development. The service mix varies from school to school, depending on need and available resources.

FUNDING

CAS community schools receive support from a wide array of public and private sources. Major public sources include Medicaid and Child Health-Plus, Early Head Start and Head Start (federal) grants, the 21st Century Community Learning Centers program, New York State Advantage After-School and Extended-Day/Violence Prevention funding, and New York City Out-of-School Time funding. Major private sources include United Way, foundations, corporations, and individuals.

IMPLEMENTATION CHALLENGES

CAS's key challenge is the ever-changing operating context, which includes such factors as principal turnover, governance and policy changes at the district level, and the vagaries of funding.

EVALUATION

Using a number of third party evaluators over a twenty-two-year period, CAS community schools have shown greater success than comparison schools in academics, student attendance, faculty attendance, school climate, parent and family engagement, mental and physical health, positive youth development, and school readiness.

FUTURE DIRECTIONS

Children's Aid recently undertook a Community Schools 2.0 strategic planning process, with strategies for strengthening its work in the following areas:

1 Whole school transformation: a commitment to serve *all* students in a community school and to address school-wide issues such as attendance, wellness, and school climate.
2 Relationships with teachers: making sure teachers understand the community schools strategy, are aware of how to connect their students with CAS

supports/services, collaborate on parent engagement, and learn together via professional development.

3 Partner coordination: addressing a full range of documented needs by identifying, enrolling, integrating, and coordinating multiple partners (internal and external).
4 Shared leadership/governance: full integration of the CAS and other partners into school governance structures and meaningful, timely involvement in school planning.
5 Data-driven decision-making: a comprehensive and regularly occurring needs assessment process and regular monitoring of key indicators as the basis for the allocation and organization of resources.

In addition, the CAS plans to continue adding schools to its portfolio in its four target neighborhoods, with an initial focus on the South Bronx (Morrisania neighborhood).

ELEV8 (Information provided by Maritza Guzman, Director, Fiscal Sponsorship and Project Management, Public Interest Projects)

BRIEF OVERVIEW

Elev8 currently operates in four states and builds on core elements that research has clearly linked with student achievement and success. Those elements, or pillars, are: extended-day learning; family and community support services; school-based health care; and family and community engagement.

ORIGINAL OBJECTIVE

Elev8's objective has been to create high-quality community schools by joining high-need communities and resources to create local solutions that support students, families, and schools.

PROCESS OF DEVELOPMENT

Elev8, a full-service community school model, was launched with financial support from the Atlantic Philanthropies in 2007 under the name "Integrated Services in Schools." Eventually rebranded as "Elev8", it currently operates in three districts in the state of New Mexico, as well as in Oakland, California, Chicago, Illinois, and Baltimore, Maryland.

Implementation began in New Mexico in 2007, with all four sites operating by 2009. Atlantic Philanthropies used due diligence to make its site selections, then gave each site time to plan, build partnerships, and create structure for running a multipronged middle school initiative. The sites were selected from among thirty-five cities and twenty-two states based on criteria that included socioeconomic need and disparity, health profiles, academic performance, and neighborhood crime data. Some participating schools represent zip codes with some of the lowest life expectancies and highest rates of asthma hospitalizations, sexually transmitted disease diagnosis and teen births in the nation. In addition, each site presented attractive potential, including strong institutional infrastructure, a history of addressing issues, a track record of success, local funding to match Atlantic's, willing school districts, and connections to political institutions for advocacy successes.

COLLABORATIVE ACTIVITIES/STRUCTURES

The Elev8 sites share a commitment to a community-school model and have many partnerships with local providers and funders. Elev8 is a flexible model that builds on local strengths. All four sites are structured differently:

1. In New Mexico, the first Elev8 site is part of Youth Development, a large nonprofit organization, and works in five schools in three widely varying school districts—in Albuquerque, on the Laguna Pueblo Indian Reservation, and the rural Gadsden Independent School District.
2. In Oakland, Elev8 is a program of Safe Passages, a nonprofit founded in 1998 that represents a unique public/private partnership committed to serve vulnerable populations in Alameda County; over forty-five public and private agencies collaborate to provide services in five school communities.
3. In Chicago, Elev8 is a program of the Local Initiatives Support Corporation's Chicago office (LISC/Chicago); services are delivered by five separate community-based organizations that have longstanding relationships with LISC, and each partners with a middle school, locally based federally qualified health center, center for working family site, and after school providers.
4. In Baltimore, Elev8 is an initiative of East Baltimore Development, a nonprofit entity overseeing the redevelopment of a large section of the city near Johns Hopkins Hospital.

TARGET POPULATION

Elev8 intentionally focuses on middle school students since research shows that the transition from middle school to high school is a particularly critical turning point. How smoothly students make this transition is strongly related not only to the likelihood of finishing high school but also to the odds of attending and succeeding in college. Young people who do well in middle school are much more likely to do well in high school, go on to graduate, and have healthy, productive futures.

FEATURED PROGRAM

Elev8 has had a long list of programmatic successes at all of its sites. In Chicago, the Parent Mentor Program provides stipends and training to parents seeking to become classroom paraprofessionals. This cadre of parents assists teachers two to three hours a day, four days a week, typically working with small groups of students who need extra instructional help. On the fifth day, these parent/mentors receive professional development, and the program encourages them to complete their high school GED or take part in college classes, training, or other career-building activities.

More than one thousand parents have participated in the program, which has proven to be a valuable part of Elev8. Teachers and principals report that having parents in the classroom has led to better discipline. Parents become more engaged in their children's schools through the program; many participants have gone on to join the school PTAs or local school councils, and some take part in advocacy efforts embraced by the schools. Finally, parents act as a cultural "bridge" to link teachers with residents of the community.

LOCATION OF SERVICES

Services are provided primarily at the Elev8 schools, although parents are sometimes referred to outside providers. This is particularly true for financial services, as parents tend to prefer receiving these services outside of the school building.

SERVICE PROVIDERS/PARTNERS

Each site has developed a long list of local partners—foundations, public agencies, non-profit service providers, federally qualified health centers, etc.

TYPES OF SERVICES DELIVERED

Elev8 sites have developed their own strategies for implementing the four pillars of the initiative—extended-day learning, family and community support services, school-based health care, and family and community engagement. Local context matters, and implementation in each school is different. Each site designed its program to specifically address issues in the community while also taking advantage of local opportunities.

For example, each of the five participating Chicago public schools is partnered with a lead agency that works with scores of local organizations on quality-of-life issues including education, family supports, public safety, healthcare, and opportunities for youth. Those agencies have been highly effective at engaging Elev8 parents and community members in all activities. Elev8 Chicago helps support the extension of the school day with afternoon, weekend, and summer programs, including the International Baccalaureate curriculum, as well as high-quality mentoring and leadership programs for youth. New Mexico and Oakland have broken down barriers to parent involvement by building new levels of trust and creating opportunities that respond to parents' schedules, draw on their talents, and respond to their concerns. For example, schools have increased parent participation by holding meetings on Saturday mornings, creating parent resource rooms in schools, inviting parents to apply their talents to minor school repairs, engaging parents in helping principals solve pressing problems, and focusing on positive aspects of their child's school experience.

In Baltimore, Elev8 provides and supports enrichment activities after school and during the summer months, as well as high-quality mentoring programs through Big Brothers Big Sisters of the Greater Chesapeake. Students receive academic support and opportunities to participate in enrichment activities ranging from soccer to debate. The program also seeks to promote a positive school climate to improve social interactions and peer relationships, including the creation of a safe space for service learning and leadership development. Elev8 Baltimore empowers students to take control of their own health needs by offering on-site health services. In partnership with Baltimore Medical Systems, offered services include immunizations and family planning, dental, vision, and mental health services; activities such as extracurricular sports programs and programs in visual and performing arts; nutrition programs and health education (including reproductive health).

All of the sites have created opportunities for parents and other family members to engage with the schools. In some cases, sites have helped organize parents to advocate for a variety of efforts such as school construction funding. The sites also provide a range of support services to parents, including connections to workforce training and tax-preparation services.

FUNDING

With major funding from the Atlantic Philanthropies phasing out, all four Elev8 sites are focused on securing new sources of funding to sustain their work.

IMPLEMENTATION CHALLENGES

Elev8 is an ambitious initiative that seeks to establish a strong model for building community schools focused effectively on middle grades. Implementing such a complex program brought many challenges that the sites have had to grapple with and overcome.

In Chicago, implementation was strengthened by an intensive community engagement process, where dozens of members of the community took part in planning sessions led by the community-based organizations overseeing the Elev8 work in each of five schools. Over three months, the planning groups, ranging in size from 40 to 125, determined goals for the academic, health, social supports, and parental engagement aspects of Elev8. The process was especially valuable in building interest and commitment among parents and community members, who had a meaningful role in shaping the initiative. The process also strengthened the relationships between the CBOs and the schools' leaders. That local buy-in has proven to be extremely important in sustaining the original vision and goals of Elev8 Chicago during the past several years, as all five original principals have moved on to new jobs and the Chicago school system has undergone repeated leadership turnover.

"A lot of the community folks who did that initial planning are still involved. They have helped maintain the fidelity to the program," says Chris Brown, who has directed Elev8 Chicago from its beginning. "They're not rigid about it, but there is fidelity to what we originally intended."

While all four sites faced obstacles, Elev8 New Mexico's implementation was especially challenging, as it was the first site launched and focused on three far-flung areas of the state. Atlantic Philanthropies initially selected the New Mexico Community Foundation to lead the implementation of what eventually became Elev8. Leaders of the effort selected the districts to move into (one urban, one rural, and one on an Indian reservation) and identified five schools to involve.

In retrospect, leaders of the New Mexico implementation have identified several lessons about the implementation:

1 A year-long planning process would have positioned the initiative better than the three-month process that was used. More time would have helped create "buy-in" by principals and others in the school systems.
2 Early on, the initiative did not do enough work to engage the local community in shaping the program; that meant, in turn, that community members had to accept a program that had been designed largely by "higher-ups" not directly involved in the community.
3 The long distances between the three school districts created logistical issues for providing technical assistance or management support.

EVALUATION

From Elev8's inception, evaluation has been a critical piece of the initiative, both to gauge effectiveness and adjust the program according to data. Atlantic Philanthropies established a two-tier evaluation process for Elev8 at both the national and local level. The foundation selected Public/Private Ventures as Elev8's national evaluator, and in later years, after the dissolution of Public/Private Ventures, Research for Action and McClanahan Associates assumed that role. Atlantic recognized that evaluations do not always reflect the complexity of a multicomponent, multiservice initiative like Elev8; that it would take time for the initiative to mature to the point where it would have measurable positive impacts on students; and that it would become even more challenging to prove that Elev8 had generated the positive outcomes.

In setting up the evaluation process, Elev8 required all parties to commit to communication and accountability, sharing information and pooling their expertise to address issues as soon as they arise.

Atlantic brought in local evaluators to three of the four Elev8 state sites to assess implementation. In Baltimore, the Annie E. Casey Foundation provided support for a local evaluation of the local Elev8 effort. The local evaluations carefully tracked implementation progress and interviewed a range of Elev8 stakeholders, including principals, parents, and program partners. These early evaluations provided rich information to site leaders looking to make midcourse adjustments to strengthen their programs.

In recent years, the national and local evaluators have begun to make more data available to the public, such as the number of children and parents engaged in Elev8 activities or the number of children being vaccinated at school-based health centers. The evaluation structure has provided, and will continue to provide, information that is critical to the grantees, as well as produce lessons for the field and decision-makers at the national level.

Beginning in 2012, Elev8 sites have been working with the national and local evaluation teams to measure and report on their progress against programmatic benchmarks in areas such as student success, school climate, and family and community engagement. Also, a new phase of evaluation began in 2013, in which the evaluation teams collect information that will demonstrate how and if Elev8 improves the lives of students. Such measures will focus not solely on educational success, because measuring Elev8's value is a more complicated and nuanced task. Instead, the evaluators will focus on understanding how Elev8 helps students advance successfully through ninth grade and what developmental supports (such as adult support, parent involvement, leadership opportunities, and healthy living) Elev8 affords them to help them succeed.

ELEV8 ACHIEVEMENTS

Student Achievement

1 More than seven thousand youth have benefitted from Elev8's out-of-school-time learning programs.
2 Seventy percent of youth say Elev8's afterschool programs allow them to practice schoolwork, while more than 80 percent say Elev8 staff challenge them to do their best.
3 Seventy-five percent of interviewed parents in Oakland reported improved academic performance when their children attended Elev8's extended-learning programs.
4 More Elev8 students in Chicago are being accepted into competitive high schools.

School-Based Health Services

1 Students who take advantage of Elev8's SBHCs overwhelmingly say that they receive services sooner and access resources that are otherwise unavailable.
2 There were nearly twenty-eight thousand visits to Elev8's school-based health centers during the 2010–11 school year.
3 There have been significant increases in compliance rates for school physicals and immunizations.

Resources for Families

1 Nearly 2,700 parents and other community members have worked through Elev8 to tap vital support services, including emergency services, and resources to help them address pressing economic needs.
2 Elev8 Baltimore helped more than one hundred parents and other family members obtain job training, financial support and counseling in the 2010–11 school year.
3 Elev8 tax clinics help families access tax refunds and tax credits. In Oakland, Elev8 secured combined tax refunds of more than $500,000 for low-income families.
4 Elev8 New Mexico returned more than $400,000 to Laguna, a small Pueblo reservation, by helping families access earned income tax credits, childcare subsidies, health insurance, and food stamps.

Transforming Schools into Better Places to Learn and Work

1. Students in Elev8 schools feel safer at school and in Elev8 activities than do students in their surrounding communities.
2. One Elev8 New Mexico school saw a 50 percent drop in disciplinary actions in the three years after Elev8's launch; youth arrests in one Elev8 community fell from sixty to one in a year.
3. Discipline referrals in one Elev8 Chicago school dropped more than 80 percent in 2009–10.
4. Elev8 has substantially broadened student acceptance and use of counseling services, which school staff link to notable declines in disciplinary problems.
5. There have been increases in attendance.

Strengthening the Whole Community

1. In Oakland, dozens of parent leaders support Elev8's family resource centers, recruit families for school events, conduct "parent patrols" to ensure safety to and from school, and lead school fundraising efforts.
2. Elev8 parents and youth have united in Washington, D.C., to share their policy priorities with federal lawmakers. They also advocate for their communities with local and state agencies and elected officials.
3. Elev8 leverages resources and encourages public and private investments that help communities thrive.

FUTURE DIRECTIONS

Along with sustaining their work, the Elev8 sites have helped create lasting change locally. Most importantly, Elev8 has shown how to create better services at lower costs by linking public, private, and nonprofit resources and activities around common goals. New Mexico, for example, has taken steps at the state level to become much better at pooling resources to support health *and* education.

In Oakland, the Elev8 experience helped generate support for the community school model, and in 2010, Oakland United School District Superintendent Tony Smith endorsed a plan to adopt the community school approach throughout the district, with schools offering health, housing, employment, and other services in a more coordinated fashion.

In Chicago, the community-based lead agencies have spread their work from the original Elev8 schools to touch an additional twenty-two schools and over seventeen thousand students. The lead agencies have used the school-based health centers as hubs to improve the health outcomes of students and families in their communities. They have also built on the out-of-school-time programs to provide safe spaces and enriching activities for students and families.

And in Baltimore, Elev8 demonstrated the value of a community school approach by helping the lead agency funding out-of-school-time activities to embrace the community school approach.

Returning to the overall topic of exemplary full-service community schools, we look now at city and school-district organized models. In Hartford, Connecticut, and Tulsa, Oklahoma, both community school initiatives receive technical assistance from the Children's Aid Society and follow its scale-up model. Both are creative in critical areas: Hartford has braided funding streams to support cohesive programming, and Tulsa is making headway with creative opportunities to provide transportation, which is a frequent barrier to service, especially in communities without strong public transport systems. Canyons School District (CSD), with support from the Utah State Office of Education (USOE), is a newer initiative, which began adopting a community school framework in its four Title I pre-K–5 elementary schools in 2012. In 2014, Canyons received the Family/Youth Partnership Award at the Center for School Mental Health national conference.

HARTFORD COMMUNITY SCHOOLS: HARTFORD PARTNERSHIP FOR STUDENT SUCCESS (Information provided by Sandra Ward, Former Director, Hartford Partnership for Student Success)

BRIEF OVERVIEW

Community schools work began in Hartford around 2007, when four youth-serving institutions and the City of Hartford came together to discuss the creation of a community schools model in the city. The organizations included the city's youth division, Hartford public schools, the Hartford Foundation for Public Giving, and the United Way, and their discussions coincided with the arrival of a new superintendent who had used the community school model in Cincinnati.

The model launched in 2008–9 at five schools. There had been a long-standing afterschool initiative at three schools through the local community foundation, so three of those sites were grandfathered in and two new schools were selected based on their low performance and interest in a redesign process. They needed a new theme selection, new curriculum, new staff (all staff were fired)—it was a whole turnaround model.

The current community school model relies on a lead agency to partner with the school in hiring a full-time community school director and a full-time staff person to oversee afterschool programming. From there, the model varies from school to school. There can be educational coordinators, family coordinators, additional staff, etc., managed by the lead agency, which does not provide all of the services but coordinates all the services at the school building. A team of people, including the principal, school staff, and parents, selects the lead agency through an RFP process that involves a written component, an interview, and a site visit.

ORIGINAL OBJECTIVE

The Hartford community schools initiative began as a strategy for organizing the resources of the community to support student success, not just academically, but socially and emotionally as well. The initiative encourages students to become civic minded, and hopes to encourage families and communities to support these goals. Situating comprehensive services within a school building makes for more efficient, cost-effective delivery. These school-based services are more easily accessible to families and more able to collaborate with each other on behalf of youths within the school building. For example, a teacher might approach the community school director and say, "Look, José told me he didn't have dinner last night because there's no food in the house," and then a staff member could help José access the school's food pantry.

Another strong characteristic of the Hartford community school strategy is its formal outcomes framework, which covers four different areas, including: student outcomes; school level outcomes, including school culture and climate; family outcomes; and community outcomes. The long-term goal is to positively impact the whole community. This has already occurred in different parts of Hartford that have well-established schools and thus increasingly stable neighborhoods.

PROCESS OF DEVELOPMENT

The local Community Foundation, the Hartford Foundation for Public Giving had a long-standing afterschool initiative that increased capacity in a few agencies and developed high-quality afterschool programs. The Children's Aid Society provided technical assistance and training in Hartford for ten years prior to the launching of the community schools model. Since then, CAS has provided even more teacher training and technical assistance at all levels: agency, principals, and district. When a school "launches," the first year is designated for planning and development, because it takes a long time to build the relationships needed for success. The CAS has a four-stage framework of exploring, emerging, mentoring, and excelling. It requires a long period of patient adjustment before all the pieces work in tandem with each other.

There has been a "memorandum of understanding" since the beginning among the core institutions, including a commitment for supportive infrastructure that includes evaluation, training, and technical assistance.

COLLABORATIVE ACTIVITIES/STRUCTURES

There are four lead agencies, each with different levels of available resources, across the seven schools. Two of the organizations provide a range of foster services, including mental health services. Every other month, the entire network comes together across all seven schools to share information and successful practices. They work on issues that affect parties across the districts wrestling with policy, data issues and other challenges.

The providers value the level of collaboration that occurs. The base of collaboration occurs between the principal and the community school director; when this relationship works well, things flow easily. If the communication is inadequate, it impacts the collaboration at other levels. Each school has collaborations with businesses in the community, with residents who do not have children in the schools, and/or with traditional service organizations and corporations. It is up to the community school director to pull all of those resources into the school and knit them together in a way that addresses the needs of the school, students, and community. The community school directors are hired by the lead agency in collaboration with the school principal.

TARGET POPULATION

Currently, the Hartford community schools are focused on grades K–8. One school is developing into a high school. The target population includes children *and* their families, based on the belief that children will face challenges in school if they are not secure and stable at home.

FEATURED PROGRAMS

There are two Village for Family and Children program sites that have special financial literacy components, food bank components, and truancy programs. They have brought in juvenile justice funding to operate a truancy prevention program. This is a large multiservice agency that offers many resources.

SERVICE PROVIDERS/PARTNERS

The four lead agencies have leveraged partnerships with the library, Connecticut Children's Medical Center, and the Hartford Symphony. There has been a range of diverse partners, including health insurance companies that provide asthma education as well as literacy and mentoring programs. The lead agencies have also leveraged multiple other partnerships with the schools. Where in the past the school principal would respond to requests for extra services, these resources are now coordinated by the community school director.

Each school has different services, depending on its primary community partner and the community and student needs. For example, one school has a food pantry in the family resource center. In addition, there is financial literacy support at a few of the schools to support parents in their savings and investments, including some Industrial Development Agency (IDA) programs happening through United Way. One lead agency is a mental health provider licensed to bring clinical services directly to the school. The agency handles billing with either private insurance or the state insurance program, so there is no cost to the families or the school.

LOCATION OF SERVICES

Services are primarily school-based. Exceptions include field trips that give youth exposure to different museums and community resources, including the library. There's also an agency that has studio performance space near a school. When it is impossible to bring certain services to the school, parents are provided with information about how to access these other community-based services.

TYPES OF SERVICES DELIVERED

The role of community schools is to think about providing whole school support for matters such as attendance. When supporting good attendance and timeliness, schools play a role in follow-up and case management. The community school looks to help with barriers to timeliness, such as lack of an alarm clock or lack of transportation. Some schools have done an attendance incentive where youths are rewarded (classrooms with good attendance get an ice cream party at the end of the month, etc.). Hartford community schools educate parents about the role of breakfast, sleep, school activities, etc. They also develop common communication tools and calendars to better coordinate their interactions with parents. Additionally, schools provide programming for parents such as ESL, financial literacy classes, parenting workshops, informational sessions about speaking to children about drugs and sex, and other activities to support parents. Afterschool programming is another critical service.

FUNDING

Initially, there were separate budgets; now, all funds are represented in each school's community school budget. The four institutional partners fund the district-level Hartford community school director. The employer of record is the Hartford Foundation for Public Giving.

IMPLEMENTATION CHALLENGES

A major challenge is keeping up with change in culture, which happens at multiple levels and affects budget demands. This requires strong communication and collaboration among parents, teachers, and administrators.

There is a challenge in managing partnerships as well, since there are four lead agencies and four institutional partners collaborating to support this work. Each agency has its own set of policies, personnel, and set of approaches.

EVALUATION

Hartford conducts process and outcome evaluations with an external evaluator. For four years, the OMG Center for Collaborative Learning in Philadelphia was the evaluator; subsequently the role was assumed by ActKnowledge, an affiliate of the City University of New York.

FUTURE DIRECTIONS

The four institutional partners recently signed a new memorandum of understanding (where expectations for each organization are clearly delineated and agreed upon) wherein they agreed to adopt the name Hartford Partnership for Student Success in order to broaden the vision of the group beyond community schools. There are two community school goals: (1) to maintain fidelity to the community schools as they exist in Hartford; and (2) to replicate elements of the community school model in other schools in Hartford. It is a very resource-intensive model, one that will require a large staff to fund and then determine the most prominent needs of a particular school. The other goals are: expansion of quality out-of-school time; creating quality summer programs for children; and increasing responsiveness to emerging opportunities that support student success.

THE TULSA AREA COMMUNITY SCHOOLS INITIATIVE (TACSI) (Information provided by Jan Creveling, Senior Planner)

BRIEF OVERVIEW

The Tulsa Area Community Schools Initiative (TACSI) identifies as a strategy, not a program, for bringing programs, services, and opportunities into schools and their surrounding neighborhoods. TASCI is both community- and school-based.

TACSI incorporates partnerships around the following seven core components:

1. Early Childhood (birth–eight years).
2. Health Services and Health Education.
3. Mental Health and Social Services.
4. Out-of-School Time and Youth Development.
5. Family Engagement.
6. Neighborhood Development.
7. Lifelong Learning for Families, Students, and Community Members.

ORIGINAL OBJECTIVE

In 2005, the community schools effort in Tulsa grew out of the Metropolitan Human Service Commission (MHSC), staffed by the Community Service Council, the umbrella organization for TASCI. MHSC, a membership body composed of city, county, and state agencies, school districts, and foundations, sought to create school reform that would focus on the whole child in the context of the school and local community. They hired a staff person, who is the current director of the community schools initiative, for an eighteen-month period to engage in extensive research—on-site visits, interviews with community school experts, review of research papers, and online investigative research. A precursor to the community schools effort came through a federal Department of Health and Human Services grant to develop a family support mechanism to fight child abuse.

PROCESS OF DEVELOPMENT

It took approximately two years to plan for rich, robust implementation. There was strong district support, which remains critical to success. TACSI functions out of a memorandum of understanding with two school districts and community partners that stipulates the management team as the decision-making body of the governance structure. There also is a steering committee that serves as the advisory group, composed of members who have long been involved in advancing educational opportunities.

Implementation teams were established for each school district, staffed by the TACSI Resource Center working collaboratively with principals, assistant principals, and community school coordinators. Each school has a site team whose composition reflects the demographics of each neighborhood and which serves as a critical component of neighborhood buy-in.

COLLABORATIVE ACTIVITIES/STRUCTURES

The TACSI Resource Center, housed in the Community Service Council, is the intermediary for pulling all of the partners together to provide joint planning, assistance, and training.

Each one of the core components has a current organization that provides leadership and structure; when a gap exists for that core component, a group is pulled together by the TACSI Resource Center to address the gap. For example, when addressing the mental health component, there is a children's behavioral consortium regarding mental health for students and their families. There is a collaborative body of all community partners that meets monthly to discuss trends and issues in program alignment with the schools. When there is already good work being done in the community, the goal is for TACSI to join those engaged in it. The total initiative is based on collective impact (see chapter 4), which relies on strong, trusting relationships among all parties involved.

TARGET POPULATION

In 2006, the Tulsa community decided to target elementary schools; Oklahoma as a whole, and Tulsa in particular, has had a good experience with the early childhood community, a component supported by local philanthropies. The target population consists of the Title I elementary schools in the Union district, which includes approximately 14,000 students, and in Tulsa, with approximately 41,000 students. There is one participating middle school in the Union district, which includes about 2,200 sixth and seventh grade students.

FEATURED PROGRAM

The Roy Clark School won the National Community School Award. Roy Clark has formal and informal partners that work collaboratively through memorandums of understanding.

LOCATION OF SERVICES

TACSI community school services are predominantly school-based; some services are provided during the school day and others after school, as well as over the summer and during intercession. There are also home visits and community-based services. Transportation is always a challenge impacting the location of services. TACSI is in the process of developing a transportation system with Tulsa Public Schools using donated buses. Transportation services can also be accessed from leveraged funds from TACSI's partners.

SERVICE PROVIDERS/PARTNERS

TACSI has a wide range of services, programs, and opportunities for students and their family members, as well as community residents. Some examples are: a global garden that promotes gardening in and out of school; yoga; bike club; and afterschool clubs. There are 160 formal and informal partners. TACSI's motto is "If there's a need identified, we fill it. The answer to any question is: 'Yes, together we can.' "

TYPES OF SERVICES DELIVERED

Schools that have school-based health clinics serve as the primary health care home for both the school and the surrounding neighborhood. For schools without clinics, TACSI uses partners to provide eye care, dental care, mental health care, and other identified services.

FUNDING

Both districts utilize Title I funds to support the community school coordinator position, as all TACSI schools are high poverty schools. The philosophy is that everyone has a passion; everyone has a gift so that everyone in the community can give in some capacity—whether it is time, talent, or money. TACSI is fortunate to be strongly supported by philanthropy and local businesses.

IMPLEMENTATION CHALLENGES

The greatest implementation challenge has been consistent principal leadership within the schools to support faculty and school staff. Tulsa Public Schools initiated Project Schoolhouse, which caused some schools to close due to under population. This necessitated training many new teachers and principals, and it has been challenging to retrain and reteach some of the second-year principals about community schools. It takes principals three to five years to hire appropriate staff and reformat their school's structural core and vision.

EVALUATION

As TACSI schools move into full-service community schools and keep fidelity with that model, there is a greater chance of achieving success with their students. Currently, TACSI is developing a data tracking system using indicators developed from the National Coalition for Community Schools' Results Scorecard. The focus of evaluation is on schools, partners, and individual students. The Roy Clark School won a national award (mentioned earlier) based partially on its high-quality data-informed work.

FUTURE DIRECTIONS

TACSI is following the National Coalition's Scale-Up guide to quality improvement.

CANYONS SCHOOL DISTRICT'S COMMUNITY SCHOOLS INITIATIVE IN TITLE I SCHOOLS (Information provided by Karen Sterling, Director of Student Advocacy and Access, Canyons School District; Carol Joy Anderson, Education Specialist,

Office of Behavioral Supports/Mental Health Needs, Utah State Office of Education; Dawn Anderson-Butcher, Professor, College of Social Work, Ohio State University; and Lauren Paluta, Graduate Research Assistant, College of Social Work, Ohio State University).

OVERVIEW OF THE INITIATIVE

Canyons School District, with support from the Utah State Office of Education (USOE), began adopting a community school framework in its four Title I pre-K–5 elementary schools in 2012. The goal of the community schools model is "Collaborating for Student Success in College, Career and Citizenship." Using the Ohio Community Collaboration Model for School Improvement (OCCMSI) as a guide (Anderson-Butcher et al. 2008; see fig. 3.1), Canyons is maximizing school and community resources during the school day and in out-of-school time through its partnership with key entities such as the Boys and Girls Clubs (BGC) of South Valley, Valley Behavioral Health (the county mental health provider), Play Works, the University of Utah College of Social Work, USOE, the Copperview Recreation Center, local government, the business sector, and others. The work in CSD is imperative: all four schools are underperforming, and youth encounter many barriers to learning. As described in the most recent Census and Fair Housing report, the surrounding county has experienced concentrated increases in poverty since 2007. Over 80 percent of the students live in poverty. The most impacted "low opportunity areas," such as Midvale, lack access to medical and dental care as well as grocery stores. Over 50 percent of families with school-aged children speak English as a second language, and 30 percent of youth report internalizing symptoms.

The CSD community schools initiative prioritizes five core pillars—academic learning, youth development and school climate, parent and family engagement/support, health and social services, and community engagement—which mirror the main components of community schools.

Academic learning strategies include quality instruction in classrooms; tutoring interventions provided after school by certified teachers for the most underperforming six to eight students from each grade; homework assistance in the afterschool hours, and value-added progress monitoring using AIMSweb. Preschool and parent as teachers (PAT) outreach programs were started to capitalize on evidence-based early interventions.

Youth development and school climate priorities focus on effective classroom management techniques and school-wide climate interventions (such as incentive programs like Shark Dollars) in school, a comprehensive BGC program that operates from 3 to 6 p.m. Monday through Friday, recess and social skills interventions taught by Play Works, and recreational sports offered by the local Parks and Recreation Department.

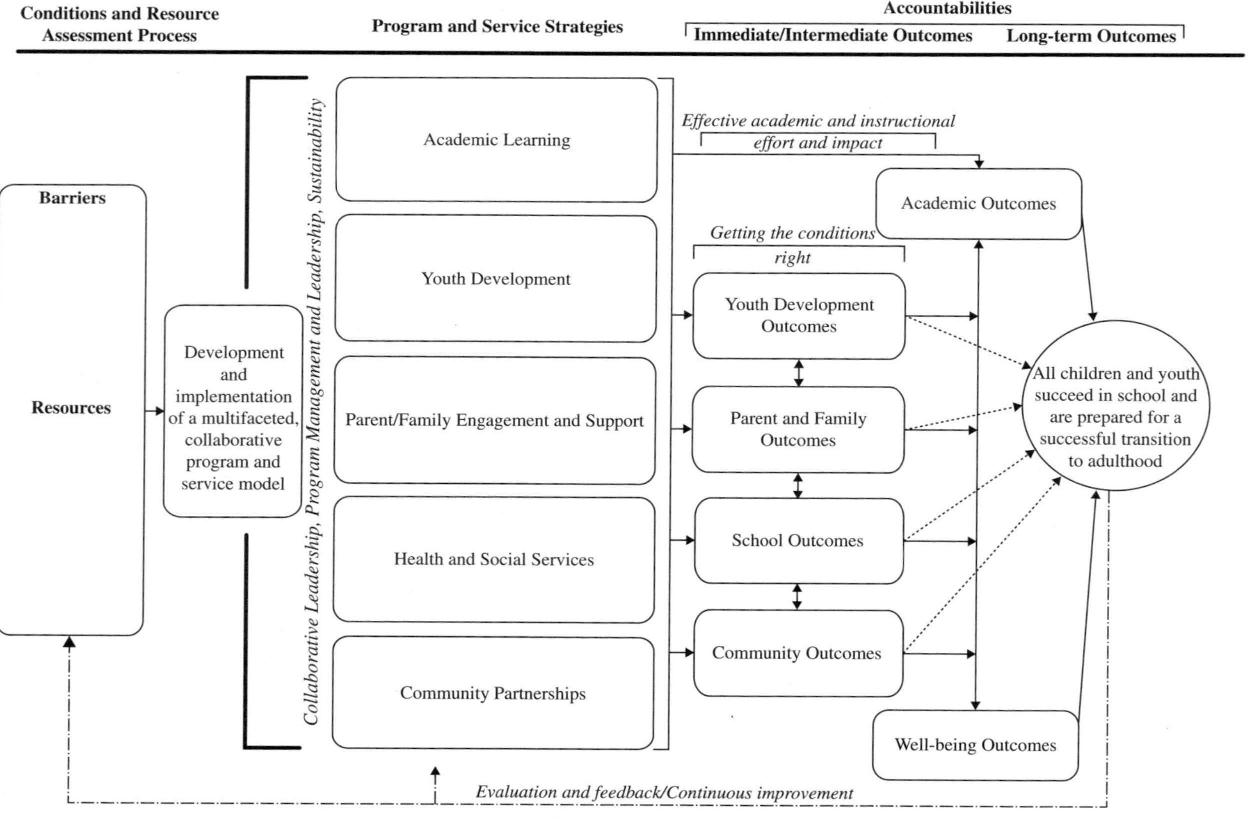

FIGURE 3.1 Ohio Community Collaboration Model for School Improvement

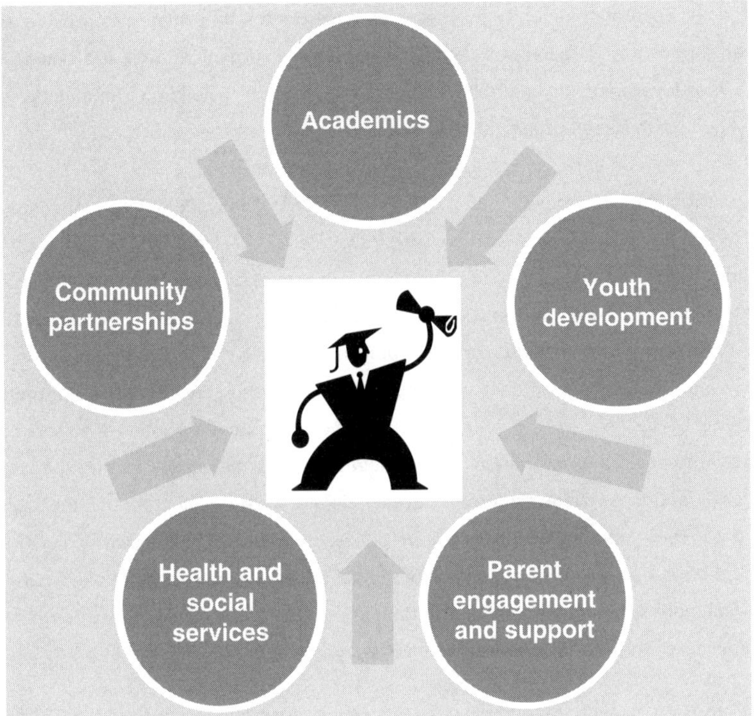

FIGURE 3.2

Parent/family engagement and support activities are offered at school-based family literacy centers during the day and in the evening. Computer, ESL, literacy, parenting, and nutrition classes are also offered at the centers. Traditional parent involvement opportunities (such as parent-teacher conferences, back-to-school nights, etc.) have been strengthened, and parents are learning new skills as they serve as volunteers in classrooms.

Health and social services are central to the community schools. Service coordination wraparound teams comprised of multiple professionals (i.e., school psychologists, school-based therapists, school social workers, principals, teachers, parents, etc.) case coordinate students and their families. School-based behavioral and mental health (SBMH) services include individual, group, and classroom interventions. Strategic linkages have been made to the local overflow homeless shelter. And the University of Utah has co-located a health clinic in the recreation center served by these four schools, allowing for easy referral and access to health care by families.

Finally, several community partnerships have been strengthened to provide additional supports and resources. Local collaboratives, organizations, and businesses have been leveraged, including the Midvale City Community Building Community Coalition, local faith-based organizations, businesses such as Savage (to fund community gardens), the food bank, and police and fire departments.

In particular, one innovation that has emerged from the work in CSD is the integration of SBMH services in partnership with Valley Behavioral Health (VBH). Through this collaboration, students have been able to more seamlessly receive mental health services. In the first year of operation, 175 students have been served through school-based services. Outcomes data are favorable, as research by the Ohio State University showcases that access to care was improved across the schools and that students receiving SBMH services significantly improved in key outcomes such as intrapersonal distress, behavioral dysfunction, and critical needs as measured by the Youth Outcomes Questionnaire (see Anderson-Butcher & Paluta 2015). The state of Utah is using the data from these innovations to drive policy to support SBMH state-wide. VBH is using the work to guide the expansion of school-based services in Salt Lake County. It now has more school-based than outpatient providers, and is offering services in thirty schools across the county (up from twelve two years ago).

COLLABORATIVE ACTIVITIES/STRUCTURES

One key reason the CSD community schools initiative is successful is due to the infrastructure. The director of federal programs in CSD leads the initiative. This person meets regularly with key leaders from each partner organization (such as the executive director of the BGC, the head of SBMH services at VBH, the mayors of various municipalities, etc.), as well as working collaboratively with other leaders in the district who are charged with school improvement (such as the director of principals, the associate superintendent, the director of special education, etc.). CSD also has ensured that the community schools work is embedded in the traditional school improvement planning processes used in each building. For instance, school improvement is now governed by the initiative's five pillars as opposed to being solely focused on "inside the school walls" strategies. Strategies in the school improvement plan are implemented for the school day and out-of-school time, with input from the school and the community. Additionally, the community school approach has been written into district school board policy, thus supporting ongoing sustainability of the work as transitions happen in the future.

Another reason the CSD community schools initiative is successful is related to the ongoing communication and capacity-building system in place. Partners meet quarterly to review progress, examine challenges, explore emergent needs, and brainstorm solutions and next steps. Likewise, professional development opportunities are offered to teachers and school staff, community providers, and partners collectively in relation to PBIS, community schools, school improvement planning, and cultural competence. Furthermore, funding agencies in the community are beginning to support community school planning and sustainability (for instance, discussions are under way in relation to securing United Way funding in support of the work).

In addition, the CSD community schools initiative also involves the creation of a comprehensive system of learning supports, involving early identification of academic challenges and nonacademic barriers by teachers and school staff, referrals to a single point of contact, and triage of individual student cases, positive intervention behavioral supports, service coordination/wraparound teams, and ongoing progress monitoring of students based on value-added data. Relationships among school and community providers are maximized as all students benefit from universal strategies aimed at creating supportive learning environments both in school and in out-of-school time, and students who need intervention and supports the most are targeted for services.

FUNDING

Funding for the CSD community schools initiative is diversified. Foremost, CSD uses federal Title I dollars to support infrastructure and the hiring of key staff including a Title I community schools specialist, four site-based coordinators, preschool staff, and certified afterschool tutors. Parent/family strategies are supported through the maximization of federal program dollars (Titles I, III, and VII) as well as competitive grants. McKinney Homeless dollars allow for additional personnel who support students in crisis, additional BCG staff for the afterschool program, and a liaison to community services. Dollars from 21st Century Community Learning Centers fund the afterschool programs' personnel, supplies, and transportation. SBMH services provided by VBH are funded through Medicaid, private insurance, and a special line-item in the state budget for mental health services for youth who do not have insurance. Gifts have been received from major corporations. Many in-kind resources also are utilized, such as space (e.g., for SBMH providers, the health clinic, the afterschool program), technology (e.g., computers used during the school day being used in the afterschool program), and people power (e.g., parent and teacher volunteers, Latinos in Action student mentors and translators, professional development support through the district, and financial/supervisory oversight).

EVALUATION

The USOE has commissioned the Community and Youth Collaborative Institute (CAYCI) at the Ohio State University to conduct a mixed-method study to examine process and outcomes associated with the adoption and implementation of the community schools framework in CSD. Analyses examined quantitative data from students and teachers at baseline (n=2,198 students; n=212 teachers; n=1,575 parents), and two years after community schools implementation (n=2,125 students; n=286 teachers; n=1,493 parents/caregivers).

Findings show significant building-level improvements in student's perceptions of improved internalizing symptomology, academic support, and school climate. Teacher perceptions of the students' readiness to learn, school climate, and learning support system were significantly more favorable after two years of implementation than at baseline. Multiple indicators of parent/caregivers involvement in the school significantly improved, as well. Additionally, academic, behavioral, and social-emotional outcomes among students were examined in terms of specific community school interventions, such as for school-based mental health and afterschool programming. Office discipline referrals have declined significantly, particularly during unstructured times during the school day (i.e., recess). SBMH outcomes were noted (as described above), as well as academic outcomes in math and reading for students served in afterschool tutoring. Additionally, student achievement data were examined across the four schools. Three of the four improved math achievement scores, whereas two of the schools improved reading achievement scores over the course of implementation.

Last, qualitative data collection strategies, including interviews and site observations, tracked key system-level innovations across the four community schools. Numerous innovations have resulted, such as improved policies and procedures, enhanced programs and evidence-based practices, and increased partnerships and funding streams. Relationships have improved, as well, among teachers, school staff, parents/caregivers, students, and the community. For instance, from 2012 to 2014, the percentage of Canyons staff who felt that their school offered accessible services and supports to families increased from 43.48 percent to 62.02 percent. It has been estimated that an average of twenty-one instructional hours per teacher were reclaimed as a result of the enhanced procedures and students' improving social skills.

IMPLEMENTATION CHALLENGES

The CSD community schools initiative has been fairly successful during its first two years of operation, with evaluation findings demonstrating positive outcomes associated with its adoption and implementation both at the student and school level. However, there have been challenges along the way. One has been a short time line for adoption of the community schools model. The Canyons School District was created in 2009 through a voter referendum. At that time, three of the four Title I schools were in the school improvement category, creating the urgency for systemic improvements even as the district itself was in its infancy. Instead of gradually growing a community school (by adding one program piece, then others), CSD chose to implement the full model focused on five pillars simultaneously. This created a lot of change for the school, as well as for community partners. School leaders, especially principals, had to learn how to do their work differently and in partnership with others. Community providers needed to learn how schools operate and are governed, and then tweak their program models to fit the school's priorities. Challenges also were evident in relation to ensuring that district-level administrators (such as curriculum directors, school board members) and local leaders (such as mayors, county commissioners, business leaders, etc.) understood and valued the community school approach. While their support is critical for ongoing sustainability, maintaining this support is challenging due to the turnover of people in key supervisory and administrative roles. For instance, an interim superintendent was in place and then a new superintendent was hired during year two of implementation. Likewise, the lead day-to-day person in charge of the community schools operation in CSD took another job at the end of the academic year. The Title I specialist for academic supports recently retired. It has taken time to hire and train the new people for these challenging but invaluable roles.

FUTURE DIRECTIONS

Future directions involve further embedding the community school framework in the school improvement planning process of the buildings, as well as strengthening the focus in each community school on the top priorities and needs of the students served. At the beginning of the 2014–15 school year, teachers, school staff, parents, and community partners all participated in a professional development conference focused on community schools, and top priorities for next steps were created for each building. For instance, one school focused on building school climate and strengthening relationships among students and teachers and school staff, whereas another school tackled internalizing symptomology among students (thus designing strategies to improve students' overall well-being and affect). All schools are focusing on strengthening classroom-based instruction and its alignment to the curriculum and state accountability system (a constant priority in all schools across the country). In the end, stakeholders in the community schools will focus on all of these aims, thus sharpening the focus of the community schools and their strategies of targeting highest needs.

Another priority is sustaining the community schools. Grants currently supporting the work will end in a few years (and others will be written) to sustain the funding. Dollars that are being used to support key components of the model will need to be protected, and ones that are not being used for top priority needs will be redeployed so that the work is further aligned to outcomes. Additionally, the CSD's schools will continue to nurture and foster relationships with current and future partners to support the maximization of school and community resources in support of learning, healthy development, and overall school success.

In addition to the nonprofit and district efforts noted in the foregoing examples, there are a handful of county-wide efforts to develop and implement community schools (see fig. 3.2). These initiatives are especially challenging because of the diversity and scope of schools and communities represented. Chapter 5 discusses a county-wide initiative in upstate New York. Here, we highlight SUN (Schools Uniting Neighborhoods) Community Schools in Multnomah, Oregon, as a leader in a county-wide approach to community school development and implementation.

SUN COMMUNITY SCHOOLS (Information provided by Diana Hall, Program Supervisor)

BRIEF OVERVIEW

Schools Uniting Neighborhoods (SUN) Community Schools is a unique partnership of city, county, state government, six local school districts, and community organizations that started in 1999 at eight public schools. Responding to community demand, system development, and positive results, the initiative has expanded over time to include seventy community schools.

ORIGINAL OBJECTIVE

Multnomah County, Oregon, includes the City of Portland and is home to approximately three-quarters of a million people. It has made youth educational achievement a priority, and in so doing, it has developed an innovative and successful model for cross-sector collaboration. Bringing together schools and partners from across the community, SUN Community Schools strive to collectively impact educational success and family self-sufficiency.

PROCESS OF DEVELOPMENT

In the late 1990s, Multnomah County community members and leaders recognized a need for a new approach to meet the needs of children, families, and schools. The environment posed multiple challenges, including shrinking budgets, a significant racial achievement gap, growing poverty, a severe shortage of affordable housing, and an increase in the number of children being left unsupervised during out-of-school hours. Demographic changes were dramatically increasing the cultural and linguistic diversity in the region, requiring schools and social service organizations to develop new skills in order to educate and support these populations effectively. Leaders recognized that an individual's level of educational attainment is the primary predictor of poverty in adulthood. The effect of family poverty on school success was also clear, as barriers such as homelessness, mobility, hunger, illness, and trauma made it impossible for many students to come to school ready to learn. Conversely, it became clear that it was not possible to talk about alleviating or eliminating poverty without talking about education. With leadership from elected officials in the City of Portland and Multnomah County, the decision was made to partner together to support schools. The initial goal was twofold: to support education and school success; and to improve the way resources for students and their families were delivered by developing a school-based delivery model.

An ad hoc committee of a broad array of stakeholders convened to determine the best strategy to accomplish this goal. The committee included leadership from an existing community building initiative and after school cabinet. After a year of research and deliberation, the full-service community school model was chosen, and the first eight SUN Community Schools were implemented in the fall of 1999, with the city and county providing core funding. Since that time, the community has chosen to expand SUN Community Schools from eight to seventy schools, with a vision for every school to be a SUN Community School. Supportive policy has been adopted in the county, city, and school districts, and a more expansive network of care, named the SUN Service System, has been developed to organize and prioritize the county's investments and partnerships to support school-age children and their families.

COLLABORATIVE ACTIVITIES/STRUCTURES

SUN Community Schools initially developed in the late 1990s out of a multijurisdictional community building initiative. The community schools initiative, and the broader system of care (the SUN Service System) it now is part of, has been developed collaboratively over the past fourteen years. The primary system partners include:

1. Multnomah County (Department of County Human Services, Health Department, library, Department of Community Justice);
2. City of Portland (Parks and Recreation, Planning and Sustainability, Transportation);
3. Six school districts;
4. Portland Children's Levy;
5. Business;

6 Nonprofit/community partners;
7 Oregon Department of Human Services; and
8 All Hands Raised (Cradle to Career backbone organization).

Multnomah County acts as the intermediary, or managing partner, for the collaboration. The partnership has defined its relationship as a collaboration including sharing decision-making, investment, risks, and rewards. Shared decision-making and guidance happens through the seventeen-member SUN Service System Coordinating Council, which has representative seats from the key systemic partners above.

The collaborative action is also evident at operational and direct-service levels. At the operational level, there is at least one SUN liaison in each district and jurisdiction that has responsibility for working collaboratively at the operational and administrative levels and overcoming systemic and bureaucratic barriers. At the school site level, SUN Community Schools build collaboration among school staff, community partners, parents, youth, and neighbors to collectively impact student success.

TARGET POPULATION

Recognizing the need for support at all ages and attention to transitions in and out of the K–12 system, as well as between grade levels, SUN Community Schools are located in elementary, K–8, middle, and high schools. The focus is on the whole child, integrating academics, social services, supports and opportunities in order to meet student and family needs. The specific services and programs offered are tailored to the individual assets and needs of a school, and community resources are organized strategically to support student success.

FEATURED PROGRAM

SUN Community Schools is considered the cornerstone of the larger SUN Service System. There are several focused initiatives within the SUN Community Schools that rely on the community school infrastructure to provide the vehicles and relationships for effectively and efficiently reaching the most vulnerable children and families. These initiatives include the Child and Family Hunger Relief Project and the Early Childhood Community School Linkage Project.

LOCATION OF SERVICES

At the school site, SUN Community Schools mobilize and strategically organize community resources to provide a strong core instructional program; educational support and skill development for youth and adults; enrichment and recreation activities; family involvement and support; social, health, and mental health resources; and family and community events.

SERVICE PROVIDERS/PARTNERS

As full-service neighborhood hubs, where school and community partners work together to ensure youth and families have what they need to succeed, SUN Community Schools serve as the vehicle to link community institutions, such as libraries, parks, community centers, neighborhood health clinics and area churches and businesses. In the SUN model, a noneducational lead agency partners with an individual school and together, with help from school and community leaders, they co-manage the community school collaboration at the site. The inclusion of nonprofit partners in the role of lead agency capitalizes on the unique capacities of these community-based organizations to provide expertise in anti-poverty services, youth and family engagement, and community development fields; relationships and standing within communities and with community leaders; and means for fund- and "friend"-raising in ways that governments and educational agencies cannot. Lead agencies receive core funding that supports the hiring of a SUN Community School site manager as well as limited flexible dollars to fill resource gaps in key underfunded services.

TYPES OF SERVICES DELIVERED

While many public schools offer activities before and after school, SUN goes further by reinventing the school as a place that addresses the full spectrum of family needs. On a typical day, the school opens early, providing students with a safe place to eat breakfast, do homework or participate in recreational and skill-building activities. During the school day, a community school site manager works with school staff, families, and community partners to identify specific student and family needs and broker services and to develop innovative partnerships that bring critical child and family supports directly to campus. Families and community members come to the school for advisory committee and leadership activities, parenting classes, health supports, food, clothing, and access to anti-poverty, mental health, and other social services. The day does not end with the school bell. Instead, the extended-day program picks up where the traditional classroom leaves off, providing students with an array of academic, enrichment, and recreational activities that complement and build on the school day. Students receive a full dinner and engage in physical activity to improve their physical health. In the evening, the school serves as a community center offering a variety of educational and recreational activities for adults and youth as well as providing space for community projects and meetings. This is SUN carrying out the vision its name so clearly describes, truly using schools to unite neighborhoods.

FUNDING

The SUN Community Schools are attracting over $23.7 million in cash, aligned services, and in-kind. In 2011–12, $6.7 million of that amount was cash contributions for "core operating costs" (roughly $100K per site). The allocation of funds is as follows:

1 Multnomah County: ~$3.2 million
2 City of Portland: ~$1.6 million
3 Portland Children's Levy: ~$800,000
4 21 CCLC grants: ~$670,000
5 Districts: ~ $400,000

School districts contribute heavily in aligned/leveraged services and in-kind. Altogether SUN values district contributions at around $10 million, within the overall $23.7 million.

IMPLEMENTATION CHALLENGES

SUN has overcome two challenges: developing agreements and systems for sharing data for evaluation and reporting; and getting community school site managers (coordinators), who are employees of nonprofit organizations to be considered as school officials within the Family Educational Rights and Privacy Act provisions so they can communicate with school staff to best align services to support the academic success of individual students.

SUN still faces two key ongoing challenges:

1 Maintaining champions and sustained funding as leadership changes in sponsoring partner organizations, particularly in local government and school districts. SUN Community Schools are a strategy for each partner organization in meeting at least part of its core mission. It is key to develop the understanding among sponsors of the benefits of community schools to a wide range of stakeholders.
2 Building capacity in a system that is going to scale. With seventy community school sites, it takes consistent attention at multiple levels to build the knowledge and skills necessary to develop community schools that are effective in fully harnessing the collective power of all partners and organizing those efforts strategically toward the goal of student success. The capacity to collaborate and lead community schools needs to be present at leadership, administrative, and community school levels (principals, school staff, nonprofit community school site coordinators, and partners). Multnomah County and its

partners provide technical assistance and training to build and sustain this capacity. It has been a challenge to provide the level of support needed as the initiative has grown from eight to seventy schools, especially as intermediary staff has not grown proportionally.

EVALUATION

SUN Community Schools' evaluation includes annual evaluation of the following outcomes for students who participate regularly in community school supports: increases in state benchmark scores in reading and math; attendance rates; credits earned (high school); retention (in grades 9–11) and graduation; and interim academic and youth asset measures (as measured through teacher and student surveys).

In the 2011–12 school year, attendance rates increased to 95 percent for participating students; over three quarters of students increased benchmark scores in reading; and high school students earned 7.8 credits on average, compared to the six needed to graduate on time. In a recently published quasi-experimental study, high school students who participated regularly in SUN supports had significantly better school attendance rates and earned a greater number of credits toward graduation than their peers who did not participate in SUN.

FUTURE DIRECTIONS

The SUN partners hold a vision for every school in the county to become a SUN Community School and are working on developing a funding model.

SUN Community Schools was initially chosen as a strategy to address critical issues its community was facing, including a growing achievement gap and poverty, as well as increasing language and cultural diversity that the public institutions and community were not equipped to support adequately. SUN has been considered a means to promoting equity ever since, and supportive policy underlying it addresses equity and culturally specific services. Recently, Multnomah County has developed an Equity and Empowerment Lens and SUN is applying the lens tool to its system.

CHARTER SCHOOLS

In addition to the public school models presented above, increasing numbers of charter schools are developing across the United States, some of which are adapting a community schools model. Today, every U.S. state has the option of contracting for charter schools, which are schools that receive public funds to educate children in lieu of the state's public schools.

Contracts differ from state to state, but most release charter schools from many regulations that govern public schools in order to allow for flexibility. Charter schools are monitored by each state for adherence to the specific goals stated in the contracts. Since the first charter school was created in Minnesota in 1991, they have grown in popularity and expanded, especially after 2002, when No Child Left Behind stated that children attending failing schools had the right to transfer to another school, including a charter school. According to the National Center for Educational Statistics (U.S. Department of Education 2014a), 31 percent of children in charter schools attend schools where at least 75 percent qualify for the government's free lunch program. From 1999 to 2012, charter schools increasingly served economically disadvantaged children.

Along with this demographic trend, there has been a movement for charter schools to partner with community agencies in order to better serve students' needs. The National Resource Center on Charter School Finance and Governance (2008) encourages partnerships with a variety of agencies, including nonprofit service organizations such as social service agencies, for-profit organizations such as businesses and educational management companies, and public organizations such as health clinics, hospitals, and local police. It points out that twenty-three states' charter school laws call for community involvement in some form, although even in states that do not have these provisions, some charter schools seek out partnerships on their own. The center also strongly suggests that all states with charter schools explicitly state that community involvement be a part of charter schools' operations. Most recently, new charter schools have developed as part of the growing number of community schools.

Charter schools fit into an array of categories including public, nonprofit, workplace, faith-based, and for-profit, each of which incorporates integrated community services in a range of ways and to varying degrees. The extent to which community involvement affects achievement in charter schools requires additional research. Some have debunked the value of community interventions (Dobbie & Fryer 2011), while others, including the Coalition for Community Schools and the Netter Center for Community Partnership, have praised charter schools when they provide integrated community-based services. Reacting to a 2010 U.S. Department of Education full-service community schools grant that went to three charter schools, Ira Harkavy, coalition chair and associate vice president and director of the

Netter Center for Community Partnerships at the University of Pennsylvania stated: "We welcome these grantees to the growing number of schools and communities that are using the community school strategy to support student success. . . . We must all work together if all of our students, particularly those at-risk, are to learn, develop and become contributing citizens of our democracy" (America's Promise Alliance, 2010). For 2014, the U.S. Department of Education solicited additional full-service community schools grants, and charter schools continued to be eligible recipients (U.S. Department of Education, 2014a,c).

Charter schools with strong integrated community services/community school models exist throughout the county. Examples include: the Green Dot Public Charter Schools in Los Angeles; East Austin College Prep Academy, a network of charter schools in the San Fernando Valley led by Bert Corona Charter School; the Children's Aid Society's College Prep Charter School in the Bronx, and, the Broome Street Academy in New York City. A number of these charter community schools maintain the same focus on equity as "regular" public community schools. For example, the Children's Aid Society's College Prep Charter School admission criteria advantages children who are low-income, English language learners, and "welfare-involved" (http://childrensaidcollegeprep.org/news/children's-aid-society's-bronx-charter-school-holds-lottery-third-academic-year).

Among other criteria, Broome Street Academy gives enrollment preference to students who: (a) are or have been enrolled in the child welfare system; (b) are homeless; and (c) are graduating from a middle school where over 50 percent of students perform below grade level on the state English Language Arts (ELA) exam (http://www.broomestreetacademy.org/sites/default/files/2014–15%20application%20for%20admission.pdf).

The Broome Street Academy is located in the same building as a social service agency, The Door. This location allows charter school students' seamless access to services that include health and mental health counseling, medical services, and recreational programs. The head of this school, Barbara McKeon, has been appointed to New York City Mayor DeBlasio's Community Schools Advisory Board to help oversee the city's initiative to create new community schools and to support those already in existence. A profile of Broome Street Academy follows, taken from a conversation with McKeon.

BROOME STREET ACADEMY (Information provided by Barbara McKeon, Head of School)

MISSION

Broome Street Academy Charter High School prepares young people for post-secondary success that leads to positive life outcomes. It values student strengths and provides multiple pathways to success through a curriculum of rigorous academic, career, and social instruction grounded in the principles of youth development. Fulfilling that mission requires ongoing evaluation of student and program success. Broome Street Academy (BSA) subscribes to pedagogy of engaging and collaborative learning; an overall culture of support; differentiation; rigorous curriculum; data-based instruction; and literacy across the curriculum. This philosophy is exemplified throughout the school in BSA's curriculum, the cycle of observation, professional development opportunities, and overall expectations of students and staff. Social and emotional support is embedded in the P.R.I.D.E. pillars: professionalism, resilience, investment, dignity, and empathy. BSA explicitly teaches and rewards points for evidence of these characteristics.

FUNDING

BSA relies primarily on per pupil funding based on state and city budgets. This includes Title I, Title II, and Special Education funding. Supplemental direct fundraising efforts also offset costs.

CONNECTION WITH THE DOOR

BSA is housed in The Door, making access to services seamless. BSA students become members of The Door upon enrollment at BSA, giving them complete access to any and all Door services, including health care (medical, dental, dermatology, vision, pregnancy counseling), mental health services (psychiatric, clinical counseling, crisis intervention), educational (college counseling, academic tutoring, high school equivalency), recreational (dance, music, life activities), and meals. During the 2013–14 school year, 254 active or former Broome Street Academy students accessed a total of 3,137 services.

Broome Street Academy has seen a great deal of recent growth in the college/career preparation sector of its services. College/career prep, health services, and food services continue to be the most commonly used services by BSA students at The Door. In March 2014, 136 students participated in a Talent Search Workshop for college planning, and thirty students attended either the college fair or a college trip. Broome Street Academy and The Door have also expanded their partnership in counseling and case management with the Statewide Planning and Research Cooperative System

(SPARCS). Between the beginning of February and the end of March 2014, nine students attended a total of thirty-seven sessions. Eighty-nine percent of the students who participated in SPARCS improved their GPA from Q2 to Q3, while discipline referrals decreased by 44 percent between the three-month period prior to the start of the intervention and a three-month period since the beginning of the intervention.

The uniqueness of The Door-BSA model is attributable to the physical proximity of services and the working relationships between Door and BSA staff (see fig. 3.3). As a community, BSA plans large activities to support both BSA students and Door members. BSA and Door staff work as team members on different aspects of service delivery (e.g., Behavior Management Team participants are from both The Door and BSA staff), and Door program-specific staff provide instruction to BSA students (e.g., counseling, college advising). Thus, while employees of each organization are separate, the two organizations have worked to integrate services as much as possible with Door staff working in the school and vice versa.

BSA is currently engaged in a research project with Yeshiva University's Wurzweiler School of Social Work to quantify the impact of Door services on attendance and

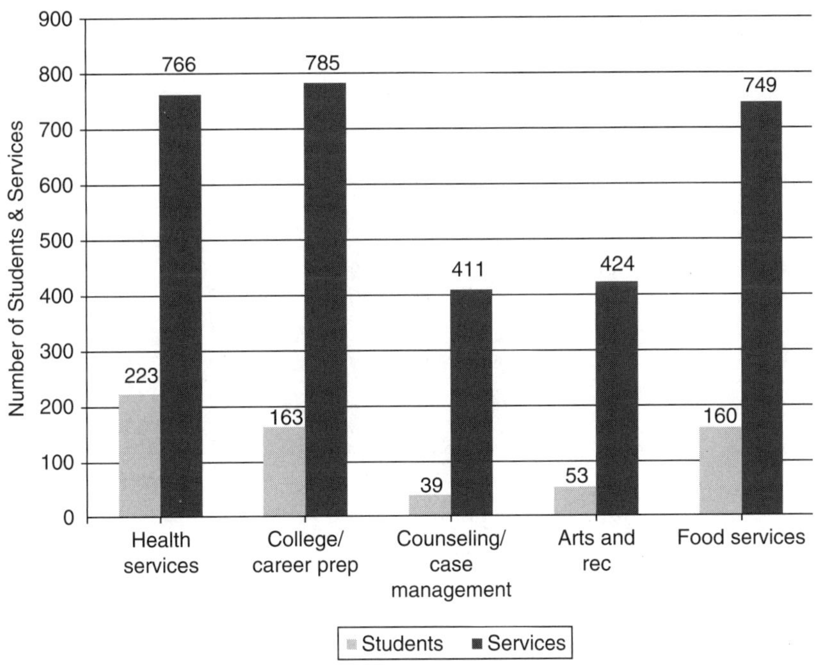

FIGURE 3.3 Number of BSA Student Visitors and Service Visits to The Door During the 2013–14 School Year

engagement. BSA staff know anecdotally that BSA students perceive The Door as a safe place where confidentiality is a priority. BSA staff know that providing seamless access improves the likelihood that students will reach out for services and that staff can refer BSA students to needed services and are able to release them during the school day for those critical appointments. Many BSA students would not otherwise find the services they needed if left to do so independently.

The challenges that BSA needs to overcome center around differences in age and expectations between Door members and BSA students. Thus, while youth of similar age as BSA students access The Door programs, they are not bound by the same behavioral expectations as BSA students (uniforms, language use, for example). Also, there are many Door members who are significantly older than BSA students, which can be intimidating to the latter and cause resistance in service use. More collaborative work is also needed, including pairing staff from each organization for specific projects.

FAMILY/CAREGIVER INVOLVEMENT

A top priority for BSA is to increase family/caregiver involvement and service offerings. Many BSA family/caregivers feel marginalized by their own school experience or are single parents without the necessary time to devote to BSA. A staff member is dedicated to improving relationships between BSA and caregivers and is working on developing monthly

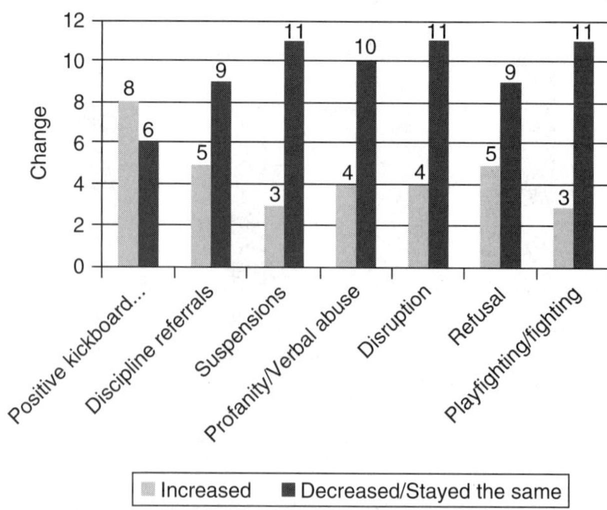

FIGURE 3.4 Number of Students in the "Check Out" Pilot Program

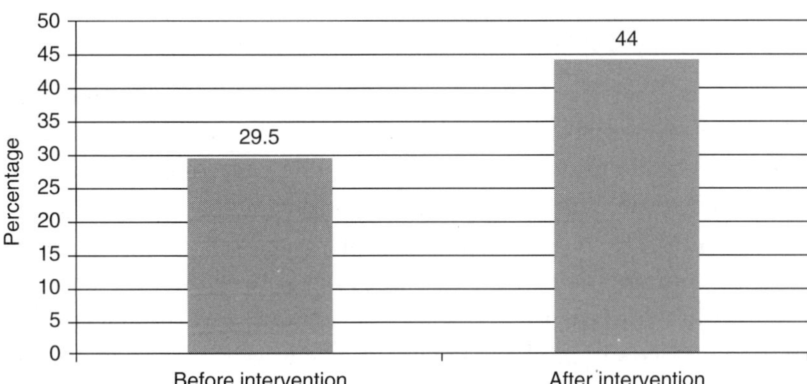

FIGURE 3.5 Average Percentage of Positive Kickboard Comments Before and After Intervention

culturally and time-sensitive activities toward that goal. BSA also offers workshops on teen development, relationships, social media, and other areas impacting caregivers.

"CHECK OUT" PILOT PROJECT

In response to the increase in challenging behavior in March 2014, BSA began a pilot project that involved fourteen students and four staff members. The goal of the project was to establish relational trust with one person in the school and teach problem-solving, decision-making, and self-advocacy skills with a view toward improving behavior. The results have been very positive and will be used along with the Harvard study results to create a model for building relational trust. Student surveys have been administered, and a full mixed methods pre-post intervention analysis is being conducted.

CRITICAL FOCI OF FULL-SERVICE COMMUNITY SCHOOLS

While the community school exemplars detailed above address a range of issues and offer diverse services, community schools do share many common aims. Each community school develops its particular focus based on needs assessments so that the integrated services provided match what is most necessary to support the success of each community's children and youth. Services that are often components of community schools include: extended hours, family engagement, solutions for attendance challenges, dropout prevention and intervention, and nutrition programs.

Extended Hours Before and After School and Summers

Researchers note that two-thirds of the achievement gap between higher-income and lower-income ninth graders is attributable to the cumulative impact of the discrepancies in summer learning opportunities during the elementary school years (Alexander, Entwisle, & Olson 2007). Friedman and Schmitt-Carey note that this occurs at least partially because "schools today still operate as they did when our grandparents headed off to kindergarten. Most educate students for six-plus hours a day from September to June as if we still need our 'children home to work the fields,' as Gov. Andrew M. Cuomo says" (2013).

Growing numbers of schools responding to the research regarding this achievement gap see the need to extend school hours for children and are doing so in a variety of ways. Extended school programs occur before and after school, on weekends, during school holidays, and in the summer. They operate in a range of settings, including schools, museums, libraries, parks, faith-based organizations, and community-based organizations. The term "afterschool" is often interchanged with "school-age care," "out-of-school time," and "expanded learning" and describes "an array of safe, structured programs that provide children and youth, ages kindergarten through high school, with a range of supervised activities intentionally designed to encourage learning and development outside of the typical school day" (Little, Wimer, & Weiss 2008:2). Afterschool programs offer safety, positive youth development, and academic enrichment and support. While they have a range of goals, they often focus on students' self-confidence, school engagement, and academic outcomes. Typical afterschool activities include "academic enrichment, tutoring, mentoring, homework help, arts (music, theater, and drama), technology, science, reading, math, civic engagement and involvement, and activities to support and promote health social/emotional development" (Little, Wimer, & Weiss 2008:2).

The National After-School Association (NAA), based in the United States, originated to foster development of, provide education about, and encourage advocacy for the out-of-school-time community. NAA supports professionals working with children and youth during out-of-school hours with the goal of developing and implementing high-quality programs that promote positive child and youth development and keep them safe (http://naaweb.org/about-us). It holds conferences and offers an array of resources on its website to support high-quality extended care.

Research and evaluation studies including meta-analyses addressing the positive educational and psychosocial impacts of extended day and summer opportunities have been ongoing for over a decade. Results show noted improvements in academic outcomes, social outcomes, higher education and career aspirations, work habits, emotional adjustment, and peer relations. In contrast, students who do not spend their out-of-school time in productive activities are shown to be more likely to be involved in violent juvenile crime, sexual activity, and smoking, drinking, and drugs (Children's Aid Society National Center for Community Schools, 2011). One large-scale study that examined the impact of student participation in programs *both* after school and in the summer revealed the importance of the continuity gained through these programs for children served during both time periods (Russell et al. 2006).

Family/Parent Engagement

Family/parent engagement requires seeing families as critical partners in children's school experiences and success and requires seeing children beyond their roles in classrooms. As Epstein (1995) states "If educators view children simply as *students*, they are likely to see the family as separate from the school. That is, the family is expected to do its job and leave the education of children to the schools. If educators view students as *children*, they are likely to see both the family and the community as partners with the school in children's education and development" (Epstein 1995:701).

As school personnel look for more meaningful and wider family involvement, implementing it becomes more challenging. In the past, "schools were content to develop a coterie of dedicated parents, willing and able to manage fundraisers and to provide volunteer help in classrooms. Today, while those contributions still matter, family involvement is seen as a primary vehicle for academic improvement—it calls on every family to actively participate in their children's education, at home and in school, and to become role models by actively volunteering and assuming leadership positions" (Berg, Melaville, & Blank 2006:16).

Parent/family engagement is a core component of successful efforts to integrate schools and communities. Replacing "parent" with "family" broadens the definition of a child's primary caregiver(s) to include grandparents, foster parents, and others who fulfill this role (Centers for Disease Control and Prevention 2013). In their efforts to improve development, learning, and health of youths, schools and community agencies engage parents in meaningful ways and in multiple settings including home, school, out-of-school programming, and the community (Centers for Disease Control and Prevention 2013). In order to be most effective, parent engagement should be "systemic, integrated and sustained"; it should involve "a shared responsibility in which families and schools play complementary roles"; it should be "continuous from birth through young adulthood"; and it "must support student learning in multiple settings" (Children's Aid Society National Center for Community Schools 2011:8).

Family engagement, though a critical component of education for all children, has been found to be especially beneficial for low-income families and students of color (Steen & Noguera 2010). Cooper and Crosnoe (2007) outline financial and time constraints that impact families living in poverty. These include long work hours with less flexibility, multiple physically demanding jobs, and limited transportation options. Additionally, these parents may be less optimistic about their children's abilities to be successful in school, less confident about their ability to intervene on behalf of their children, and less knowledgeable about the educational system. In addition, teachers can unintentionally pass on lower expectations and negative perceptions about both children in poverty and their parents. It is critical to understand and value the unique contexts of families in order to engage them successfully. For example, engaging with Native Americans, Latino/a, and Haitian immigrants needs to be understood in relation to each family's languages spoken and read, cultural beliefs, and immigration status (if relevant), in addition to income and race (Berg, Melaville, & Blank 2006; Bronstein & Kelly 1998; Lawson & Alameda-Lawson 2011; Olivos & Mendoza 2010). Other critical variables, such as transportation, combine with economic issues and differently impact successful engagement with rural families (Blitz et al. 2013). Therefore, while principles of engagement apply across populations and settings, different emphases may be needed for certain population groups and individuals to develop a successful family engagement program.

Family engagement comes in an array of forms, but a critical component of all effort on the part of schools is outreach. Families who have the interest and ability to participate in the life of the school already do so. In order to engage more families, especially those identified as "hard-to-reach," new methods must be employed. Sometimes a simple invitation will suffice. For example, the program director of Citizen Schools in Massachusetts individually called parents of 146 sixth-graders to invite them to an open school night at Garfield Middle School. This effort yielded a jump from the usual ten to fifteen families to participation by 200 people (Pappano 2010). Staff at Gardner Pilot Academy in Boston have also seen dramatic improvements in family participation in typical "parent events" since the school became a community school. Whereas only 25 percent of families participated in parent-teacher conferences in 1997, 98 percent of families participated in the 2010–11 school year (Chang & Lawyer 2012).

While time-consuming, home visits are an optimal way to engage and build trust with families. "Parents who feel wanted, needed, and appreciated tend to become more involved" (Berg, Melaville, & Blank 2006:20). When teachers conduct home visits, they have a chance to see where and how their students live. Berg et al.'s focus groups with principals revealed that home visits are most effective when a parent liaison or community partner arranges them. The authors encourage principals to provide release time for teachers so that home visits do not take away time from their classroom duties. Blitz et al. (2013) found home visits by community partners not employed by the school to be advantageous, especially where families have had negative experiences and distrust school personnel. In this model, community partners develop relationships with family members on the family's "turf" and then serve as liaisons between families and school personnel in the school buildings (Blitz et al. 2013; Bronstein & Kelly 1998).

The National Education Association (2008) outlines Joyce Epstein's six-component framework on the breadth of family engagement, which has been a guide for many school programs:

1 *Parenting.* Assist families with parenting skills, family support, understanding child and adolescent development, and setting home conditions to support learning at each age and grade level. Assist schools in understanding families' backgrounds, cultures, and goals for children.
2 *Communicating.* Communicate with families about school programs and student progress. Create two-way communication channels between school and home that are effective and reliable.
3 *Volunteering.* Improve recruitment and training to involve families as volunteers and as audiences at the school or in other locations. Enable

educators to work with volunteers who support students and the school. Provide meaningful work and flexible scheduling.

4 *Learning at Home.* Involve families with their children in academic learning at home, including homework, goal setting, and other curriculum-related activities.

5 *Decision-Making.* Include families as participants in school decisions, governance, and advocacy activities through school councils or improvement teams, committees, and other organizations.

6 *Collaborating with the Community.* Coordinate resources and services for families, students, and the school with community groups, including businesses, agencies, cultural and civic organizations, and colleges or universities.

Within each of Epstein's categories is a wide range of activities that occur at schools, each of which has its own particular structure. Similar connections with families are called for and occur in school-linked services across the globe. For example, Scotland's government mandate for extended schools states: "Schools will want to work closely with parents to shape these activities around the needs of their community and may choose to provide extra services in response to parental demand. . . . There is no blueprint for the types of activities that schools might offer. How these services look and are delivered in or through a particular school will vary" (Cummings, Dyson, & Todd 2011:20). So while the shape of a set of programs is expected to depend on child, family, school, and community needs and resources, the core role of the importance of parents in shaping them is clearly stated in this mandate from Scotland, which parallels the perspective and approach of those U.S. schools that function as components of well-integrated family-school-community partnerships.

While family engagement can have a range of benefits, a primary one is its impact on student attendance. Research with hundreds of students who ultimately dropped out of school reported that in the majority of cases, parents were not contacted when their children missed school, or even when they dropped out. Surveys with youth who had dropped out revealed that most believed that "communication between schools and parents needs to be greatly strengthened—that schools need to do more to invite parents in and be part of the solutions, and that parents need to do more themselves to be involved. One of the ways this deficit of parent involvement shows up is in truancy, where parents can be more involved simply by making sure their child shows up each day at school" (Bridgeland, DiIulio, & Morison 2006:14). As the section below reveals, attendance problems often begin at very early ages.

Attendance

According to the National Center for Children in Poverty, over 11 percent of children in kindergarten and almost 9 percent in first grade are chronically absent. Because chronic absence in the early years of schooling has deleterious outcomes for future success (Chang & Romero 2008), high-quality early childhood education programs are important components of addressing chronic absenteeism.

Attending school regularly is obviously a prerequisite to any and all kinds of school achievement, yet too many students have difficulty getting to school every day or even most days. Chang and Romero (2008) argue that attendance is higher when schools provide an engaging learning experience, have a stable core of experienced, skilled teachers, and actively engage parents in their children's education. Chronic absence decreases when schools and communities actively reach out and communicate early and consistently to families when their children begin to show patterns of excessive absence. Attendance is a complicated issue, impacted by factors in the family, school, and community. When families have difficulties impacting chronic absence it is often due to variables including unreliable transportation, "long work hours in poorly paid jobs with little flexibility, unstable and unaffordable housing, inadequate health care and escalating community violence" (Chang & Romero 2008:4).

Not surprisingly, chronic attendance issues are closely linked with high school dropout rates, with 43 percent of dropouts claiming that a major reason they withdrew from school was because they "missed too many days and could not catch up" (Bridgeland, DiIulio, & Morison 2006:3). Because dropping out of school is rarely a sudden decision and most often a gradual reflection of disengagement, attendance patterns should be attended to at all grade levels.

A number of effective efforts have emerged across the country to address chronic attendance problems. In order to target interventions, schools need to have reliable data about their students' attendance. Unfortunately, "many schools in America can't tell . . . on any given day who's in school and who's not" (Bridgeland, Dilulio, & Morison 2006:1). Attendance Works (http://www.attendanceworks.org/about/) provides a forum for sharing information about the range of effective approaches to improving school attendance. The organization generates and provides information so that school districts understand the value of tracking chronic absence data beginning before or at entrance to kindergarten and also have access to resources to support partnerships with families and community agencies to intervene when attendance is a problem. The objectives of Attendance Works include building public awareness of and political will for the importance of addressing chronic absence; developing coalitions that advance state and local policies for tracking and intervening to improve student attendance; and providing technical assistance and tools to help schools and communities to address chronic absence. Attendance Works has found that critical strategies for school sites involve: recognizing good and improved attendance; engaging students and parents; monitoring attendance data and practice; providing personalized early outreach; and developing programmatic responses to barriers.

Attendance Works' website includes innovative approaches that have proven effective in reducing absenteeism around the country. Examples include the approach used by City Year, a national nonprofit that places AmeriCorps members ages seventeen to twenty-four in 160 high-need schools in twenty U.S. cities. As part of City Year's Attendance Initiative, Corps members welcome each individual student on arriving at school every morning. "We're personalizing the school environment," says Jeff Jablow, City Year's vice president of strategy and operations. "Students know that there is someone waiting to greet them by name every morning, who cares about them, and who will support them throughout the day" (http://www.attendanceworks.org/what-works/multi-site-programs/city-year/). Another example comes from Diplomas Now schools, which offer incentives to encourage all students to come to school every day, such as breakfast in a VIP room or Diplomas Now dollars to use in a school store (http://www.attendanceworks.org/what-works/multi-site-programs/diplomas-now/). Check & Connect focuses on building trusting relationships. Student levels of engagement (as reflected in their attendance, grades, and behavior) are "checked" regularly by mentors and used to guide their efforts to increase and maintain students' "connection" with school (http://www.attendanceworks.org/what-works/multi-site-programs/minneapolis/).

Dropout Prevention and Intervention

"Once the global leader—after World War II the United States had the highest high school graduation rate in the world—the country now ranks 18th among the top 24 industrialized nations, with more than 1 million secondary school students dropping out every year" (Kania & Kramer 2011:36). High dropout rates in the United States "disproportionately affects young people who are low-income, minority, urban, single-parent children attending large, public high schools in the inner city." Approximately one-third of all public high school students in America fail to graduate; for minority youth (black, Hispanic, or Native American) the rate is closer to one-half (Bridgeland, Dilulio, & Morison 2006:1). Once these students withdraw from school, their trajectory continues to diverge from those who do graduate, and they are more likely than their peers "to be unemployed, living in poverty, receiving public assistance, in prison, on death row, unhealthy, divorced, and ultimately single parents with children who drop out from high school themselves" (Bridgeland, Dilulio, & Morison 2006:2).

A study conducted with more than five hundred ethnically and racially diverse students from around the country who had dropped out of school revealed that only a minority of youth claimed academic failure as the reason for their leaving school and that this held true whether they lived in urban, suburban, or rural areas. Of these dropouts, 70 percent were confident that they could have graduated if they had tried. While they cited a complex array of issues involved in their decisions to drop out, most related predominantly to a lack of engagement with school, as well as to a number of non-school variables, including needing to get a job and make money, becoming a parent, and/or needing to care for a family member (Bridgeland, Dilulio, & Morison 2006). In conversations with these students, researchers found them offering their own recommendations for schools looking to help youths graduate, including:

1 Improve teaching and curricula to make school more relevant and engaging, and enhance the connection between school and work;

2. Improve instruction and access to supports for struggling students;
3. Build a school climate that fosters academics;
4. Ensure that students have a strong relationship with at least one adult in the school; and
5. Improve the communication between parents and schools (Bridgeland, Dilulio, & Morison 2006:iv–v).

These youths' voices regarding reforms to support more successful graduates echo the need for a multisector approach addressed throughout this book. Clearly stated, "strategies for dropout prevention work best when built on a foundation of school-community collaboration and implemented in the context of a strategic plan" (Smink & Schargel 2004:66).

A vital element of dropout prevention is mentoring, as highlighted above by the youths' emphasis on the importance of students having a strong relationship with at least one adult in the school. When asked what led to the choice to drop out, students typically respond with: "No one cared if I stayed or left" (Smink & Schargel 2004:139). In reference to dropout prevention, Milliken says, "Programs don't change kids—relationships do. Every child needs one adult who's irrationally committed to his or her future. . . . A good program creates an environment where healthy relationships can occur" (2007:7). While mentoring is not a novel concept, it has emerged as an increasingly effective support for twenty-first-century youth whose families are geographically dispersed and/or less able to be involved in their children's education and lives for a host of reasons.

While traditional mentoring occurs between one youth and one adult, other forms of mentoring have developed that include group mentoring (one adult with up to four youth), team mentoring (several adults with a small group of youth), peer mentoring (youth mentoring other youth), intergenerational mentoring (matching an older adult with youth), and e-mentoring (mentoring through electronic means) (Smink & Schargel 2004). Simply put, "a mentor is . . . a wise and trusted friend with a commitment to provide guidance and support" (Smink & Schargel 2004:139).

Initiatives from a variety of public and nonprofit entities effectively promote and support mentoring. A national program, America's Promise, joins statewide mentoring programs from California, Connecticut, Texas, and Massachusetts, and both older and newer nonprofit organizations like Big Brothers Big Sisters, 100 Black Men, and Communities in Schools (detailed below) to implement widespread, important mentoring programs. Regardless of format, mentoring relationships benefit by structure and adherence to best practices. Two large meta-analyses that collectively evaluated close to eight hundred mentoring efforts have found the following to be the most critical components of successful mentoring programs:

1 Engaging in social activities;
2 Engaging in academic activities;
3 Number of hours per month that youth and mentors meet;
4 Decision-making about the use of time;
5 Pre-match orientation and training;
6 Post-match training and support;
7 Mentor youth with similarity of interests;
8 Age of the mentee;
9 Monitoring of program implementation;
10 Access to community setting for mentoring activities;
11 Mentors whose background includes a helping role or profession;
12 Expectations for frequency of contact;
13 Ongoing training;
14 Structured activities for the mentors and youth; and
15 Parental support and involvement (Smink & Schargel 2004:147).

The final section of Smink and Schargel's (2004) book on dropout prevention argues the importance of evaluation and of implementing what we know to be effective in minimizing the numbers of youth dropping out of school. This includes the following components: early education; mentoring; alternative education for a diversity of learning styles; professional development for teachers; individualized instruction; instructional technology; community collaboration; and safe, supportive, and nurturing school environments.

Milliken (2007) presents a three-sided triangle critical for eliminating school dropouts. While he says the United States is actively engaged in reform efforts targeted at two sides of the triangle—the content of education including the curriculum and pedagogical strategies; and the form of education including school management and governance—what is missing is "the community component that will meet the nonacademic needs of children" (Milliken 2007: xxvii). An exemplary dropout prevention initiative, Communities in Schools (CIS) is profiled below.

COMMUNITIES IN SCHOOLS (CIS) (Information provided by Dan Cardinali, President; Heather Clawson, Vice President, Research, Evaluation, and Innovation)

BRIEF OVERVIEW

Communities in Schools is a national dropout prevention network with the stated mission of empowering students to "stay in school and achieve in life." The CIS model is premised on surrounding at-risk youth with a community of support, including local businesses, social service agencies, health care providers, and parent and volunteer organizations. A trained site coordinator, often a professional social worker who is based in the school building, manages these integrated student supports. Working with other members of the school management team, the site coordinator conducts a needs assessment at the beginning of each school year to determine risk factors for the student population in general, and in particular for the 5–15 percent of students identified as most in need of support. Next, the site coordinator works with the school to develop a comprehensive prevention/intervention strategy serving 75 percent of students, along with intensive, individualized case management plans for the subset of students deemed most "at-risk."

In short, the primary elements of the CIS model include:

1. A site coordinator assessing needs at the beginning of the year;
2. The use of evidence-based community resources;
3. A public health model with two levels of prevention/intervention services; and
4. Constant monitoring and adjustment over the course of the year to ensure service delivery is driving outcomes.

Coordination is a key factor in the success of this model; the goal is to ensure that all services are being delivered in an integrated and collaborative way.

OBJECTIVE IN DEVELOPING THE INITIATIVE

As CIS has evolved, two fundamental goals have emerged: meeting the needs of the most at-risk students through integrated supports tailored to their individual needs; and increasing the scale of broader preventative programs (currently 1.3 million students in 375 school systems) in order to establish integrated student supports as a critical part of the design of public education.

Succinctly, the goal is to have the best model with the best outcomes, and to use these results to impact policy in order to make the benefits available to all students.

PROCESS OF DEVELOPMENT

The original organization was started about thirty-five years ago by a group of adults, some of whom were dropouts themselves, while others were successful students convinced that the public school system was not serving them or their peers well. For the first dozen years or so, CIS was in the social entrepreneur innovation phase, when "crashes and burns" were not uncommon. By the early 1990s, a more focused CIS realized that as a community-based nonprofit, the best way to bring resources to schools was through partnerships with the local business and social service community. This hyper-local approach met with mixed results: by the mid-1990s, when CIS and the Justice Department performed an evaluation in forty-five communities, the inescapable conclusion was that CIS programming was excessively heterogeneous.

In response, national leadership agreed upon a more standardized system in order to ensure fidelity to the model and encourage its replication. The upside to this was the development of a collective identity across divergent communities. A strong evaluation component was introduced in the late 1990s, helping CIS to better understand its network, students, partners, volunteers, and outcomes. For the first time, CIS had reliable data on attendance, behavior, course performance, dropouts, and graduation rates across the network.

In 2005, CIS launched a five-year evaluation aimed at learning what was going right and wrong and what practices were yielding the best results. Analysis of school-level outcomes as well as individual student outcomes demonstrated the impact of integrated student supports. Placing schools along a continuum of fidelity to the CIS model helped to identify the inflection points where a noticeable difference in outcomes occurred.

Currently, CIS is engaging in yet another major national evaluation with the goal of learning even more about implementation, identifying what works and what does not, and where to achieve the greatest cost efficiencies while still maximizing results. The national office is working to assist all CIS affiliates to become compliant with the evidence-based standards gleaned from these evaluations.

COLLABORATIVE ACTIVITIES/STRUCTURES

Today CIS operates urban, suburban, and rural programs in kindergarten through grade 12—more than 2,200 sites total. There are about 187 local affiliates in twenty-six states and the District of Columbia. Nearly half of those affiliates have been accredited under the Total Quality System, which seeks to ensure consistent business and site operation practices linked to measurable outcomes throughout the network, and all remaining affiliates are in the process of accreditation.

In every local affiliate, site coordinators are the front-line service providers connecting students with the resources they need to stay in school. The site coordinator is typically a full-time, paid employee of CIS, though part-time employees and repositioned personnel are sometimes used. Depending on the size of the school, a single site coordinator may lead multiple staff in providing targeted case management services. All CIS site coordinators are attached to the local affiliate, and they typically have a toolbox full of community resources that they can bring to bear on individual cases, including public health departments, social service agencies, rural clinics, etc. In addition, many affiliates have a program director responsible for resource mapping across multiple sites.

The vast majority of local CIS affiliates are partnering with local organizations that meet basic needs such as food, shelter, and housing. Affiliates may also seek out organizations that provide enrichment, life skills, social/emotional learning, family engagement, and other broad prevention services. In addition, the national office maintains relationships with leading national nonprofits such as YMCA, AmeriCorps, Boys and Girls Clubs, and Big Brothers/Big Sisters, helping to ensure efficient delivery of services at the local level. In all of its myriad relationships, CIS sees itself as the lead coordinating agency, ensuring the kind of integrated services required for successful outcomes.

TARGET POPULATION

Approximately 1.3 million students receive support from CIS each year, including a subset of 134,000 highest-need students of whom 80 percent are students of color and 97 percent are economically disadvantaged. The majority of CIS schools are Title I, and many have been designated "in need of improvement."

FEATURED PROGRAMS

Some accredited affiliates with comprehensive sites and highest levels of fidelity to the CIS model have programs working at a remarkably impressive scale. In Richmond, Virginia, for instance, CIS operates in fully 85 percent of public schools, and the CIS model is present in a huge preponderance of schools in Austin and Houston, Texas.

SERVICE PROVIDERS/PARTNERS

The provision of services comes from the community—from the most evidence-based intervention and prevention programs that meet the need portfolio of the school. Service delivery is routinely monitored so that quick action can be taken if it is not working or if dosage and/or content needs to be changed, as well as to learn from providers where service delivery is and is not working well.

LOCATION OF SERVICES

Because it is located inside the school, CIS can identify at-risk students in a timely manner and quickly connect them to a mix of external partners chosen to meet their individual needs. All work is done in collaboration with the school district and the leadership team at individual schools. Services are delivered primarily on school grounds, with the exception of mental health and some other services. For example, an established program like the Boys and Girls Club may be delivered at a partner site in the community and not on school grounds.

TYPES OF SERVICES DELIVERED

With specific goals in place for improved attendance and academic performance, the CIS site coordinator seeks out and manages the needed supports. Level 1 services, including clothing or school supplies, parent engagement, attendance initiatives, topic-specific assemblies, career fairs, health screenings, and grief counseling, are accessible to all students within a school. Level 2 services are targeted, holistic interventions tailored to specific students and usually require an enrollment procedure. These services may include counseling, mentoring, tutoring, free or low-cost health/dental care, and safe housing.

FUNDING

At the local level, CIS affiliates are funded through numerous sources, including school district budgets, state grants, federal programs such as Title I, and private donations from individuals and businesses. As individual 501(c)(3) entities, affiliates have their own board responsible for local fundraising, while the statewide organization works on funding at the state level. In addition, the national office maintains an active and successful development effort, with a significant portion of donations returned to affiliates through challenge grants and other programs.

IMPLEMENTATION CHALLENGES

Communities in Schools runs a large network, with many of the same management challenges and financial pressures faced by other national nonprofit organizations. But the labor-intensive nature of the CIS model, with its emphasis on one-on-one relationships, means that issues related to human capital tend to present the biggest challenges to implementation.

In every community in which it operates, CIS faces demand that far outstrips its capacity for delivering integrated supports. In many schools, 60–70 percent of students could benefit from more intensive service—a constant source of stress for site coordinators who are passionate about their work, yet already spread too thin. Turnover further complicates this chronic imbalance between supply and demand. Although low in comparison to other nonprofits, CIS has a five-year average turnover rate on the front lines. As a result, CIS must constantly manage its talent pipeline, attracting site coordinators who are deeply passionate about the mission and professional in outlook. Currently 88 percent of site coordinators have post-secondary degrees, and many are licensed or certified social workers; 42 percent are bilingual.

Another challenge is dealing with great variation in economic resources in a community. Most affiliates use public dollars to sustain their work. Because of the increasing pressure on public budgets, CIS has worked overtime at the national level to attract funding from foundations and other private sources as part of an effort to reduce budgetary uncertainty so employees are not constantly worried about losing their jobs or earning a livable wage.

EVALUATION

As mentioned previously, evaluation efforts began relatively early in the history of Communities in Schools, and constant feedback is considered a part of the network's DNA. The most recent comprehensive national evaluation included up to ten different studies designed to identify which aspects of the CIS model correlate most strongly with positive results for schools and students. A new evaluation was launched in 2012 under the auspices of a Social Innovation Fund (SIF) grant, with the goal of better understanding the optimum dosage and mix of services for differing student populations, ideal caseloads for site coordinators, etc. In addition, a first-ever longitudinal study is in the works to track the long-term success of students, years after their CIS experience. Because improved practice is a primary goal of CIS evaluation efforts, the national office is currently investing in new information systems to ensure that site coordinators and other local staff can access relevant data on demand, giving them the ability to make programming decisions and corrections based on real-time information.

In this challenging environment, CIS has consistently achieved remarkable results, with 97 percent of case-managed students in grades K–11 being promoted to the next grade and 96 percent of eligible seniors graduating.

FUTURE DIRECTIONS

Communities in Schools has three clear goals for the future. One is continuing a national proof point that makes it impossible to deny the need for integrated student supports throughout the public education system. The second goal involves branding the network to increase awareness of student supports and to impact public dialogue on the issue. Finally, CIS is working intentionally and tirelessly on policy initiatives at the federal and state level to ensure that integrated student supports are present in the implementation of the Common Core or in the architecture of other school reform efforts.

Nutrition

The last component of full-service community school initiatives we address in this section is nutrition since good nutrition is universally agreed to be a core component in promoting readiness to learn. "Learning to eat and eating to learn are opportunities that schools can provide today's students to help them maximize education achievements, develop healthy lifestyles, and lower their risk of chronic disease" (Caldwell, Nestle, & Rogers 1998). With emphasis from First Lady Michelle Obama, nutritional efforts have increasingly become a focus of school-community initiatives to promote healthy students, families, and communities. This is, in part, in response to the fact that "obesity has reached epidemic proportions in the United States" and that behaviors established in childhood often continue across the life span, making preventing and reducing childhood obesity "a major public health priority" (Fagen et al. 2014:96); in addition, most young people "have unhealthy eating habits" (Caldwell, Nestle, & Rogers 1998:196).

Caldwell, Nestle, and Rogers advocate a school-community approach to improving nutrition and overall health, with the following essential components:

1. Access to a variety of nutritious, culturally appropriate foods that promote growth and development, pleasure in healthy eating, and long-term health, as well as prevent school-day hunger and its consequent lack of attention to learning tasks;
2. Nutrition education that empowers students to select and enjoy healthy food and physical activity; and
3. Screening, assessment, counseling, and referral for nutrition problems and the provision of modified meals for students with special needs (1998:197).

Critical to the success of these three components is a coordinated health effort promoted by a supportive school environment and reinforced by school staff, families, and the local community. This is especially critical where efforts are targeted to students from low-income homes, so that stigma does not get in the way of their taking advantage of services like free meals. It also requires providing adequate time and space for students to eat meals in a safe environment. "Improving the quality of school meals will have little effect if students do not eat the school meals" (Caldwell, Nestle, & Rogers 1998:200).

Caldwell, Nestle, and Rogers highlight an array of partnerships that can support healthy eating. For one, classroom health education can be supported by food service managers who involve students in planning menus and preparing recipes, educate students about preparing healthy meals, display nutrition information about foods served, and offer specific foods that complement class lessons. Second, physical education teachers and foodservice managers can work collaboratively to teach students about the importance of an approach to health that combines physical activity with healthy eating, so that these messages are not singularly delivered. Third, collaboration with families can occur in a range of ways, including inviting families to eat at school with their children, sending school menus home with other school messages, and including family input into school meals. Fourth, community organizations can provide schools with guest speakers, educational materials, and other targeted interventions. Fifth, involving school staff in these efforts is one of the best ways to promote adult role modeling of healthy eating. Sixth, coordinating with school social workers and other school mental health professionals provides a bridge for addressing psychosocial issues that impact healthy eating. And last, "all school personnel can foster a healthy school environment by supporting policies that ensure a variety of healthy food choices wherever food is available in the school" and by "involving the entire school community in efforts that promote good nutrition" (1998:210).

In February 2014, First Lady Michelle Obama joined U.S. Department of Agriculture Secretary Tom Vilsack to announce proposed guidelines for local school wellness policies. "The food marketing and local wellness standards proposed today support better health for our kids and echo the good work already taking place at home and in schools across the country. The new standards ensure that schools remain a safe place where kids can learn and where the school environment promotes healthy choices. USDA is committed to working closely with students, parents, school stakeholders and the food and beverage industries to implement the new guidelines and make the healthy choice, the easy choice for America's young people," Secretary Vilsack said (U.S. Department of Agriculture 2014).

Currently there are a number of federal programs that support good nutrition through school-community collaboration. One initiative is the USDA Farm to School Program, through which an increasing number of schools and districts are utilizing local foods and providing related programming to students about food, farming, and nutrition. This effort includes grants, research, training, and technical assistance to bring local and/or regionally produced foods into school cafeterias; implement hands-on learning such as school gardening, farm visits, and culinary classes; and the integration of nutrition-related education with standard curriculum (Food and Nutrition Service 2014). In Kentucky, for example, Owsley Elementary School has a Farm to School grant that supports a pizza garden, which children grow to provide vegetables for the school cafeteria. Another Farm to School grant supports a high school gardening project. Produce from both gardens is "Kentucky Proud" certified and sold in the local famer's market (Williams 2010).

A federal program that addresses out-of-school time, the At-Risk Afterschool Snack and Supper Program, provides nutrition assistance so that afterschool programs serving children and teens in low-income neighborhoods can offer free snacks and suppers. When children are well nourished, they have the energy to focus on homework, socialize with peers, and participate in physical activities;, children and teens who eat these free, healthy snacks and suppers are also discouraged from eating junk food. Since afterschool programs often provide food for students, taking advantage of government support means that they have more funds left for programming and other purposes (New York State Afterschool Network & Hunger Solutions New York 2010).

A third program that supports community-school partnership for better nutrition is the U.S. Centers for Disease Control and Prevention (CDC) Communities Putting Prevention to Work (CPPW) initiative, funded by the American Recovery and Reinvestment Act of 2009 and the Patient Protection and Affordable Care Act of 2010. One recipient of this support, suburban Cook County (Chicago area), awarded mini-grants to thirty-eight local school districts, governments, and community organizations to make healthy foods more available and unhealthy foods less available in communities and schools; create convenient, safe places for walking, biking, and other physical activities; increase opportunities for physical activity in schools; and support children walking and biking to school (Fagen et al. 2014).

Many other initiatives exist, supported by state and local efforts, nonprofit organizations, colleges and universities, and local and national foundations. Two notable Vermont programs include the University of

Vermont's Expanded Food and Nutrition Education program, a six-week program that encourages parents and caregivers to prepare healthy, affordable meals; and the Stanford Vocational Culinary Arts Program, which is housed in Noble High School in Bennington and has students in the two-year program operate a fifty-person restaurant that is open during school hours. The restaurant functions not only as a place for obtaining nutritious food, but also as a gathering space for students, teachers, and community members (Williams 2010).

Another successful school-linked nutrition program, the Agatston Urban Nutrition Initiative (AUNI), is part of the Netter Center's university-assisted community schools initiative (see chapter 4), which grew out of a University of Pennsylvania anthropology course. "While AUNI's emphasis is on nutrition education and food access in West Philadelphia, it works in a total of 20 Philadelphia public schools, serving more than 10,000 students every month. Hands-on cooking and gardening clubs and youth-run fruit stands connect school day and afterschool learning activities for K–12 students, as well as connect to the academic work of Penn students and faculty" (https://www.nettercenter.upenn.edu/programs/auni).

Currently AUNI has two major program initiatives that include the EAT.RIGHT.NOW program, and the Youth Development program. In addition to providing nutrition education in twenty Philadelphia schools, EAT.RIGHT.NOW conducts hands-on afterschool cooking and gardening clubs to reinforce content learned during the school day and to provide students with opportunities for practical knowledge and experience. AUNI's signature project is a youth-run afterschool fruit stand that empowers youth to become agents of change in their own community and increase access to fruits, vegetables, and healthy snacks (https://www.nettercenter.upenn.edu/programs/auni).

The AUNI Youth Development program provides paid internships to more than sixty high school students during the school year and over one hundred students each summer. Working hand in hand with EAT.RIGHT.NOW, students teach healthy cooking classes, tend school gardens, and operate local farmers' markets, thereby increasing access to local, organic, affordable, and culturally relevant food; creating tools for self-reliance; providing a space to deepen relationships with the land, food, and each other; improving community and school health; and developing leadership capacity and academic and job-related skills. AUNI's Youth Development interns have opportunities to develop professional relationships and showcase their expertise through participation in regional and national networks and conferences (https://www.nettercenter.upenn.edu/programs/auni).

LINKING OUTCOMES AND GOALS IN COMMUNITY SCHOOLS

Kenning (2011) reports on one of the Cincinnati public schools where in the late 1990s less than 20 percent of students reached tenth grade, and where, after implementing a community schools model, in 2010, 82 percent of students graduated from high school (Jacobson, Hodges, & Blank 2011). More details on outcomes of community schools are presented in chapter 9, as well as through the exemplars. However, it is important to state here that while primary desired outcomes are those that positively impact student learning, community schools have shown a broad range of outcomes in addition to and beyond student academic learning, such as improved relationships among peers, better health and school attendance, stronger family engagement through opportunities for parents, improved school climate and safer neighborhoods (Children's Aid Society 2011). Community schools overtly state that their goals extend beyond academics; for example, the Cincinnati community schools' goals are "to support student achievement, revitalize neighborhoods and maximize the community's return on their financial investments" (http://www.cps-k12.org/).

Scotland, discussed in chapter 6, has been among the leading implementers of community schools. Smith (2004) outlines benefits in Scotland that extend beyond students and their academic careers and directly benefit schools, community-based agencies, and communities. These benefits are also relevant for community schools in the United States. *Benefits to children and youth* include improved early intervention and early warning action; improved attendance rates; improved academics; improved employment prospects; less drug abuse; and reduced teenage pregnancies. *Benefits to schools* include expert services and counseling in schools, which support teachers and pupils and improve efficiency by staff collaboration; the "one-stop" school-based service center, which enhances the role of the school as a central place in the community; improved communications between school and home; reduction in parental alienation from schools and mistrust of parents by schools and teachers; and engagement of previously disaffected young people in the school system through school-based services. *Benefits to community-based agencies* include working more closely with schools, especially when based in them, allowing greater collaboration and attention to the whole child; and improved communication between agencies, resulting in more efficient and effective service provision. *Benefits to communities* include reduction in crime and violence; improved health of families; better access to services and resources that might not otherwise be readily available; and more productive partnerships among schools, parents, and the wider community.

MOVING ON THE CONTINUUM FROM SINGLE OR MULTIPLE SERVICES TO AN INTEGRATED SYSTEM OF SCHOOL-LINKED SERVICES

In schools and communities interested in moving from a single or multiple service to an integrated system, the Children's Aid Society has developed the following four-stage, nonlinear model reflecting this process:

1. *Exploring*: This stage begins with discontent about the current way a school operates and a desire to improve or change it. Creative large-scale thinking, high energy, and optimism mark this stage. These thoughts, dreams, and emotions contribute to the shaping of a shared vision.
2. *Emerging*: This stage is characterized by a commitment to jump in and do something. An assessment helps determine initial program design. As a shared vision and clearly defined goals emerge, some of the groundwork is laid. A decision is made to start the transformation of a school or schools by introducing some services, securing initial funding, and establishing partnerships. The success of this stage is based on a shared commitment to the vision and goals, clear communication around roles and responsibilities, dynamic responsiveness to documented needs, and taking time for recognition and celebration. This phase commonly lasts about two years.
3. *Maturing*: The hallmark of this stage is steady, intentional progress toward goals. The vision becomes clearer, and, consequently, there is greater internal and external support. The community school begins functioning better; service utilization increases and improves; and relationships between the school and its community partners deepen and become more natural as partners realize that their work requires continuous and significant effort.

4 *Excelling*: At this stage, high-quality programs are fully integrated into the fabric of the school. The school culture focuses on addressing the needs of the whole child and invites increased parent involvement, establishing strong relationships within the school, community, and school district. The entire school staff values the partnerships that transform the school (2011:33–34).

* * *

Using literature and profiles of exemplary school-linked services programs, strategies, and services, this chapter has illustrated the diverse and wide range of ways that different communities and schools engage in partnerships to support student success. Primary concerns addressed through these efforts have been described, such as chronic absenteeism, high school dropout rates, and challenges in family engagement. A broad array of community school efforts have been profiled to illustrate the range of ways opportunities for pursuing these efforts develop and come to fruition. Chapter 4 addresses barriers and supports for the boundary-crossing work that is required to make these efforts successful, specifically describing how services integration, interprofessional and interorganizational collaboration, and collective impact provide the foundation for school-linked services.

4

Working Effectively Across Systems

BECAUSE THERE ARE MANY ORGANIZATIONS and professionals developing and providing services when schools and communities join efforts, an integrated approach to service delivery is a critical framework. Adams uses the term *cross-boundary leadership* to describe an arrangement where principals and other educators maintain their leadership authority even as "all school role groups" are empowered to "share responsibility for student and school performance and to work collectively toward common outcomes" (2010:13).

While most professionals today espouse the importance of using an integrated, collaborative team-based approach, this is easier said than done. This is especially important in an era characterized by financial constraints, which require strategic approaches to resource sharing. All agency professionals worry about the security of their own programs and jobs. Despite the challenges, Horwath and Morrison (2007) note that the manner in which the process of moving toward greater collaboration is handled is as important as any of the decisions about goals, governance, or structures. They suggest attention to building trust and nurturing relationships in the process of building partnerships.

The recent recommendation signed by U.S. Department of Education Secretary Duncan and American Federation of Teachers (AFT) president Randi Weingarten states: "Improving student learning and educational equity require strong, consistent, and sustained collaboration among parents, teachers, school boards, superintendents and administrators, business leaders, and the community. And such improvements require that we all take responsibility for the academic and social well-being of the students in our charge" (2013:1). What follows is an outline of the challenges, strategies, and benefits of working across organizations and across professional lines in linking and integrating services, communities, and schools.

SERVICES INTEGRATION

A major impetus for the school-linked services movement grew from the program development model of *services integration*, defined as the "systematic effort to solve problems of service fragmentation and of the lack of an exact match between an individual or family with problems and needs, and an interventive program or professional specialty" (Kahn & Kamerman 1992:5). Whereas the roots of services integration in the United States reach back to charity organizations and settlement houses, this approach to service delivery reemerged in the early 1970s from Secretary of Health, Education and Welfare Elliot Richardson. In the late 1980s, the approach again emerged as a vehicle to counter a system of services for poor families characterized by a categorical nature, fragmentation, inaccessibility, and inadequacy (Hare 1995).

Kagan et al. (1995) highlight the following functions of service integration: to bring together previously unconnected services; to overturn past practice, policy, or bureaucracy; to create mechanisms that work to promote and sustain integrative strategies; and to change relationships for and among people and institutions. They outline the following elements as components of a comprehensive service integration effort:

1 Integration efforts within and across disciplines;
2 Multiple approaches seeking "broad based reform that affects clients, programs, policy, and organizational bureaucracy" (1995:145);
3 Efforts involving multiple levels of government;
4 The existence of clear avenues of reciprocity and communication between different levels of government;
5 Creative, broad-based involvement, including consumers, the private sector, media, etc.; and
6 A results orientation, with clearly identified goals and accomplishments.

Services integration has been a preferred means to address children's services (especially in the health and social service sectors) in the United

Kingdom under the New Labour government. It includes a range of services that require collaborative efforts, from early interventions for children, to criminal justice and education (Hood 2014).

COLLABORATION

Collaboration can be described as the preferred "how-to" of service integration, a method of creating and sustaining a seamless system of human services and education. The literature on linking schools and communities suggests that effective collaboration is essential for success (Adelman & Taylor 2000; Kline & Brabeck 1999) and should occur at both the organizational level (interagency/interorganizational collaboration) and at the professional/individual level (interdisciplinary/interprofessional) collaboration. In the United Kingdom, the term *integrated working* is used to refer to collaboration at a range of levels: interpersonal, interprofessional, and interagency (Hood 2014). Bruner describes the process of collaboration as jointly developing and agreeing to a set of common goals and directions; sharing responsibility for obtaining those goals; and working together to achieve those goals, using the expertise of each collaborator (1991:6).

Several authors have distinguished between collaboration and other closely related terms describing how individuals and organizations work together. Bruner (1991) makes a distinction between collaboration and communication; he describes the latter as helping people do their jobs better by providing each with more complete information, but not requiring any joint activity (p. 6). Kagan describes the concepts of collaboration, coordination, and cooperation as a pyramid, with cooperation at the base, since it is "the most widespread and easiest to achieve" (1992:59). She describes cooperation as involving informal relationships that exist in the absence of any defined structure or understanding of mutual goals. Coordination, at the middle level of the pyramid, involves individuals and organizations coming together to fulfill a shared goal. "At this level, agencies retain their autonomy, though they engage in sustained joint planning" (1992:59). Collaboration, at the apex, is the most complex and difficult to actualize. "Here, joint goals and strategies are agreed on, resources and leadership are shared, and an identifiable durable collaborative structure is established" (1992:60). Horwath and Morrison identify collaboration on a spectrum encompassing the following five levels:

1. *Communication*, where individuals from different disciplines talk together;
2. *Cooperation*, involving joint working on a case-by-case basis;
3. *Coordination*, involving formalized joint working, but without sanctions for noncompliance;
4. *Coalition*, involving joint structures where agencies give up some autonomy; and
5. *Integration*, where organizations come together to create a new joint identity (2007:56).

Melaville and Blank (1991) provide examples of successful cooperatives and collaboratives. In cooperative arrangements, partners assist each other in meeting their own organizational goals, without requiring any substantial alterations in basic services or in the policies or funding streams that govern their respective agencies. In contrast, collaborative initiatives create fundamental changes in the way services are designed and delivered. Cooperative efforts may be "a reasonable starting point for change," but "efforts must become increasingly collaborative if they hope to achieve the goal of comprehensive service delivery" (1991:14). This is especially true for services geared toward "fragile families" (Bruner 1991). For the fortunate, the family serves as the collaborator of services, but "fragile families" confront a host of difficulties in taking on this role: they have a harder time assessing and using all the services they need; they are more likely to be involved with a variety of services; and when "system failures" occur, these families often lack the necessary resources to combat the problems (Bruner 1991:7).

While services integration represents a type of program to be built, and collaboration represents a preferred way of building and implementing it, occasionally the terms are used interchangeably. Looking at the research on successful characteristics of each reveals the following elements common to both: clear values and goals, broad community support, flexibility in funding, effective communication (verbal and/or electronic), and overall flexibility and clear professional roles balanced by porous interdisciplinary/interprofessional boundaries. As attributes of both services integration and collaboration, these elements are critical in the development and carrying out of school-linked services programs at both the organizational and individual professional levels.

Interagency Collaboration

"We live in an era of partnering, of joining institutional forces to accomplish complex societal changes through finding common ground" (Noam 2001:4). Schools and communities partner together in a range of ways to improve the lives of children, families, and neighborhoods. While a side-by-side partnership is at one end of the spectrum, an integrated collaborative partnership at the other end of the spectrum, has the best opportunity to reduce fragmentation and duplication of services and thus to more adequately meet the needs of a community's children and families.

A report from the Centers for Disease Control states that interagency collaboration is a core component of "coordinated school health" and describes this process as "identifying appropriate partner organizations and cultivating relationships with those organizations to meet mutual goals" (n.d.16). Appropriate partners have knowledge and skills for identifying people and resources to help meet programmatic needs, which they carry out by "linking with strategic partners both within and across agencies. They must be familiar with various organizations' policies and protocols, as well as applicable federal, state, and local laws, regulations, and codes. They also possess the ability to recognize when they need help, where to get it, and how to utilize it" (n.d.:16).

Despite the strong beliefs that interagency collaboration should characterize school-linked services, the process of effectively carrying this out is fraught with challenges. These difficulties arise in all aspects of the process, including the development of new forms of leadership, breaking down boundaries between service delivery and service recipients, legitimizing interprofessional collaboration, and developing and negotiating interagency agreements and other contractual arrangements (Mooney, Kline, & Davoren 1999).

Weist, Ambrose, and Lewis (2006) delineate guidelines for collaboration across organizations, which together form the building blocks of successful school-linked services partnerships. The process begins with strong alliances between and among the leaders of the community organizations and the school. As leaders affirm their commitment to collaboration, it is important to involve as many school and community-based staff as possible in the development and goal-setting process. Caruso suggests an "asset inventory" (2000:111) as a way to bring community and school service providers together to assess both resources and gaps. Such alliances should be followed up and formalized in memoranda of understanding (MOU) in which expectations for each organization are delineated and agreed upon. LaCour (1982) suggests that the MOU should guide and reflect a "system of care" that supports all organizational partners and should indicate:

1 The purpose for the agreement;
2 The responsibilities of each agency along with the method for performing those responsibilities;
3 Standards each agency will meet when performing an activity;
4 Procedures for exchanging information on common clients; and
5 The method for modifying the agreement.

Casto et al. describe the critical components of an ideal functional system of care that is built on effective interorganizational collaboration:

> A functional system of care would be conversant with the language and culture of different agencies; it would have mechanisms for integrating work involving multiple providers; it would have a means of making decisions involving multiple decision-makers and working out funding of care involving multiple sources; it would have a mechanism for defining standards against which to program and evaluate comprehensive interventions; and it would have a means for holding the community and its families in primary focus even as the administrative rigmarole demands near-total attention. (1994:8)

Finding strong collaborators is critical in successful interorganizational collaborations. Caruso (2000) makes the case that universities are often excellent organizational partners in school-linked services collaborations and systems of care, and indeed they are increasingly partners in these efforts. They can supply interns from a wide variety of relevant professional schools, including social work, education, nursing, counseling, occupational therapy, psychology, and others, while university faculty and researchers may be available to assist with consultation, grant writing, and program evaluation (see page 130 on public school–university partnerships). In addition to universities and colleges, the Children's Aid Society (2011) notes that potential school-linked services agency partners can include child welfare authorities; local hospitals and other health providers; local businesses and corporations; vocational schools; community foundations; police and other law enforcement agencies; libraries; arts and cultural institutions; legal assistance organizations; local elected city and county offices; and state government agencies.

Smink and Schargel (2004) describe the "educative community" that can grow out of strong school-community interorganizational collaborations. These educative communities include schools, homes, places of worship, media, museums, libraries, and the workplace and are partnerships where all participants share responsibility and accountability. High-quality interagency collaborations that support educative communities need to be built upon, and by, professionals who operate outside of silos and practice interprofessional/interdisciplinary collaboration.

Interprofessional/Interdisciplinary Collaboration

A critical requirement of working in any role in and with schools today includes an understanding that the process of education requires a variety of professionals to interact with each other (Forbes & Watson 2009). Given that school-linked services involve an array of professionals, whether we use the term "interdisciplinary," "interprofessional," "trans-," or "multidisciplinary," the practice of working effectively across professional lines is integral to this effort.

Interprofessional collaboration has been said to be "fundamental" to the process of creating full-service schools, along with understanding the complexities that it brings (McInnis-Dittrich, Neisler, & Tourse 1999). Anderson-Butcher and Ashton (2004) outline the ways that collaboration among different professionals working with schools, children, and families can improve school mental health interventions. Such collaboration improves other interventions too, including those geared toward physical health, academic success, etc., and involve:

1. Increasing access to services for students and families;
2. Broadening the range of prevention and intervention services in schools;
3. Reducing service duplication;
4. Providing professional support and decreasing burn-out among school professionals; and
5. Increasing the professional knowledge and skills of team members.

Just as there tends to be consensus that interagency collaboration is a requirement for implementation of school-linked services, so, too, is there consensus about the need for collaboration among professionals across disciplinary lines. In both cases, collaboration is a complex endeavor. Professional differences in socialization, role perceptions and definitions, and terminology are typical barriers to interprofessional collaboration in school-linked services (Bronstein & Abramson 2003; Mellin, Anderson-Butcher, & Bronstein 2011). Additional challenges include: divergent perceptions and "rules" about confidentiality (Bronstein & Terwilliger 2007; Mellin & Weist 2011); time constraints; space constraints; and personal relationships (Bronstein 2002, 2003).

Researchers have developed, tested, and expanded theoretically sound models to guide helpful, interdisciplinary collaboration in school-linked services (Bronstein 2002, 2003; Mellin, Anderson-Butcher, & Bronstein 2011; Mellin et al. 2010). These models highlight the following components of interdisciplinary collaboration, all of which are essential for success:

1. *Interdependence* refers to the reliance upon interactions between professionals, where each is dependent upon the other to accomplish his or her goals and tasks. Some behaviors that characterize interdependence include: time spent together, communication among professional colleagues, and respect for colleagues' professional opinions and input.
2. *Newly created professional activities* refer to collaborative acts, programs, and structures that maximize the expertise of each collaborator and ultimately amount to more than could be achieved when professionals act independently. They result in services that are fundamentally and structurally different from what can occur in the absence of collaboration.
3. *Flexibility* addresses the deliberate occurrence of role-blurring. Behaviors that characterize flexibility include the ability to reach productive compromises in the face of disagreement and the alteration of roles as professionals respond creatively to address the best interests of the client—whether that client is a child, a family, an organization or a community—even if so doing takes them outside their "traditional" professional role.
4. *Collective ownership of goals* refers to shared responsibility in all aspects of reaching goals, including joint design, definition, development, and

achievement. Those who work to define, achieve, and evaluate goals include colleagues from different professional disciplines, students, families, and communities.

5 *Reflection on process* refers to attention paid to the collaborative process. This includes behaviors whereby collaborators think and talk about their working relationships and processes and incorporate feedback about their process to strengthen relationships and outcome effectiveness.

These aspects of collaboration can be measured using scales such as the Index of Interdisciplinary Collaboration (Bronstein 2002) or the Index of Interprofessional Team Collaboration for Expanded School Mental Health (Mellin et al. 2010). As components of collaboration are identified as weak, they can be strengthened to enhance the overall collaborative experience. Influences on collaboration can also be enhanced to improve interactions. Areas where support and/or barriers to the collaborative process influence the components presented above include: structural characteristics, professional role, history of collaboration, and personal characteristics (Bronstein 2002, 2003; Mellin et al. 2010).

1 *Structural characteristics* relevant to interdisciplinary collaboration include: a manageable workload, an agency culture supportive of collaboration, administrative support for collaborative work, professional autonomy, and time and space for collaboration to occur.
2 A strong sense of *professional role* includes: holding the values of one's own profession, a commitment to the goals of one's organization, respect for ones professional colleagues, a holistic, client-centered view of practice, and a similar and/or complementary (not an opposing) perspective to one's collaborators.
3 A *history of collaboration* refers to prior, positive experiences with interprofessional collaboration, which are correlated with recurring positive collaborative experiences.
4 *Personal characteristics* relevant to interdisciplinary collaboration include the ways collaborators view each other as people outside of their professional role. This includes respecting and trusting one's colleagues. Personal characteristics are often found to have the most significant impact on collaboration.

Despite new models for the development, implementation, and evaluation of interprofessional collaboration, it continues to be a difficult concept to put into action. Even in the United Kingdom, where there are stronger national policy mandates for collaboration than in the United States, Allan voices the concern that "joined up working . . . appears to be more of a cliché than a policy, ordered by government departments which are themselves disconnected and function within cells" (2012:144). She goes on to state that in many parts of the United Kingdom the actual implementation of interprofessional collaboration is quite slow. Additionally, "the lack of knowledge about what interprofessional practice entails is a serious omission which must be addressed with urgency" (2012:147). She calls for more research dedicated to finding the best way to obtain this knowledge. Therefore, even where mandates at the highest level of government outline policy for collaborative practice, the details of its implementation (and a research base to guide it) need further development.

In a recent paper, two Scottish researchers (Forbes & McCartney 2014) outline steps that should be taken to build and support bridges across the silos of children's services, including:

1 A focused, rigorous audit and review of governance and policy directed at all professional groups across the child sector, to understand the knowledge, skills, and cross-sector relationships that are required;
2 The institution of policy production arenas and processes aimed to deliver coherent, continuous, and connected cross-profession and cross-agency policy texts and policy enactments underpinned by values of child well-being and social justice;
3 An understanding of the needs of practitioners for reeducation for effective inter- and transprofessional work, leading to enlisting university institutions to redesign practitioner education programs to educate practitioners in the necessary transdisciplinary knowledge, skills, and relational capabilities for collaborative practice with children; and
4 A clearer understanding by government agencies, professional registration and accrediting bodies, and university disciplines who design and implement practitioner education that to achieve an overarching child policy vision of social justice, education and practice must be informed by a conceptual framework that is transprofessional and transdisciplinary in nature.

The exemplary school-linked initiatives in the United States that are highlighted throughout this book have all struggled with, and found mechanisms to encourage, successful collaboration across organizational and professional lines. Each program's collaborative activities are delineated in each of the exemplars discussed. Below we address the concept of *collective impact*, which takes the notion of collaboration to a new level; the term was coined in 2011 in an article in the *Stanford Social Innovation Review* and became a focus of the 2012 White House Council on Community Solutions. Its application to school-linked services is described below.

COLLECTIVE IMPACT

Collective impact relies on a "commitment of a group of important actors from different sectors to a common agenda for solving a specific social problem" and operates on the assumption that "substantially greater progress could be made in alleviating many of our most serious and complex social problems if nonprofits, governments, businesses, and the public were brought together around a common agenda to create collective impact" (Kania & Kramer 2011: 36, 37).

The term is meant to turn our attention from isolated interventions of individual organizations to broad, cross-sector coordination as a much more effective, albeit more labor and time-intensive approach. Collective impact has been successful in an array of efforts, including the Elizabeth River Project (an environmental initiative), Shape up Somerville (to prevent childhood obesity), and even the Mars Corporation's work with NGOs, local governments, and business competitors to improve the lives of impoverished cocoa farmers in Côte d'Ivoire (Kania & Kramer 2011). Noting that addressing failures of our public school system can benefit from a collective impact approach to reform, Kania and Kramer observe that in reality "the heroic efforts of countless teachers, administrators, and nonprofits, together with billions of dollars in charitable contributions, may have led to important improvements in individual schools and classrooms, yet system-wide progress has seemed virtually unobtainable" (2011:36). Both TASCI and SUN Service Systems (highlighted in chapter 3) demonstrate how collective impact is a central component of their community schools approach to partnership.

Kania and Kramer outline five conditions for developing collective impact:

1. Common agenda where all participants agree on the primary goals for the collective impact initiative as a whole;
2. Shared measurement systems to assess the common agenda;
3. Mutually reinforcing activities where each participant undertakes the specific set of activities in which he or she excels in a way that supports and is coordinated with the actions of others;
4. Continuous communication over "several years of regular meetings to build up enough experience with each other to recognize and appreciate the common motivation behind their different efforts"; and
5. Backbone support organizations with "dedicated staff separate from the participating organizations who can plan, manage, and support the initiative through ongoing facilitation, technology and communications support, data collection and reporting, and handling the myriad logistical and administrative details needed for the initiative to function smoothly." (2011:40).

While Kania and Kramer effectively make the case for collective impact as an approach to large-scale issues like educational reform (because it is so labor and time-intensive), they also point out that this approach is not required for technical problems, which are well defined and can be addressed by one or a few organizations. In contrast, adaptive problems are complex, with no universal answer and no single means to bring about change. Reforming public education, restoring the environment, and improving community health—these tasks are all adaptive problems requiring a collective impact approach. Below we highlight StriveTogether, a successful school-community collaboration based in collective impact, which is being implemented in a range of communities in the United States.

STRIVETOGETHER (Information provided by Geoff Zimmerman, Associate Director of Data Utilization)

BRIEF OVERVIEW

Every year, billions of dollars are invested in education. Yet, our education system is falling short. Completing high school and earning a college degree or credential are now prerequisites for a growing number of jobs in our increasingly diversified economy. Educators, businesses, and communities across the nation are looking toward a new strategy for education reform that maximizes investments for greater student success.

COMMUNITY EFFORTS

It was a realization that demanded the attention of leaders from three school districts across two states: 25 percent of Cincinnati public school students were failing to graduate, and only 52 percent of Northern Kentucky students had post-secondary education plans. The districts partnered with StriveTogether, a nonprofit subsidiary of KnowledgeWorks, to establish a different approach. This approach, called *cradle-to-career collective impact*, replaced competing agendas, siloed funding streams, and duplicative programs with a shared vision for education reform.

Established in 2006 under an entity known as the StrivePartnership—a fusion of about three hundred local, nonprofit social service agencies, foundations, school districts, universities, and private businesses—StriveTogether has produced positive results. Through its alignment of these entities and commitment to improving outcomes, StriveTogether helped communities attain higher retention rates at participating universities, increased high school graduation rates of all subgroups, and improved reading levels at local schools.

Before StriveTogether, each of these entities operated independently, with little coordination and no central database to highlight the problems that needed tackling most urgently. From the beginning, StriveTogether focused on engaging the community and convening the right community stakeholders—from educators who worked directly in the schools to the nonprofits that provided services for students' educational, emotional, and physical well-being; from the philanthropists who offered various funding options to the corporations who needed skilled labor and a strong workforce pipeline. This broad cross section came together to work toward a common goal: that every student would have the opportunity to enter a meaningful career.

Together, the leaders invested their time and talent to engage executive and grassroots partners in the vision, work through "turf" issues among service providers, and encourage funders to move existing resources to proven strategies. StriveTogether focused its resources and efforts on key strategies believed to "move the needle" on outcomes throughout the cradle-to-career continuum. By establishing indicators for student success, such as kindergarten readiness, early grade reading, high school graduation rates, and college graduation, StrivePartnership focused on outcomes that matter and strategies that work.

A NATIONAL MOVEMENT

Since its start in Cincinnati and North Kentucky in 2006, communities in thirty-seven states and the District of Columbia have embraced StriveTogether's collective impact approach.

From the experience in greater Cincinnati, StriveTogether learned that in order to create an appropriate infrastructure, each new community must balance strong leadership with authentic partner engagement. Key sectors, such as education, nonprofit, civic, and business, need to be represented in the planning, engagement, and implementation process.

The principle behind the partnership is simple and adaptable to local circumstances: put concerned people in one room, agree upon statistically definable goals, and coordinate action and spend the dollars to hit the targets.

Partners need to establish shared responsibility and accountability early in the convening process, while engaging all education stakeholders in strategic planning. Perhaps the most difficult task is building credibility through clear and open communication of success and failures.

Most importantly, all partners need to have a common vision for improving education outcomes for students. Within communities, StriveTogether continually focuses on evidence-based decision-making to inform the community's efforts and priorities in improving student outcomes. Networks select community-level outcomes from the cradle-to-career continuum and ensure accountability to stakeholders. They also work with school districts and partners to create the necessary processes and mechanisms to effectively access and share data necessary for this decision-making. And finally, they must have the capacity to analyze student and community-level data to improve efficiencies and effectiveness of processes and action.

ENSURING LONG-TERM SUCCESS AND SUSTAINABILITY

Individual networks take ownership of creating civic infrastructure and resources to sustain improved student outcomes, while receiving backbone support and strategic assistance from StriveTogether, along with sets of assessments and benchmarks to ensure quality and success. The StriveTogether team also advocates aligning a collective agenda at local, state, and national levels aimed at improving community-level outcomes.

StriveTogether designed a strategic-assistance approach to help groups build on opportunities, solve issues, and overcome challenges impacting education in their communities. The approach brings experienced, hands-on, solution-oriented staff to communities to help with framework, curriculum, and communication and to offer other tools to build on existing strengths. StriveTogether thus helped build capacity for cradle-to-career education partnerships while impacting student success across the country.

Nearly fifty communities nationwide have already made a bold commitment to join the StriveTogether Cradle to Career Network, adopting the rigorous definition of quality collective impact and achieving critical early quality benchmarks in StriveTogether's

Theory of Action guide. Each of these communities is focused on sustainable improvements on student outcomes across the educational continuum. StriveTogether also continues to provide strategic assistance to a number of additional sites, helping communities establish a rigorous work plan and accomplish quality benchmarks.

StriveTogether continues to support investment in education in a way that helps students get ahead instead of falling short. With the right strategic vision, shared goals, and collaborative action of the entire community, we can ensure all students are supported from cradle to career.

For more information: http://www.strivetogether.org

EXAMPLES OF COLLABORATIVES LINKING SCHOOLS AND COMMUNITIES

There are a number of organizations (and relationships between and among them) that are involved in community-school partnerships and support school-linked services. Below we focus on universities, cross-sector collaborations, and partnerships between schools and child welfare organizations.

Universities

Collaboration between universities and public schools has a long history, especially with internship requirements for professional degree programs in education, nursing, psychology, and social work. However, university–public school collaborations increasingly extend beyond practical experience for students to include service to the community, applied research, and workforce development (Baskind & Briar-Lawson 2005; Briar-Lawson & Zlotnik 2003).

Since the mid-1960s, institutions of higher education have taken on a more central role at the juncture of universities and communities, helping to encourage a "civic consciousness" and promoting the university as "mission driven" (Harkavy & Puckett 1994). Harkavy and Puckett describe the form these partnerships should take, such that "academic researchers learn from and with the community, do research collaboratively with and not on people and contribute to the solution of significant community problems" (1994:313). These include a range of issues, from different disciplinary and professional perspectives and goals (i.e., agreeing to and achieving the "right" balance of student education and service to the community), to concrete matters (i.e., scheduling when an interdisciplinary group from the university and community attempt to carry out collaborative projects), to sustaining efforts when university students leave, to a university's role in economic development and community revitalization (Bringle & Hatcher 1996; Bronstein 2002; Bronstein, et al. 2012; Harkavy & Puckett 1991, 1994; Lewis 2004; Kezar & Rhoads 2001).

The University of Pennsylvania's Netter Center has been the leader in developing a model of university-assisted community schools, which many other universities have adapted and followed. Details of their work are provided below. Following a description of the Netter Center, we highlight City Connects, developed at the Lynch School of Education at Boston College. The efforts of Broome County Promise Zone, out of the State University of New York, Binghamton, are discussed in chapter 5 as an example of an emerging university-assisted urban-suburban-rural initiative.

NETTER CENTER FOR COMMUNITY PARTNERSHIPS; UNIVERSITY-ASSISTED COMMUNITY SCHOOLS (Information provided by Rita Hodges, Assistant Director)

BRIEF OVERVIEW

Begun in 1985 by the University of Pennsylvania (Penn) and its school and community partners, the university-assisted community schools (UACS) program (led by what is now the Netter Center for Community Partnerships) supports existing neighborhood schools to function as centers of education, services, engagement, and activity for students, their parents, and other community members. Service linkage between schools and communities is a component of a wider mission for simultaneously improving the quality of life and learning in the community while improving research, teaching, learning, and service at the university.

Because local context is critical, each higher education institution (whether a community college, four-year college, or university) has different needs, strengths, and resources just as local public schools and communities have distinct assets, needs, and interests. However, we suggest that there is a framework that helps to produce an optimally functioning university-assisted community school and that its key elements are:

1. A central office on campus that coordinates university resources and helps UACS work to become integrated into the mission of the higher educational institution, rather than remaining the effort of a few faculty members;
2. Engagement that involves multiple schools and departments across the campus;

3 A school principal who welcomes and encourages the partnership and conveys this philosophy to the school faculty and staff;
4 A coordinator from the university, the school, or the community who works at the school site to link the school, the community, and the higher educational institution;
5 Community school staff who are integrated into the school's operation, so that planning for and provision of supports for students, their families, and the community are as seamless as possible; and
6 Parent/community involvement through advisory boards or other mechanisms to provide input on supports needed in the school and on delivery of services.

ORIGINAL OBJECTIVE

Founded in 1992, the Barbara and Edward Netter Center for Community Partnerships is the University of Pennsylvania's primary vehicle for bringing to bear the broad range of human knowledge needed to solve the complex, comprehensive, and interconnected problems of the American city so that West Philadelphia (Penn's local geographic community), Philadelphia, the University itself, and society benefit. The Netter Center's work is based on three core propositions:

1 Penn's future and the future of West Philadelphia/Philadelphia are intertwined.
2 Penn can make a significant contribution to improving the quality of life in West Philadelphia/Philadelphia.
3 Penn can enhance its overall mission of advancing and transmitting knowledge by helping to improve the quality of life in West Philadelphia/Philadelphia.

The Netter Center works to achieve the following objectives:

1 Improve the internal coordination and collaboration of all university-wide community service programs;
2 Create new and effective partnerships between the university and the community; and
3 Create and strengthen local, national, and international networks of institutions of higher education committed to engagement with their local communities.

A major component of the Netter Center's work is mobilizing the vast resources of the university to help transform traditional public schools into innovative university-assisted community schools. UACS focus on the school as the core institution, the "hub", for community engagement and democratic development, as well as for linking school-day and afterschool curricula to solving locally identified, real-world community problems. This initiative is called *university-assisted*, because universities constitute the strategic sources of broadly based, comprehensive, sustained support for community schools. UACS engage universities as lead partners in providing academic, human, and material resources. Sustainability is achieved through a mutually beneficial approach that is integrated with the core mission of the educational partners.

PROCESS OF DEVELOPMENT

The history of Penn's work with West Philadelphia public schools has been a process of painful organizational learning and conflict, characterized by many mistakes and by understanding and activities changing over time. Penn is only now beginning to tap its extraordinary resources in ways that could mutually benefit both Penn and its neighbors and result in truly radical school, community, and university change.

When the work on university-community-school relationships began in 1985, West Philadelphia was deteriorating, with devastating consequences for community residents as well as the university. These included increased blight, crime, and poverty, as well as diminishing Penn's ability to continue to attract and retain outstanding faculty, staff, and students. Committed to undergraduate teaching, the Netter Center's founding director, Ira Harkavy, and distinguished Penn historian Lee Benson designed an honors seminar aimed at stimulating undergraduates to think critically about what Penn could and should do to remedy its "environmental situation".

Intrigued with the concept, the president of the university, Sheldon Hackney, himself a former professor of history, agreed to join them in teaching the seminar in the spring semester of 1985. The seminar's title suggests its general concerns: "Urban University-Community Relationships: Penn-West Philadelphia, Past, Present, and Future as a Case Study." Unwittingly, during the course of the seminar's work, they reinvented the community school idea. They developed a strategy based on the following proposition: universities can best improve their local environment if they mobilize and integrate their great resources, particularly the "human capital" embodied in their students, to help develop and maintain community schools that function as focal points for creating healthy urban environments.

Over time, the seminar's increasingly successful work stimulated a growing number of academically based community service (ABCS) courses (Penn's term for service learning) in a wide range of Penn schools and departments, developed and implemented under the auspices of the university's Netter Center for Community Partnerships. ABCS courses focus on action-oriented, community problem-solving and the integration of research, teaching, learning, and service, as well as reflection on the service experience and its larger implications (e.g., why poverty, racism, and crime exist). To date, over 160 such courses, spanning six schools and twenty-three departments, have been developed to work with schools and community organizations to solve strategic community problems.

In July 1992, President Hackney created the Center for Community Partnerships, which was renamed the Barbara and Edward Netter Center for Community Partnerships in 2007 in recognition of the generous support provided by Barbara and Edward Netter. To highlight the importance Hackney attached to the center, he located it in the Office of the President and appointed Ira Harkavy as its director. By creating the center, the university formally committed itself as a corporate entity to finding ways to use its enormous resources (particularly its student and faculty "human capital") to help improve the quality of life in its local community—not only in respect to public schools but also to economic and community development in general. A major component of the center's work is to identify, mobilize, and integrate Penn's vast resources to help transform traditional West Philadelphia public schools into innovative university-assisted community schools.

COLLABORATIVE ACTIVITIES/STRUCTURES

Penn, through the Netter Center, is the "lead" organization for its university-assisted community schools. This work would not be possible without a partnership that involves parents, teachers, principals, community members, elected officials, community organizations, faith-based organizations, businesses, the Philadelphia Federation of Teachers, and the School District of Philadelphia.

Each university-assisted community school site has, at minimum, one full-time site director (a Netter Center at Penn employee), who works closely with the school and the community to determine activities that best serve the specific needs and interests of that area. In addition to organizing and overseeing programs, site directors serve as liaisons between the university and the school, as well as between school-day teachers and afterschool programs. University students taking ABCS courses, work-study students, and student volunteers provide vital support for these programs, serving as tutors, mentors, classroom fellows, or activity and project leaders.

The Netter Center has a community advisory board that guides its programs and activities, in addition to a faculty advisory board, a student advisory board, and a national advisory board.

TARGET POPULATION

The Netter Center's university-assisted community school programs in West Philadelphia focus on a set of schools within three high school catchment areas. The targeted West Philadelphia neighborhood is marked by extreme poverty, violence, unemployment, homelessness, obesity, and low educational attainment. Effective partnerships and comprehensive approaches, such as university-assisted community schools, are needed to address the multiple disadvantages impacting youth and families.

FEATURED PROGRAM

Moelis Access Science is an example of the reciprocal, democratic partnerships that Penn has developed through University-Assisted Community Schools and ABCS courses. Begun in 1999 with initial support from the National Science Foundation, Moelis Access Science works to improve science, technology, engineering, and math (STEM) education of both K–12 students and undergraduate and graduate students at Penn. Faculty and students from across campus provide content-based professional development for teachers and direct classroom support for implementing quality hands-on and small group activities. For example, Community Physics Initiative is an ABCS course taught by Department of Physics and Astronomy chair Larry Gladney that links the practical and theoretical aspects of fundamental physics, and is aligned with the School District of Philadelphia's curriculum for introductory high school physics. By creating and teaching weekly laboratory exercises and classroom demonstrations at a nearby high school, Penn students are learning science by teaching science to high school students while making contributions to physics education research and practice.

LOCATION OF SERVICES

Programs, activities, and services coordinated through the Netter Center are located primarily within the public schools.

SERVICE PROVIDERS/PARTNERS

In addition to the university and public schools, a number of additional partners are involved in programming, service provision, etc., particularly community-based organizations. For example, parent services, offered during monthly parent update meetings, use partner organizations that offer workshops and drop-in clinics in such areas as employment assistance, social service benefits screening/enrollment, and other family resources, as well as parenting and life skills. Services are also provided by the Sayre Health Center, a school-based, federally qualified health center offering fitness activities, health education, and access. The UACS school site director, who is a Netter Center employee, coordinates these various resources and services at the school.

TYPES OF SERVICES DELIVERED

Through collaboration among school, university, and community partners, each UACS site has a variety of locally determined activities and programs. In addition to academically based community service courses, Netter Center programs that are key components of the UACS model include:

1. The Agatston Urban Nutrition Initiative (nutrition education and food access through school gardens, afterschool fruit stands, and cooking clubs); College Access and Career Readiness (college and career preparation through internships and leadership opportunities);
2. Community Arts Partnership (mural arts, music, and cultural activities); Community School Student Partnerships (undergraduate tutors, mentors, and classroom leaders);
3. Extended Learning / Afterschool / Out-of-School Time (academic, extracurricular, and recreational activities);
4. The Health Sciences Educational Pipeline Program (engaged learning and multitiered mentoring in medical sciences);
5. Moelis Access Science (hands-on STEM education); Penn Reading Initiative (literacy tutoring); and
6. The West Philadelphia Recess Initiative (interactive play and fitness).

FUNDING

Federal funding, together with state and local government funding, private foundations, and university resources, are integrated at university-assisted community school sites to provide a range of school-day, afterschool, and summer programs and services.

The development of the Netter Center for Community Partnerships' school- and community- based programs has benefitted greatly from funding from diverse federal departments (including the Departments of Education, Labor, Health and Human Services, Agriculture, Housing and Urban Development; the Corporation for National Service; the National Science Foundation; the National Institutes of Health; the Centers for Disease Control), from the Commonwealth of Pennsylvania, and from the City of Philadelphia.

In addition to university and government funding, contributions from Penn alumni, families, and friends, as well as gifts from corporations and foundations, play a critical role in supporting the work of the Netter Center.

IMPLEMENTATION CHALLENGES

The volatility of working in the public school system (including superintendent, principal, and teacher turnover) and high-stakes testing pressure have caused some starts and stops over the years.

The culture of higher education institutions, particularly the fragmentation of specialized disciplines and pressure to publish, has also prevented the work from realizing its full potential. A long history of university-community conflict presents a further challenge. Universities have a tendency to act as if they have the "answers" rather than working in genuine partnership and valuing community members' knowledge.

Indeed, UACS now being developed at Penn and elsewhere have a long way to go before they can fully mobilize the powerful, untapped resources of their own institutions and of their communities, including those found among individual neighbors and in local institutions (such as businesses, social service agencies, faith-based organizations, and hospitals). Among other things, this will require more effective coordination of public and private funding streams and services.

EVALUATION

Problems like poor nutrition, under-resourced urban schools, and poverty are complex and systemic. However, studies of the Netter Center's work have found important and positive outcomes for both Penn and West Philadelphia. For example, one study that compared Penn undergraduates taking ABCS courses to those in similar courses without a community engagement component found that 47 percent of ABCS students reported an increase in research skills versus 36 percent of non-ABCS students. Additionally, students in ABCS courses more often reported an increase in their desire to act morally and ethically, to become effective community leaders, to develop a meaningful philosophy of life, to be concerned about urban communities, and to volunteer in the community.

Penn students participating as classroom fellows (paid interns, work-study students, or volunteers working in K–12 schools) through the Netter Center's Moelis Access Science program also reported positive outcomes: 95 percent reported an increased ability to present science and math ideas; 100 percent reported an improvement in communication skills; 95 percent reported greater ability to work with children and adolescents; and almost half (45 percent) of new undergraduate fellows indicated that their experience with the program would be influential in their thinking about their careers, including the possibility of teaching or entering the field of education.

Surveys were conducted of teachers and 466 K–8 students enrolled in one of four afterschool programs operated by the Netter Center during the 2009–10 school year. Teachers reported that, of the participating students who needed to improve, 72 percent showed improvement in their academic performance, and 66 percent of students improved their participation in class. The majority of K–8 students indicated that involvement in the afterschool program helped them with homework (95 percent), increased their confidence (92 percent), helped them do better in school (91 percent), and increased their interests in school-day learning and school-day attendance (83 percent and 73 percent, respectively).

In 2011–12, Netter Center staff operating the Student Success Center at University City High School mobilized ninety Penn and Drexel University students as graduation coaches to work one on one and with small groups of high school students. Four-year graduation rates at the school hovered below 50 percent. Yet this team was able to help 94 percent of the 2011–12 senior class graduate, 70 percent of whom had post-secondary plans, and secure over $740,000 in scholarship and grant awards. During the three years of the Student Success Center's operation, the school's AP and honors course participation increased by 66 percent across grade levels and subject content. In addition, average daily attendance rose from 71 percent in 2008–9 to 83 percent in 2011–12.

Through a generous naming gift in 2007 from Barbara Netter and the late Edward Netter (a Penn alumnus), the Netter Center has, among other things, been able to make a significant commitment in recent years to comprehensive evaluation of its work with the community by hiring a full-time evaluator. Also part of this naming gift, in 2008, the Netter Center began supporting the development of multistate regional training centers on the university-assisted community school model.

FUTURE DIRECTIONS

Looking ahead, the Netter Center for Community Partnerships will focus on:

1. Increasing academic engagement and collaboration across the university, including mobilizing additional faculty members and students to work in West Philadelphia;
2. Having a more positive impact on the community, including through better integration of university and community resources, as well as other agency resources, at the school sites; and
3. Strengthening the national and global reach of UACS as an effective strategy for university-community-school partnerships.

CITY CONNECTS—A MODEL OF OPTIMIZED STUDENT SUPPORT (Information provided by Mary Walsh, Executive Director, Boston College Center for Optimized Student Support, and Sarah Backe, PhD Candidate)

BRIEF OVERVIEW

City Connects was designed to address the out-of-school factors that impact learning for children living in poverty. The mission of City Connects is to have children engage and learn in school by connecting each child with a tailored set of prevention, intervention, and enrichment services he or she needs to thrive.

To accomplish this mission, City Connects relies on the rich services and enrichments provided by community agencies. To link schools with community agencies, City Connects has developed a school-based infrastructure and systematic practice that coordinates comprehensive supports for learning and healthy development. The intervention identifies each student's strengths and needs in academic, social-emotional, health, and family domains and works with community agencies to deliver a tailored set of services to every child. This infrastructure transforms existing student support structures in schools. It is evidence-based and aligned with researchers' and educators' recommendations for best practices in student support.

ORIGINAL OBJECTIVE

It has long been recognized that in high-poverty urban school districts, children face challenges outside of school that impede academic success. In the 1960s, the Coleman Report concluded that students' socioeconomic and home backgrounds are significant factors affecting academic achievement. Current research confirms that larger social structures and contexts beyond the school are critical, accounting for up to two-thirds of the variance in student achievement. Schools cannot close the achievement gap without a systemic approach to addressing out-of-school factors. While the challenge of poverty may be society's to solve, and while some nonacademic barriers to learning cannot be addressed by schools, in the absence of a large-scale societal solution, schools can, and must, provide supports that mitigate the negative effect of poverty.

The objective of City Connects is to provide and sustain a systemic approach within schools that effectively addresses the out-of-school needs of children living in poverty and thereby leads to measurable improvements in their achievement.

PROCESS OF DEVELOPMENT

City Connects was initiated collaboratively in the context of a wider partnership between the Lynch School of Education at Boston College and the Boston public schools. The university-school partnership reached out to families and community agencies and engaged in a two-year planning process to design a system that would address out-of-school factors that impact learning and thriving. The program has been rigorously evaluated since its introduction to Boston public schools in 2001. The program currently exists in multiple school districts.

COLLABORATIVE ACTIVITIES/STRUCTURES

Collaboration is core to City Connects' approach: the organization was developed in a two-year planning process that involved collaboration among local school staff, school district administrators, the university, families, and community agency representatives. The implementation of the City Connects intervention in each school involves structures and processes that require collaboration across school staff, families, and community agency personnel. The City Connects organization is supported by a school-community-university partnership, and includes staff collaboration across professions and disciplines.

TARGET POPULATION

The initial target population for City Connects was students in K–5 urban schools. The organization has since expanded the practice to include students in pre-K–8. City Connects is currently developing and evaluating a high school model.

FEATURED PROGRAM

In addition to the Boston public schools, City Connects is also implemented in five other school districts.

SERVICE PROVIDERS/PARTNERS

Community agencies are the primary providers of tailored supports (prevention and enrichment, early intervention, and intensive intervention) for students and families. In Boston, for example, City Connects partners with 286 community agencies. Schools offer an important but more limited range of services, to which City Connects adds tailored referrals. Overall, students may be connected to services and/or enrichment opportunities with a wide variety of school- and community-based providers.

LOCATION OF SERVICES

City Connects partners with community agencies and the school district to provide services and enrichment opportunities to students and families. These services can be located in the school, home, community, or a combination of the three. City Connects staff also directly provide a limited number of services in schools, including crisis intervention, psychoeducational groups, and focused health and social skills education.

TYPES OF SERVICES DELIVERED

The services and enrichment opportunities that are delivered by City Connects include academic, social/emotional/behavioral, health, and family services. They include a range from prevention and enrichment (e.g., afterschool arts or sports programs), to early intervention (e.g., academic tutoring, family support), to intensive intervention (e.g., mental health counseling, crisis management).

IMPLEMENTATION CHALLENGES

Implementing City Connects in new districts has not presented significant obstacles. Principals, teachers, and school staff are generally eager to incorporate systematic strategies for addressing the out-of-school factors impacting learning and thriving. Funding innovative and evidence-based interventions in this and other areas is always a challenge to the budgets of urban school districts. Collaborative efforts at fundraising have been successful.

EVALUATION

The City Connects intervention is evaluated by researchers and statisticians in the Boston College Center for the Study of Testing, Evaluation, and Educational Policy. A cadre of independent experts serve as external reviewers. The ultimate focus of the evaluation is measuring the intermediate and long-term impact of the City Connects intervention on the academic achievement and overall well-being of students in City Connects schools. The evaluation also addresses the process of implementation in order to continually refine the practice. Measuring fidelity of implementation to the City Connects model is one of the critical foci of the evaluation.

A decade of rigorous research demonstrates that the City Connects approach to student support significantly improves academic performance and substantially narrows the achievement gap. The positive effects of City Connects mitigate many of the harmful effects of poverty and are especially beneficial to students most at risk for academic underachievement, such as English Language Learners. The impact of City Connects lasts long after students have left the intervention at the end of grade 5. Students who have been in a City Connects elementary school have significantly higher scores on statewide standardized tests in math and English/language arts in grades 6, 7, and 8, have a lower probability of being chronically absent through grade 12, and, at ages sixteen and older, are significantly less likely to drop out of school than students never in City Connects schools. Annual surveys of teachers, principals, and community partners indicate high levels of partner satisfaction as well.

FUTURE DIRECTIONS

City Connects' goal is to scale the model to urban districts around the country, and it has developed the systems, processes, and technology to make that expansion possible.

While the City Connects evaluation will continue to examine the impact of the intervention, it increasingly focuses on understanding why and how the intervention is making a critical difference for children's achievement and thriving.

Cross-Sector Collaborations

Many of the exemplary initiatives described in this book benefit from city-wide cross-sector collaborations. Indeed, as discussed throughout this book and especially in this chapter, strong collaboration is critical for the success of all community-school partnerships. For example, Say Yes to Education (Say Yes) is a nonprofit organization that has made great advancements in a number of communities with a unique approach to supporting student success, centered on its commitment to removing financial barriers to post-secondary education for all youth, and is profiled below.

SAY YES TO EDUCATION (Information provided by Mary Anne Schmitt-Carey, President, and Eugene Chasin, Chief Operating Officer)

BRIEF OVERVIEW

Say Yes to Education is a nonprofit organization that seeks to galvanize and organize entire cities around two key goals: increasing high school graduation and making a post-secondary education accessible, affordable, and attainable for every student in a community's public school system.

While the goals that drive Say Yes's work focus on postsecondary access and success, the Say Yes strategy offers a uniquely nuanced and comprehensive approach to redesigning the civic infrastructure around urban public education. Instead of working at the edges of existing school districts, Say Yes helps facilitate ongoing collaboration among school district leadership, city and county governments, and community groups in order to sustainably fund and effectively coordinate the holistic support services that students, especially those coming from low-income families, need in order to succeed in school. Specifically, based on extensive research on the predictable barriers to student success, Say Yes is committed to providing access not only to academic supports, but also to social/emotional and physical health services to students and their families.

Moreover, the Say Yes strategy works to remove financial barriers to post-secondary access for students through a district-wide post-secondary scholarship program, available to every graduate of the school district, and through partnerships with over sixty-five private colleges and universities. By removing financial barriers, the scholarship aims to create a sense of hope and promote the goal of college completion for traditionally underrepresented groups.

ORIGINAL OBJECTIVE

At its core, the Say Yes mission is based on a commitment to supporting individual children as they seek to realize and actualize their potential. Since 1987, Say Yes has worked to ensure that all students within its reach have access to the personalized supports and financial resources they need in order to succeed in preschool, primary school, high school, and post-secondary education, and that comprehensive services are delivered in a personalized, coordinated way. Beyond the practical financial assistance, the Say Yes scholarship incentive has sought to change the overall perception of opportunity and possibility among the students and families it serves.

Over its twenty-seven-year history, Say Yes has grown from a single, school-based cohort to a district-wide implementation. In the process, the strategy has evolved significantly and many additional objectives have emerged. Through its efforts to build a sustainable collaborative governance structure—one that brings together representatives from the school district, city and county governments, local philanthropy and business, teachers' and administrators' unions, community-based service providers, parents, and other community leaders—Say Yes focuses on the assets that exist within communities. It then helps foster a citywide sense of commitment and responsibility to the success of the public school district.

Through this focus on strengths, communal investment, and shared accountability, Say Yes aims to create a sea-change in the culture of expectation and hope in public education at the city level, and ultimately to promote a vibrant college-going culture throughout school districts. By investing in the construction of this collaborative and data-driven civic infrastructure, Say Yes also seeks to create an efficient system that can successfully outlive the tenure of single dynamic leaders. Indeed, after an intensive six-year introduction of the strategy in close partnership with the national Say Yes organization, responsibility for sustaining the strategy over the long haul transitions to the local community.

While Say Yes does not directly impact classroom structure or practice, the goal is that through collaboratively established outcome metrics and improvement and growth of support services, there will be meaningful changes in the school system, which, in turn, will impact classroom activities. Essentially, the transparent and public reporting of progress toward the established outcome measures is designed to become a lever for accountability—an accountability that is explicitly focused on support and improvement rather than punitive measures.

The Say Yes strategy is also based on the conviction that quality public education systems contribute to the overall economic health of geographic regions. As the collaborative works together to improve the success of public school students, Say Yes aims to draw more families to urban centers through higher-quality educational options and to increase the educational attainment levels throughout these cities. More-educated citizens are less likely to participate in criminal activity, are more likely to attract business and industry, and carry greater earning potential that can feed back into the local economy. In the long term, Say Yes hopes to be part of a wider process of urban revitalization nationally.

PROCESS OF DEVELOPMENT

While Say Yes to Education was founded in 1987, its story dates back to the days when its founder and chairman, George Weiss, attended the University of Pennsylvania with the help of a generous scholarship. While a student there, Weiss mentored a group of Philadelphia public high school students as they worked toward graduation. He was so moved by his experience that he committed, throughout his life going forward, to do what he could to remove barriers to success for as many children as possible.

After achieving success as a young money manager, Weiss began the first Say Yes cohort chapter with a pledge to 112 sixth-graders at the Belmont School in Philadelphia that he would pay their way through college if they graduated from high school. Following those early days, Say Yes grew significantly in size and scope, serving more and more children through chapters in Hartford, Connecticut (1990), Cambridge, Massachusetts (1991), a second in Philadelphia (2000), and another in Harlem, New York (2004). As the program evolved, these chapters incorporated lessons learned about the social/emotional, physical health, and academic supports that made the most difference in student outcomes; the types of services that families need in order to support their children effectively; and the most critical ages for starting services.

While Say Yes was able to support about 750 children through these smaller chapters, the organization began looking at ways that its approach could be brought to greater scale and sustainability. Given that funding for student and youth support services comes not only from the school district, but also from the city and county governments (in the form of prevention, youth development, and family services funding streams), Say Yes began to develop a strategy for coordinating student supports and scholarships for public school children throughout entire cities.

Since 2008, Say Yes has expanded to serve more than sixty-thousand students through two citywide partnerships: one in Syracuse, New York (initiated in 2008), and another in Buffalo, New York (2012). These citywide chapters are characterized by a district-wide scholarship incentive, collaborative governance of implementation, and coordination of wraparound supports, all built upon a sustainable fiscal framework. The Syracuse partnership acted as a vital co-creator in the early days of bringing Say Yes to scale, including designing the governance structure and identifying sustainable funding streams, and Buffalo has also provided critical implementation lessons that have facilitated the iterative development of the Say Yes Citywide Turnaround Strategy.

COLLABORATIVE ACTIVITIES/STRUCTURES

When Say Yes enters a new city, it offers not only a comprehensive strategy and technical support (including fiscal audits and expert consulting support), but also a $15 million initial investment designed to leverage the reallocation of public dollars in sustainable ways. By putting this investment on the table, Say Yes helps incentivize active collaboration among government, private sector, and public sector leaders in order to identify and organize city assets around the same goal of post-secondary completion for the city's youth. These collaborative bodies include:

1 A Community Leadership Council (CLC): The CLC includes a wide cross section of local leadership that meets quarterly. The CLC includes over sixty members, and its quarterly meetings are typically attended by about 250 members of the body and the public. It allows for regular, transparent accountability, and provides a public forum for addressing policy issues related to the coordination of services and the scholarship. The CLC is cochaired by the mayor, county executive, school board president, and other key local leadership.
2 An Operating Committee (OC): The OC includes key local leadership: the district superintendent, high-ranking representatives from the mayor's and county executive's offices, philanthropic leaders, higher education leaders, teacher and administrative union leaders, and parent representatives. Meeting biweekly, the OC is responsible for monitoring the delivery and quality of services, scaling services, and ensuring long-term sustainability of services.
3 Task Forces: These are directly overseen by the OC, and they work to implement the many facets of the programming. In Buffalo, the task forces focus on the following areas: community mobilization; health and wellness; legal services; "Say Yes to Teachers"; post-secondary pathways (higher education); birth to grade 8; religious leaders; business partnerships; and community-based organizations.
4 A Scholarship Board: This leads local fund-raising for the scholarship fund and manages policies for the distribution of the scholarships.

TARGET POPULATION

Say Yes works in urban centers with large minority and low-income student populations. While one of Say Yes's central goals is to ensure that students living in poverty have access to middle-class supports and opportunities, it does not work exclusively with any particular demographic subset. Rather, the Say Yes citywide strategy works to provide responsive, tailored supports and services to every single student within the public school district. Ultimately, Say Yes aims to impact the overall culture around post-secondary expectation and accessibility throughout cities.

FEATURED PROGRAMS

Say Yes employs a case management approach to organize an array of services throughout a district. One of the key sources of information that drives the work of the collaborative is the Student Monitoring and Intervention System (SMIS). The SMIS is a data system that uses inputs from teachers, service providers, school-based Say Yes site facilitators, parents, and students themselves. SMIS breaks down the key barriers to student success across four main domains: academic, social-emotional, health, and financial support for postsecondary attainment. The SMIS acts as an "early warning system," which tracks all students in a district across thirteen indicators and thirty-six subindicators. Each student receives a continuously updated personalized growth plan that indicates whether he or she is "on track to thrive," "on track," or "off track" on each of the subindicators.

Aggregate reports are also derived for individual schools and for subgroups across the district. Say Yes site facilitators work as case managers with student support teams (SSTs) at each school to connect students to community service providers and personalized school or district-based interventions. These interventions include school-day academic supports, extended day and year programs, counseling, college preparation, and family, health, and legal services. The SMIS ultimately advances an innovative and necessary way for educators to think about students beyond test scores and supports schools and communities in developing students holistically. It also significantly expands the identification and growth of the resources that exist across communities.

LOCATION OF SERVICES

Say Yes works to ensure that services are as accessible and easily utilized as possible. Most of the time, this means that services are provided within each school building. School-based services include health clinics, afterschool and summer programs, college coaching, tutoring, and mentoring, all of which are coordinated by site facilitators within each building. The school-based approach to service provision has resulted in significant increases in service utilization; in Syracuse, physically moving wraparound services from community centers and other organizational offices increased program utilization from 21 percent in 2007–8 to 70 percent in 2012–13. Additionally, other family support services are delivered in students' and families' homes.

SERVICE PROVIDERS/PARTNERS

Partnerships with community-based service providers are also a central aspect of the Say Yes strategy. In every city, community-based organizations (CBOs), such as Catholic Charities, United Way, and numerous others, have well-established and highly significant roles in working with children and youth.

A major goal of the Say Yes strategy is to tap into the assets and skill sets of these organizations to increase capacity for preparing students for post-secondary education and careers. As Say Yes enters a new city, it seeks established service providers to work with the public school district to administer services that address academic, social-emotional, and health needs. As pictured in figure 4.1, services include afterschool and summer programming, family support services, tutoring, and legal services, among others.

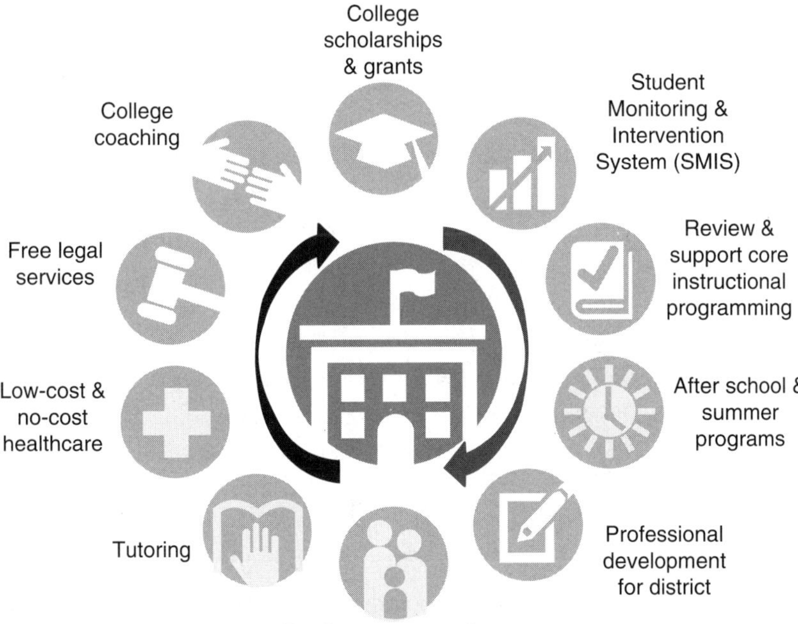

FIGURE 4.1 Types of Services Delivered

While respecting the history and accomplishments of the CBOs, Say Yes also recognizes the reality that the programming provided by the CBOs, both individually and collectively, might not optimally address the needs that exist in the community. Through a core competency review process (CCRP), the Say Yes collaborative focuses on assisting CBOs in establishing and improving services and supports that address the four major barriers to student success tracked in the SMIS. The primary components of the CCRP are:

1 A site visit to interview CBO leaders and observe exemplary services in action;
2 Evaluation using the Youth Program Quality Assessment (YPQA), a validated assessment instrument that looks at performance across seven dimensions;
3 A portfolio submitted by the CBO describing relevant programs; and
4 A feedback session where findings and next steps are discussed.

Over time, the SMIS system also allows for assessment of the efficacy of certain programs by tracking the outcomes for students who received services. This data is intended both to inform the improvement process for individual CBOs and to guide funding decisions based on evidence of efficacy.

FUNDING

A direct startup investment of $15 million from Say Yes allows the work of scaling services to begin in new cities without immediate pressure to raise all of the necessary operating funds. This investment, paired with an in-depth analysis of school district, city, and county spending, leverages the development of a six-year financial plan to scale up local funding streams to sustain services beyond Say Yes's consulting and financial support. The key community partners, including the school district, city, county, unions, parent leadership, and local philanthropy, develop and commit to this spending plan.

As the Say Yes strategy has been refined, it is more widely sought after in cities nationally. With growing recognition, the organization is better able to generate the necessary energy to secure up-front local financial commitments for seeding the scholarship endowment. Currently, Say Yes seeks an up-front commitment, primarily from foundations, business, and individual contributors, of $1,000 per student in the district toward the scholarship.

IMPLEMENTATION CHALLENGES/LESSONS LEARNED

Among the many factors that differentiate Say Yes is its identity as a learning organization over the course of twenty-seven years of growth and refinement. Furthermore, Say Yes uniquely incorporates the lessons of promising but unsustainable reform efforts of the past. These past efforts, including "break the mold" reform models such as Comprehensive School Reform and the New American Schools' approach, offered many important lessons about what works and needs to be in place to produce sustainable and impactful educational reform. Some key guiding lessons are:

1. Reforms that deal exclusively with academic improvement address only some of the barriers preventing educational success, and reforms that focus primarily on immediate test score increases rarely succeed.
2. Reforms associated with particular leaders (e.g., a charismatic superintendent or principal) usually do not last much beyond the tenure of that individual.
3. Reforms restricted to particular contexts (e.g., one or several schools) often lose staying power by being out of sync with school district initiatives.
4. Reforms championed solely by K–12 educators (e.g., school districts) often lose staying power by failing to become rooted in and supported by the broader community.

Through the work that Say Yes has done at the city level in Syracuse and Buffalo, New York, several additional key lessons have emerged:

- It is necessary to gather explicit work and financial commitments from every stakeholder group up-front, so there is complete clarity of expectations throughout planning and the rollout of services.
- School district leadership must demonstrate a true commitment to and a good track record of collaboration in order to make the strategy effective.
- Trust needs to be built among the stakeholder groups, including the city, the county, and the district leadership, in order to secure the working and financial commitments needed to do the work sustainably. Early patient efforts to build relationships within the community are vital. Even the best intentions can be met with skepticism, and Say Yes must address misunderstandings and incorporate feedback early.
- Shared commitment to jointly developed outcome metrics is essential in order to drive and focus the collaborative work. Without outcome metrics, there is no clear road map to drive the work of the partnership, and thus there is the risk of veering into micromanagement of school-based programs. Though these outcome metrics are co-created through the partnership based on local context needs, the core metrics are: post-secondary completion, post-secondary matriculation, high school graduation, advanced course taking (indicative of college-readiness), and proximal indicators of post-secondary

readiness (including select outcomes for pre-K, kindergarten, and grades 3, 5, and 8).

- While Say Yes as an organization possesses a deep understanding of research on best practices (in relation to afterschool, physical, and emotional health services, etc.), it has learned that in order to have programs implemented effectively, it cannot be too prescriptive. It is vital to take time to listen to and partner with school staff, to respect their knowledge, and to build commitment and ownership at the school level.
- It is essential to complete the financial analytics (specifically, the value chain analyses of all school district spending, and all funding streams related to education, youth, prevention services, and family services from the city and county) very early in the process. These analytics enable the design of a strong long-term plan for scaling up services and leveraging the initial Say Yes investment into a locally sustainable funding model within six years.

EVALUATION

As described in the Lessons Learned section above, some of the key Say Yes nonnegotiables when it enters a new city are joint commitments to data collection and sharing through the SMIS and to outcome metrics to drive the work of the collaborative. These measures are shared publicly through an online dashboard, as well as quarterly through the public community leadership council meetings.

The Maxwell School of Public Policy at Syracuse University has been engaged since the outset of the Buffalo implementation to do a long-term study of its impact, both in terms of academic and regional economic gains. Additionally, evaluation of the project is independently performed each year by the Center for Research and Reform in Education (CRRE) at Johns Hopkins University. CRRE is an experienced third-party evaluator, specializing in studies involving educational reform from preschool through high school. The evaluation study plan focuses on both project implementation fidelity and attainment of project goals.

FUTURE DIRECTIONS

Given the promising early indicators in the first two citywide implementations, Say Yes is currently in the process of planning its expansion to at least one new city outside New York State in the near future. The process of selecting future cities is significant in that it reflects the deep internalization of lessons learned throughout the organization's history. Based on considerations such as school district size, political factors, and geographic location, Say Yes created a list of twenty-six districts nationally for consideration. It then further narrowed the list through an extended internal due-diligence process and through contact with local stakeholders to determine the quality, stability, and commitment of district and local leadership and the capacity for building financial sustainability.

Based on this deliberative process, Say Yes was working during the summer of 2014 toward releasing a request for proposal (RFP) to three or four cities, and then began working closely with local communities to support the development of their proposals. After releasing the RFP and prior to the naming of the next Say Yes city, the process involves several steps.

First, Say Yes must establish a sense of buy-in and commitment from all partners through city visits and comprehensive presentations. Local commitment must emerge from a full understanding of the strategy and clarity of expectations among all stakeholder groups.

Second, financial analytics and value-chain analyses of the school district budgets and city and county spending on prevention, youth development, and family services are necessary. These analytics provide insight into reallocation opportunities and inform the creation of a more efficient and effective fiscal plan.

Finally, the foundation of the collaborative must be created through a memorandum of understanding (MOU) with each individual stakeholder group, a fiscal pro-forma, and identification of outcome metrics. The MOUs lay out the roles and responsibilities of every stakeholder group regarding financial and other commitments toward the scholarship and programming and active participation in governance. The fiscal pro-forma is the six-year funding plan that allows the initial $15 million Say Yes investment to leverage the scaling-up of wraparound services in such a way that the services can be locally sustained within six years. The outcome metrics are the benchmarks and timelines that drive the work of the entire collaborative.

After all of these components are in place, Say Yes then plans to announce the selection of a third and possibly a fourth city and begin to establish the cross-sector collaborative governance structures. Once they are in place, the operating committee will then spearhead the process of developing a rollout plan and establishing a dashboard of outcome metrics for ongoing public accountability.

Ultimately, Say Yes's plans for national growth represent a natural next step after decades of disciplined expansion and thoughtful program development. At its core, Say Yes is a learning organization, consistently rooted in a belief in the rich potential of every child and the conviction that communities have much to gain through a shared commitment to the future of all children.

While there is much still to be learned as Say Yes adapts to new contexts, the future is profoundly hopeful. As summarized in a piece by the *Buffalo News* editorial board in

2014: "Something fundamental is happening here. Expectations are rising. Students and their parents are lifting their sights. They are starting to understand that their possibilities are far greater than they had counted on. A larger world is opening up. That's magical. And it's a standard that, properly nourished, can be passed on from generation to generation. That's the real promise of Say Yes to Education."

Partnerships with Child Welfare

Partnerships between schools and the child welfare system make sense for the health of children, families, and communities. For one, schools are a logical place for child maltreatment to be identified in the process of prevention of and early intervention in abuse and neglect. The U.S. Department of Health and Human Services (HHS) addresses the intertwined roles of schools and communities in the prevention of child abuse and identifies the need for evidence-based prevention efforts. HHS suggests that schools initiate and participate in community public awareness programs and team up with child welfare agencies to offer community members training on identifying and reporting abuse. Schools can also contribute their resources—including meeting space for community conferences on child maltreatment—and school staff can serve as consultants for prevention and awareness programs (U.S. Department of Health and Human Services 2003).

School staff are required by state laws to work closely with child welfare; they are mandated to report suspected child abuse and neglect, with laws and penalties attached to noncompliance varying among states (American Bar Association 2014). Educators and other professionals working in schools and with school children need to be acquainted with their state's specific requirements. Prevention programs such as mental health counseling, anger management groups, and anti-bullying campaigns can bring school, child welfare, and juvenile justice partners together for holistic responses to issues related to abuse.

In addition to preventing increasing numbers of children from entering the child welfare system, schools and child welfare agencies must work together to assure the well-being of children *already in* the child welfare system, including the appropriate use of special education placements. Federal law requires that schools comply with the Individuals with Disabilities Education Act (IDEA) by working with the designated "parent" in out-of-home placement situations for special education placements and individual education plans (IEPs) (American Bar Association and Casey Family Programs 2014). In most states, foster parents are deemed the designated "parent," who then must be contacted by the school for collaborative work on all IDEA matters (U.S. Department of Health and Human Services 2012).

The U.S. Office of Child Abuse and Neglect's Children's Bureau describes the negative effects of exposure to trauma that many children in the child welfare and foster care systems experience and suggests interventions that include mental health counseling and programs that screen for and intervene in emotional problems when trauma and maltreatment are suspected (U.S. Department of Health and Human Services 2012). Many of these programs can be accessed through linkages with social service agencies, including through co-locating child welfare workers at schools.

Mental health services are one example of services that schools can provide for children in foster care. Research reveals a high percentage of children in the child welfare and foster care system in need of mental health services. According to one study with a sample of 3,803 children ages two to fourteen with histories of child welfare investigations, 47.8 percent were found to have significant mental or emotional or behavioral problems (Burns et al. 2004). Additional research indicates that not all children who need these services actually receive them (Shin 2004). Although there are federal programs in place that assure payment for mental health services for children in child welfare systems (U.S. Department of Health and Human Services 2012), service provision is not consistent and needs improvement (Burns et al. 2004; Glisson & Green 2006; Shin 2004). Increasing access to mental health services in the schools as part of a school-linked services approach could ensure children in the child welfare system have access to needed services.

Schools partnering with child welfare can go a long way to help children in the child welfare system to obtain quality education. In New York City, for example, the city's department of education in collaboration with the child welfare agency host a weekend fair, where seventh- and eighth-grade children in foster care or recently adopted children learn about high school choices and receive special assistance in making educational decisions (New York City Administration for Children's Services 2014). A program in the state of Washington showed that providing extra tutoring and mentor programs for foster care middle school youth translated to positive academic results (Tyre 2012).

Foster care children participate in numerous in- and out-of-school programs offered through school-linked services; because their needs are often greater than those of other children, close collaborations between schools and child welfare can assist these children in succeeding academically and combating the challenges they face. Along the same vein, child welfare services linked with and based at schools also support prevention efforts aimed at limiting the numbers of youth that enter the child welfare system.

An important factor in partnerships between child welfare and schools are laws regarding confidentiality and information-sharing. For example, a recent court ruling provides for certain circumstances where schools can release education records without parental consent. Another law assuring foster care children an appropriate and stable education, the Fostering Connections to Success and Increasing Adoptions Act of 2008, has now been coupled with a 2014 amendment to the Family Educational Rights and Privacy Act (FERPA) whereby schools do not need the consent of a parent to release education records when there is a court order that involves parents (American Bar Association 2013). The following section addresses a range of laws and ethical issues that impact confidentiality and information-sharing between schools and organizations with which they partner.

Ethical Challenges in Partnerships: Confidentiality and Information-Sharing

"Public schools are complex practice environments that generate thorny ethical conflicts for practitioners from all disciplines" (Kline & Brabeck 1999:285). When attempting to integrate community services with schools, ethical issues are exacerbated merely because of the multiple layers of added agencies with their own mandates, policies and governance, and added practitioners with their own socialization and professional ethical codes. For collaboration to be successful, organizations and professionals must find ways to balance allegiance to their own agency/profession with allegiance to school and educational professionals, with the primary mission of providing quality educational services. Such collaboration requires a holistic child-centered approach and means that various agencies and different forms of professionals' expertise need to be prioritized at different times. As stated earlier, reflecting on the collaborative team process is a core component of collaborative activity; accordingly, Kline and Brabeck (1999) encourage deliberate reflection on ethical practice to enrich and expand opportunities for action.

A wide range of legal, policy, and professional codes come into play in serving children through school-linked services, with contrasting views and guidelines about confidentiality. Families feel safe and respected when they know their rights to privacy are protected and are more apt to engage with services where this is the case. At the same time, professionals view the limits on the flow of information (and potentially on the delivery of services) imposed by confidentiality regulations as major impediments to collaboration across agency and professional lines. Balancing confidentiality and information-sharing in family-school-community partnerships is complicated by a diverse array of service providers and a multitude of conflicting regulations (Jonson-Reid 2000).

Linking schools with other organizations involves not only differing views of confidentiality and information-sharing, but also different rules and regulations. School staff are covered under the Family Educational Rights and Privacy Act (FERPA), which states that student records may be accessed by family and relevant school staff; therefore school staff are used to open access to student records. On the other hand, community physical and mental health professionals are bound by the Health Insurance Portability and Accountability Act (HIPAA), which requires a child's parent or guardian to sign a release before a physical or mental health professional can access a child's health records. Both FERPA and HIPAA can hinder school-community collaboration in different ways. FERPA can limit community health professionals' ability to participate in meetings focused on a child's IEP. Meanwhile, HIPAA constrains what community health staff can share with school leaders seeking information about individual students (Weist et al. 2012).

While it is easy for professionals to become frustrated with confidentiality provisions, such provisions aid children and families by supporting their privacy in a variety of ways. These include:

1 Protecting embarrassing personal information from disclosure;
2 Preventing improper dissemination of information about children and families that might increase the likelihood of discrimination against them;
3 Protecting personal security;
4 Protecting family security;

5 Protecting job security;
6 Avoiding prejudice or differential treatment; and
7 Encouraging individuals to make use of services designed to help them (Greenberg & Levy 1992; Soler & Peters 1993).

On the other side of this issue are equally valid rationales in support of sharing information. These include:

1 Conducting comprehensive assessments;
2 Providing all necessary services;
3 Avoiding duplication and encouraging efficiency;
4 Encouraging coordinated and continuous service plans;
5 Facilitating the monitoring of services;
6 Helping to make services more family-focused;
7 Serving the needs of the broader community; and
8 Promoting public safety (Greenberg & Levy 1992; Soler & Peters 1993).

Confidentiality provisions come from a variety of sources, including the U.S. Constitution, state constitutions, federal and state statutes, agency regulations, professional practice standards, and ethical standards. It is critical to understand which provisions govern information-sharing in each particular agency and community and to identify which clients they serve. The focus should be on ways to meet legitimate service goals within what is possible under the law.

One suggestion for information-sharing in interagency partnerships is the creation of a "superorganization." Such a structure requires that "agencies involved in the team actually share employees, jointly assign portions of their time to the collaborative effort and thus creating a single agency with free exchange of information between members" (Jonson-Reid 2000:36). As noted in the previous chapter, SUN Service Systems community schools have negotiated a way for employees of their community partners who are intimately involved in the community schools efforts to be considered part of FERPA. This serves to open up communication between school district employees and employees of CBOs with collective goals serving the same children.

Another way to address confidentiality in school-community partnerships is with a consent form that provides for sharing of information among all agencies that are part of the interagency collaborative. The foundation of sharing information that is otherwise protected by confidentiality provisions is *informed consent*, meaning that consent "must be given voluntarily and must be 'informed'—that is, the individual must understand fully what information will be exchanged, with whom it will be shared and how it will be used. Consent must be documented in writing, usually on a signed release form" (Greenberg & Levy 1992:13). When a person is not old enough for a consent form to be legally binding, a parent or guardian may sign. Some state statutes allow minors to consent to release information. In addition, some states have "mature minor" rules whereby minors found by a court to be sufficiently mature may consent to medical care and to release records. Other states allow minors who are legally emancipated or are themselves parents to consent to care and the release of records. Sometimes minors may refuse services that they need or want because they do not want their family members to have to sign for consent. On the other hand, even when children's signatures are not legally binding, some collaboratives request them as a way to encourage children's involvement and sense of ownership.

Oftentimes, children's ages are a factor in decisions about their right to make decisions about information-sharing. Yet, views about the age at which children are able to understand the issues of confidentiality and information-sharing differ. Because of this, and because there is value in empowering children in decisions about their well-being, Berman-Rossi and Rossi (1990) suggest explaining consent to children and having them sign forms allowing sharing, even when their ability to understand the complexities of such actions is uncertain. Adelman et al. (1985) found that involving children in decisions of informed consent positively impacted outcomes of services. In order to protect adolescents' confidentiality and expand their use of preventive health care at SBHCs, the School-Based Health Center Alliance has joined with other like-minded organizations to dispute the use of explanations of benefits statements (EOBs) for adolescents seeking preventive health care for sensitive issues that are provided free of charge (http://www.sbh4all.org/site/c.ckLQKbOVLkK6E/b.7697107/apps/s/content.asp?ct=11675171). In addition to adolescents, immigrants of all ages are another population that may forego needed services due to fear of signing releases, concerned that information shared may put them at risk of deportation. Whenever this is an issue, release forms should state clearly that no personal information would be given to the Immigration and Naturalization Service (Greenberg & Levy 1992; Soler & Peters 1993).

While confidentiality is an issue to address in all agency work, it is critical in school-linked services, where the best collaboratives are often the most far reaching, and where issues of information-sharing are frequent and complex. Greenberg and Levy (1992) recommend that information-sharing not be among the first tasks of a developing collaborative. They argue that it is important to first have strong working relationships and commitment to joint efforts, and that holding off on the question of information-sharing allows a basis of trust to develop. They do, however, advise that participants clearly put this issue on the agenda as a way of asserting its importance and ensuring that it will not be ignored after other aspects of planning for joint action have been addressed. Confidentiality, when handled thoughtfully, can add, rather than reduce, collaborative efforts to build and integrate school-community connections.

* * *

Collaboration underpins the ability of schools and communities to come together to serve children. Despite agreement on the need to work together, many barriers make collaborative work challenging. This chapter has addressed components required for collaboration across an array of organizations and professional disciplines. Exemplary programs that have placed collaboration and collective impact at the core of their efforts have been highlighted and relationships between schools and likely partners in this work, such as universities and child welfare agencies, have been discussed. Lastly, we addressed the challenges of supporting both privacy and information-sharing—two values that are important to school-linked services but that often come into conflict with each other.

In the next chapter we address the various settings where school-linked service strategies are being implemented and the supports and barriers in each of these settings. We focus on low-income disenfranchised communities as the places where school-linked services can make the most difference and how to implement them in rural and urban settings serving children from pre-K through high school.

5

Settings

WHILE MAKING SCHOOLS the hubs of community services can be advantageous for *all* children, families, schools, and communities, it is the underserved communities that are most in need of this integrated model. These underserved communities exist most often in urban and rural areas; families in suburban communities are more often able to negotiate systems and link children with needed services themselves, given their higher incomes. Although this is clearly not always the case, children growing up in more affluent suburban communities are more likely to be "ready to learn" and succeed academically. "Low income students are more likely than students from wealthier families to have lower test scores, fall behind in school, dropout, and fail to acquire a college degree" (Southern Education Foundation 2013:10). Even beyond educational outcomes, Pappano (2010) notes that the contrast between poor cities and rich suburbs is also at the heart of the disparity between whites' and minorities' access to quality jobs, health care, and even life expectancy and cancer death rates.

While school-linked services, especially full-service community schools and school-based health centers, operate most often in major metropolitan areas, they are increasingly emerging in rural communities. They are less frequently in suburban communities where there tend to be fewer families in poverty. Because urban and rural communities differ from each other along a range of variables, we consider the distinctions between them, the different challenges that arise in these contexts, and the strategies that prove to be successful. First, however, we review evidence that the most effective way to improve academic achievement across school settings and communities is to address disadvantage. Then, following discussion of distinctions between urban and rural schools, we examine grade-level challenges at the preschool, elementary, middle, and high school levels, and the implications for school-linked services in these settings.

DISENFRANCHISED LOW-INCOME COMMUNITIES

Recent legislation has focused on schools rather than students in addressing academic underachievement. No Child Left Behind (NCLB; see chapter 8), for example, ignores the link between low socioeconomic status and low school performance by holding all schools to the same standard irrespective of whom they serve, and then labeling schools that do not meet the standard as low-performing (Ladd 2012). Similarly, the Coalition for Civil Rights and Education, led by the unlikely partnership of former New York City Schools Chancellor Joel Klein, Newt Gingrich, and Al Sharpton, argue that "shifting the focus of school reform toward reducing poverty or improving the health and welfare of children would be nothing more than an attempt to use poverty as an excuse for not educating all children at high standards" (Noguera 2011:13). However, the data do not support these policies and beliefs. As Noguera shows, while "schools-alone" has been the strategy of choice for thirty years, even with billion-dollar budgets, it has not successfully impacted academic and developmental outcomes for children.

In contrast, there is mounting, multidimensional evidence supporting Rebell and Wolff's claim that "America doesn't have a general education crisis; we have a poverty crisis" (2012:62). In 2011, 60 percent of students in urban schools (cities with populations over 100,000) and 44 percent of students in rural schools were eligible for free and reduced-price lunch. These figures correspond to a rise in the percentage of students from low-income families in public schools from 38 percent in 2001 to 48 percent in 2011. These growth rates, however, have not been met with growth rates in educational expenditures (Southern Education Foundation 2011). Research documents a wide array of factors that are associated with poverty and impact children's educational outcomes, a major one being health. Theis, Krawczyk, and Gaspard (1999) believe that poverty is the number one public health issue for children. Basch argues that reducing health disparities "must be a fundamental part of school reform" (2010:4).

Low-income urban minority youth are disproportionately impacted by an array of educationally relevant disparities that are not affected by educational innovation, requiring us to look beyond what happens inside the classroom to improve outcomes for children. For example, children from low-income families have poorer health outcomes than their more affluent counterparts (Starfield, Robertson, & Riley 2002; Larson & Halfon 2009) both in childhood and in adult life (Galobardes, Lynch, & Smith 2004; Russ, Garro, & Halfon 2010). These disparities manifest in conditions that include poor vision, asthma, teen pregnancy, aggression and violence, low birth weight, lack of physical activity, lack of breakfast, and untreated inattention and hyperactivity (Ladd 2012). In addition to disparities in general health, children living in poverty are also more likely to be overweight or obese, to have worse oral health, and to have social and emotional challenges (Larson et al. 2008). Children growing up in low-income households are also more likely to have functional limitations resulting from their chronic health conditions (Russ, Garro, & Halfon 2010). School-based health centers are specifically designed to interrupt the cycle of poverty and the interrelationship between health and academic outcomes (Brimfield, Ammerman, & Juszczak 2012).

In addition to health, there are numerous other income-related variables connected to academic success. They include the degree of enriched linguistic and other opportunities at home; high-quality preschool opportunities; neighborhood and housing stability, safety, and quality; nutrition; family stress; learning resources and participation in activities in the summer; and afterschool activities that middle-class families take for granted, such as tutoring, camp, travel, and extracurricular lessons in the arts, music, sports, etc. (Ladd 2012; McInnis-Dittrich, Neisler, & Tourse 1999). Discrepancies in educational outcomes between high- and low-income families are also a reflection of behaviors and abilities of families and teachers, as well as their varying kinds and degrees of social capital. For example, affluent families are better able to negotiate the education system to their advantage and to ensure that their children attend the best schools and get the best teachers (Ladd 2012).

Data on achievement outcomes show that when state test scores and state poverty rates are compared, 40 percent of the variation in reading scores and 46 percent of the variation in math scores are correlated with child poverty rates. This is compounded for children who are members of minority groups, where the numbers climb to 50 percent in reading and 51 percent in math (Ladd 2012). More affluent suburban schools boast achievement levels that rival those of countries with higher overall educational outcomes, illustrating again the centrality of income as a predictor of academic success. Even countries touting higher overall educational outcomes than the United States (e.g., Korea, Finland, Canada, the Netherlands) reveal that achievement levels of low-income children are far below those of children from more advantaged backgrounds (Ladd 2012). Cummings, Dyson, and Todd state that "a smattering of full service and extended schools will change little in societies where social and economic inequalities are rampant, and poverty is allowed to grow" (2011:111). The fact that low-income students in private schools have learning gaps similar to those in public schools (Southern Education Foundation 2011) underscores the point that what happens *inside* of schools is not sufficient to overcome all that poverty does to children.

These data support the idea that addressing the unmet needs of children in poverty is the single most significant intervention to increase academic achievement. In the United Kingdom, linking schools and services through the extended schools model is seen as "a key vehicle for delivering the Government's objective of lifting children out of poverty and improving outcomes for them and their families" (Cummings, Dyson, & Todd 2011:16). As stated in a 2013 report to then U.S. Secretary of Education Duncan, regarding the link between educational and income disparities that continue to jeopardize large numbers of children living in poverty, "Given that low-income students, English-language learners and students of color together form a majority of our young people and the fastest-growing population in the nation—and that America's future economic and civic vitality depends on their success in an age of global competition—this practice is not only unjust but also unwise" (U.S. Department of Education 2013).

Linking schools with health and social services is an important way to address these disparities; the methods of program implementation need to be considered as well. Cummings, Dyson, and Todd state that schools need "to move away from a model of delivering support to 'needy' people. Instead, they have to work alongside children, families and communities in ways that are characterized by relational power, mutual respect, and the coproduction of solutions to the problems they face" (2011:131). Below we address key ways to collaboratively and respectfully implement school-linked services in underserved areas and highlight some of the discrepancies in delivering these services in rural as opposed to urban areas and for younger as opposed to older children.

URBAN AND RURAL SCHOOLS AND COMMUNITIES

School-linked services have developed largely to address issues that plague low-income communities in major metropolitan areas. Due to the concentration of poverty and the accessibility of services, large urban areas continue to be the major setting for these efforts. Nonetheless, school-linked services are beginning to emerge in rural America, where many communities are also plagued by poverty. Lacking the concentration of services that characterizes urban life, these communities face different and often greater challenges in leveling the playing field that supports academic achievement for all. Yet, as Williams (2010) argues, in rural areas, community schools might be the most economically feasible way to mitigate the negative influence of poverty on children's ability to succeed.

When considering linking schools with services for children and families in rural areas, environmental context is critical. For one thing, rural schools and districts vary greatly in size from small one-room schoolhouses to larger schools and districts. They vary in affluence, with high-poverty communities disproportionately serving students of color. A major challenge in rural schools is hiring and retaining high-quality teachers in these communities, especially since the salaries and benefits are routinely lower than elsewhere, while at the same time staffing limitations mean that teachers must teach multiple subjects, requiring more certifications and more time devoted to course preparation. Another recruitment and retention challenge is that teachers are often the most highly educated people in these communities, with limited options for housing, recreation, and social lives, and limited jobs for spouses/partners (Williams 2013).

This context frames a number of interrelated challenges unique to service utilization in rural areas. These include the fact that services are often geographically spread out; that transportation options are limited; that the number of providers is often not adequate to meet needs; and that stigma is often attached to accessing services (especially mental health services) in close-knit rural communities. While the social networks of rural communities can sometimes provide support, they can also prevent community members from seeking professional care due to a lack of trust in "outsiders" (Owens, Watabe, & Michael 2011). This reluctance to utilize services is compounded by the limited amount of services. For example, currently, there are 2,157 health professional shortage areas (HPSAs) in the rural United States, as compared to 910 urban HPSAs. Moreover, while approximately 25 percent of the U.S. population lives in rural areas, only 10 percent of physicians practice in these areas. The same short-supply issues relative to urban areas occur with mental health services and supports, case management, and dental services in rural areas (North & Kjolhede 2012:360).

Despite the challenges, school-linked services are beginning to emerge in rural communities. Rural school-based health centers (SBHCs) account for 27 percent of SBHCs in the United States, although they are still in less than 2 percent of rural schools. Only about 15 percent of these centers currently utilize telemedicine (North & Kjolhede 2012), but technological advances do represent promising approaches to expanding access to physical and mental health and dental services in rural communities. Though rural SBHCs are still small in number, many believe that they may provide a better "medical home" for rural children than traditional medical offices due to increased access on school grounds, which also increases the potential for continuity of care. SBHCs have the ability to partner with schools and public health officials in population and individual health interventions such as vaccinations, exercise programs, smoking cessation, etc. (North & Kjolhede 2012).

Another promising school-linked practice in rural areas is the university–rural school partnership that utilizes social work and other professional interns in intensive family engagement outreach. In one example of such a partnership, sponsored by Binghamton University (of the State University of New York) and described in more detail below, social work interns team up under the supervision of licensed social workers and travel to families' rural homes to build relationships and learn about ways to support children's success in school. Interning with the masters-level social work students are undergraduate students interested in careers in nursing, education, law, social work, public administration, and psychology. Such interns have created avenues for previously isolated parents in a mobile home community almost ten miles away from the school to build relationships with teachers and school administrators, which school leaders describe as "transformative" (Blitz et al. 2013).

Another successful rural community school effort in Owsley County, North Carolina, has attracted national attention for its ability to truly make schools hubs of the community. There, Title I funds are leveraged for workshops for parents and community members on health, academics, scholarships, and other topics, while a back-to-school event includes a health fair and health screening. When asked about school-community relationships, Superintendent Melinda Turner notes that "the school *is* the community" and that "nearly every important event in Owsley is held in the schools, including weddings, receptions, theatre performances, and emergency management" (Williams 2010:17).

Among the seven standards promoted by the Rural School and Community Trust (2004) for community-school partnerships at the high school level are multilevel school and community connections and collaborations to make the school and community good places to live, learn, and play (standard 2); and policies, calendars, and resources arranged to maximize community involvement (standard 4). To support the implementation of these and other goals of community schools in rural areas, Williams outlines the following challenges and potential solutions:

1 The challenge of attracting highly effective teachers: model opportunities after the Model Teacher Education Consortium, which offers counseling, professional development, and financial assistance to employees of partnering school districts so that they can pursue initial licensure or a first degree in teacher education or other avenues to achieving educational expertise and opportunities.
2 The challenge of parental and community engagement: partner with community-based and faith-based organizations and agencies to offer diverse opportunities and venues for involvement in decision-making and interactions with children.
3 The challenge of better utilization of facilities: consider co-location opportunities prior to building new structures for schools and agencies and include needs assessment for all stakeholders when planning for publicly funded construction of facilities.
4 The challenge of negotiating agreements and reducing risks among partners: rely on local and state governments to implement formulas for allocating space costs or construction costs to multiple service providers and their separate funding sources.

5 The challenge of establishing community support and consensus: support rural communities exploring needs and finding common visions for youth, families, and schools.
6 The challenge of making federal turnaround models relevant for rural schools: since the turnaround model (see chapter 8) being implemented in urban districts is not feasible in many rural districts, have Congress and state legislatures provide incentives for community schools in rural areas, as they currently do for turnaround schools.
7 Bolstering federal funding for community schools: increase federal funding for the Full Service Community Schools Program and provide technical assistance to rural districts by the Department of Education to help "level the field in this and other competitive grant competitions". (2010:32)

Here we profile Broome County Promise Zone, an example of an emerging county-wide system of community schools that crosses urban and rural districts in upstate New York.

BROOME COUNTY PROMISE ZONE (Information provided by Laura Bronstein, Dean, College of Community and Public Affairs, and Executive Director, Institute for Multi-generational Studies, Binghamton University)

BRIEF OVERVIEW

A team of faculty at Binghamton University (BU), State University of New York (SUNY), led by its College of Community and Public Affairs (CCPA) in collaboration with a range of local organizations including the Broome County Department of Mental Health (BCDMH), Broome-Tioga Boards of Cooperative Educational Services (BOCES), and many other community agencies is working to launch a system of community schools throughout Broome County, New York. More recently, BU's Division of Student Affairs has worked to support the university-assisted community schools model through a student affairs–academic affairs partnership, with community schools having been designated the university's signature civic engagement initiative. Currently, Broome County Promise Zone community schools can be characterized as "emerging," according to the Children's Aid Society's stages of development.

ORIGINAL OBJECTIVE

Work in the university, public schools across the county, and community agencies takes a holistic approach to address educational, health, and psychosocial needs of children and families, while also promoting economic revitalization and capacity-building in Broome County.

PROCESS OF DEVELOPMENT

BU CCPA, BCDMH, BOCES, Broome County school districts, and community agencies came together with their separate but overlapping missions to serve children and families, especially those with high needs. After working collaboratively with BU CCPA and other partners on a number of initiatives, BOCES was awarded a Safe Schools-Healthy Students (SS-HS) federal grant in 2009. This grant, in turn, led to the development, implementation, and evaluation of a range of county-wide activities geared to decreasing violence and tobacco and alcohol use, supporting psychosocial development and mental health, and increasing support for early childhood education throughout the fifty-three schools and twelve school districts located in the small city of Binghamton and the surrounding suburban and rural areas of Broome County.

Throughout the work of the grant, a large, productive collaboration was built across the county with community leaders, a New York State assemblywoman, the Binghamton University president, school superintendents, and others to present state leaders with reasons why Broome County should be designated a New York State Promise Zone and receive yearly funding to better coordinate schools and mental health services. With receipt of the Promise Zone designation in 2013 and in response to Governor Cuomo's Education Reform Commission recommendation to build community schools, Broome County has engaged in the development of a county-wide system of community schools. In addition, BU has made the community schools the centerpiece of its civic engagement efforts and its signature academic affairs/student affairs collaboration.

COLLABORATIVE ACTIVITIES/STRUCTURES

Broome County collaborative structures include shared funding and joint activities. State Promise Zone funding flows to BCDMH, which contracts for services with BOCES and BU CCPA for staff (mostly community school coordinators) and other needs. BOCES also supports an additional coordinator and the university provides support for a coordinator to facilitate the involvement of university interns and volunteers. In addition, BCDMH contracts with the Family and Children's Society for satellite mental health clinics based at schools. The local community foundation recently provided a grant for supplementary materials and summer programming. Some school districts, including urban Binghamton and rural Whitney Point have utilized other funds (e.g. Title I) to support the community school efforts in their districts. The leaders of the three primary partners, BCDMH, BOCES, and BU CCPA, assemble often to provide unified guidance to community school staff and to expand capacity and resources.

TARGET POPULATION

The goal is for all community members to benefit from the community schools. In its current early stage, each district selects one school to begin with. These selections span elementary, middle, and high school.

FEATURED PROGRAM

Successful family engagement work in rural Whitney Point Central School District began under the Safe Schools-Healthy Students grant. Interns in the social work master's degree program used a "windshield assessment" to target a high-poverty mobile home community for outreach. Many families in this community are without transportation, and some are without plumbing. Many have learning and/or developmental delays, having had negative school experiences themselves while growing up, as well as in regard to their children's and, in some instances, their grandchildren's education.

With a progressive administration, the superintendent and her leadership team have supported efforts to reengage these families and to help staff view them from a strengths perspective. These families now provide parent leadership training to community members, with a graduation ceremony presided over by the mayor. Recently, a team of rural poverty-stricken family members, none of whom had graduated from high school or ever previously stayed in a hotel, drove four hours to Penn State University to present their efforts at building family-school relationships to a team of school mental health researchers from around the country (see Blitz et al. 2013).

LOCATION OF SERVICES

Services provided as part of the Broome County Promise Zone community school initiative are available in schools, in homes, and elsewhere in the community.

SERVICE PROVIDERS/PARTNERS

Service providers and partners represent the county, cities, school districts, state of New York, local foundations, nonprofit organizations, and BU. Local Rotary Clubs have also recently become interested, as have local individual citizens. A recent family literacy effort includes SUNY Broome (the local community college), with expectations to expand the involvement of all types of organizations, including higher education and businesses.

TYPES OF SERVICES DELIVERED

Currently student interns working on bachelor's, master's, and doctoral degrees, along with volunteers, provide the bulk of services; efforts are made to link the students' service work with their major areas of study. The following services were provided according to students' majors during spring semester 2014:

1. Computer science
   - Website building
2. English
   - Creating a documentary that tells the Promise Zone story
3. Human Development (HDEV) with aspiration for graduate degrees in public administration and/or education
   - Developing afterschool and summer programs
4. HDEV with interest in human resources
   - Reviewing and developing policy and procedure manual
5. Master's in social work (MSW), HDEV, psychology, and sociology
   - Engaging in individual and group social and emotional support with parents, grandparents, and students
   - Developing high school peer mentoring program
   - Developing activities for group work
   - Push in to special education classroom
   - Facilitating parent leadership workshops focusing on parenting, child development, and conflict resolution
6. Nursing students and family nurse practitioner
   - Facilitating parent leadership workshops and addressing such topics as diabetes and nutrition, medication management, communicating with a doctor, and working with a school nurse
   - Educating and supporting students with asthma
   - Engaging in child development education
7. Philosophy, politics, law
   - Mandarin-speaking intern tutoring Mandarin
8. Across disciplines
   - Academic support
   - Mentoring
   - Binghamton High School talent show
   - Family engagement/home visits
   - Community outreach
   - Afterschool programs
   - Participation in and support of documentary
   - Creating promotional materials
   - University-wide Community School Awareness Week campaign

FIGURE 5.1 Broome County Promise Zone Evaluation Logic-Model

RESOURCES	ACTIVITIES	OUTPUTS	SHORT-TERM OUTCOMES	LONG-TERM OUTCOMES	IMPACT
Community school coordinators (CSC) Sufficient staff (expertise and availability) Sufficient resources (e.g., funding, facilities) Relationships with local service providers Leadership and program infrastructure Support from schools Support from community Support from local university and college	1. Extended learning opportunities and youth development	• # of students in afterschool programs • # of students in summer programs • # of students in drop-in tutoring during the school day	• Number of courses passed • Increased academic motivation • Improved college and career aspirations • Decreased disciplinary referrals	• Increased GPA • Improved graduation rates	A model of service delivery in high-need communities in Broome County that builds the necessary supports and structure around children to equip them to be successful in school, work, and life.
	2. Family engagement	• # of caregivers in parent mentoring program • # of caregivers attending parent cafes • # of caregivers attending healthy multigenerational family project • # of caregiver contacts through community outreach	• Increased perceived ability to engage and perceived caregiver support • Increased perceived support for caregiver engagement • Increased opportunities for caregiver involvement • Increased caregiver participation in school events and activities	• Increased representation of caregivers in school decision-making • Increased GPA • Improved graduation rates	
	3. Health, mental health, and social service referrals	• # of referrals made for mental health services • # of referrals for community support and other health services	• Enrollment in mental health services • Retention in mental health services • Increased school and community support services for caregivers • Increases in attitudinal and physical access to services	• Decreases in childhood internalizing and/or externalizing MH symptoms • Decreases in alcohol, tobacco, and other drug use • Caregivers are able to provide for basic needs	
	4. Attendance support	# of contacts made regarding attendance	• Reduction in chronic absenteeism • Decreased tardiness • Increased attendance	• Increased GPA • Improved graduation rates	

Technical assistance from Children's Aid Society Culturally, linguistically, and trauma-informed approaches	5. Early childhood education	• #of referrals to PACT • # of contacts with Head Start and other preschool programs	• Enrollment in high-quality 0–3 programs • Enrollment in high-quality pre-K programs	• % of K-3 attendance above 95%	
	6. Social and emotional learning	• # of groups • # of planned activities • # of drop-ins	• Improved grades in identified subjects • Improved social skills • Improved relationships with peers • Increased prosocial activities • Decreased disciplinary referrals	• Increased GPA • Improved graduation rates	
	7. Professional development	• # of workshops/trainings provided • # of committees on which CSC and/or interns serve	• Feedback that information presented was beneficial and/or useful • Implementation of strategies presented • Improved classroom management		
	8. Linkages between schools and partners	• # of community partners involved in school activities • # of outreach activities from school to community partners • # of services and resources needing coordination	• MOAs for space and resources • Partnerships with community partners are valued as a resource for school improvement • Improved coordination of services between schools and community partners	• Increased number of community services co-located at schools • Increased representation of community providers in school improvement initiatives (i.e., membership on school leadership committees) • Interoperable electronic data management systems for children and their families engaged with multiple systems	

FUNDING

As stated above, the bulk of the funding comes from New York State, with supplementary funds and in-kind support from Broome County BCDMH, BOCES, the university, school districts, and local foundations. Additional funding is expected to come from other community clubs (e.g., Rotary) and individual donations. A community fund-raiser held at the University Downtown Center yielded greater awareness of the initiative, a front page story in the local newspaper, and individual donations.

EVALUATION

As an emerging community school initiative, the Broome County Promise Zone began by conducting needs assessments and collecting baseline data in the schools where service provision has begun. Each district participates in a county-wide evaluation plan based on the logic model (figure 5.1), which was designed by Elizabeth Mellin, PhD, following the Children's Aid Society's model.

FUTURE DIRECTIONS

The goal is to have coordinators for all fifty-three schools in the county that wish to participate in the community school initiative. To that end, the immediate goal for involved schools is to provide services that match each school's needs assessment, which, in turn, necessitates broadening the list of partners. The university is expanding its support for this effort and increasing its offerings of courses and civic engagement opportunities for university students at all levels. Staff continue documenting and assessing progress and sharing lessons learned at conferences and through publications.

Just as rural communities require different visions and implementation strategies than do urban communities, implementation challenges of school-linked services varies by primary or secondary school level. While school-community relationships and services occur throughout the pre-K–high school continuum, there are considerations and factors that must be considered when implementing services with younger versus older children.

AGE AND GRADE LEVEL CONSIDERATIONS

Early Childhood

Early childhood education has become synonymous with Head Start, the nation's largest early childhood initiative, designed specifically to support low-income families. "Head Start is a comprehensive early learning program for preschool-aged children of families in poverty, designed to meet children's cognitive, emotional, social, health, nutritional, and psychological needs" (Severns 2012: 3). Currently, Head Start is administered by the Office of Head Start, a division of the Administration for Children and Families in the U.S. Department of Health and Human Services (HHS). To be eligible to enroll in Head Start, children's families must, in most cases, have incomes at or below 100 percent of the federal poverty level. Additionally, children in foster care or with special needs may qualify, or in some cases, where there is room, children whose families are at 130 percent of the poverty level may enroll. The vast majority of Head Start children live in families where a parent works full-time (Severns 2012).

Head Start was launched in 1964 as the centerpiece of President Johnson's "War on Poverty." In 1965 Head Start began as a nationwide, eight-week summer program serving roughly half a million children ages three through five. In 1966, it grew quickly into a half-day program available during the school year. Details of its implementation and requirements have changed over its history, including the addition of a National Reporting System requirement for testing four year olds that was mandated in 2003 and then eliminated in 2007. Another important change in Congress's 2007 reauthorization of Head Start mandated that all Head Start lead teachers have a minimum of an associate's degree in early childhood or a related field by 2011, and that half of them have at least a bachelor's degree in early childhood by 2013. In 1995, Early Head Start was established for even younger children (from birth to age three) in order to serve pregnant women and families of economically disadvantaged children, a move supported by evidence that children's growth and development in early childhood is crucial to learning capacities later in life (Severns 2012).

In addition to the education requirements added in the 2007 reauthorization, the amended Head Start Act directed HHS to "re-compete" certain Head Start grants through a process called the *designated renewal system* (DRS) "to determine if a Head Start agency is delivering a high-quality and comprehensive Head Start program that meets the educational, health, nutritional, and social needs of the children and families it serves" (Severns 2012:5). While the National Head Start Association, Head Start's largest membership organization, supports re-competition, it is too early to evaluate its impact as an effective policy.

Although Head Start and Early Head Start are the largest federal early childhood education programs, there are increasing numbers of state, local, nonprofit and for-profit early childhood initiatives. As of 2012, it is estimated that 42 percent of four-year-olds in the United States participate in some kind of early childhood education program (Guernsey et al. 2014). While some research produces mixed results regarding the large-scale longitudinal impact of Head Start (Severns 2012), early childhood education continues to be cited along with routine and preventive physical and mental health care; afterschool, summer, and expanded learning time, and family engagement as the most critical factors in leveling the playing field for students in poverty (Ladd 2012; Rebell & Wolff 2012). The idea of early childhood education stretches beyond the pre-K classroom. Critical components of quality early childhood include high-quality interactions and conversations between very young children and their parents, high-quality childcare, and immersion of children in "language-rich" learning environments (Guernsey et al. 2014:6). Given these multiple components, it is not surprising that interprofessional collaboration is an increasingly critical component of early childhood education (Berzin et al. 2011; Flaherty et al. 1998) and is even termed the "glue" that holds inclusive classrooms together (Snell & Janney 2000).

Although there is a large amount of data supporting the advantages of early childhood education, more large-scale, longitudinal research is needed. Nonetheless, some of the data are enlightening. Promoting school success and emphasizing parent involvement during preschool and kindergarten years, as well as implementing first- through third-grade follow-ups, have been found to correlate with fewer juvenile arrests, less need for remedial services, and higher educational attainment for poor children a full fifteen years after the intervention (Jozefowich-Simbeni & Allen-Meares 2002; Reynolds et al. 2001). Additionally, the impact of poverty and income disparities is especially glaring at the pre-K level. Fewer than half of poor children have been found ready for school at five years of age, as compared with 75 percent of children from middle- and upper-class homes (U.S. Department of Education 2013). This, again, is an area where the United States lags behind other countries in educational outcomes. The world's best performing school systems are characterized by universal access to early childhood education (U.S. Department of Education 2013). Specifically, research has shown that early childhood education makes a difference in:

1 Academic success, particularly for disadvantaged children;
2 Reduced need for special education;
3 Healthier lifestyles;
4 Lower overall social costs, including a decreased crime rate;
5 Increased high school graduation; and
6 Higher rates for college attendance and completion.

Cost-benefit analysis reveals that for each dollar invested in high-quality early childhood education, there is a 7–10 percent per annum return on investment. "This means that taking early action to address the effects of adverse environments on young children can not only reverse some of the harm of disadvantage, but can also result in high economic return" (U.S. Department of Education 2013:28). The 2013 U.S. Equity and Excellence Commission states that "ensuring universal access to high-quality early learning programs is a matter of the highest national priority, with a special focus for children in our poorest communities" (U.S. Department of Education 2013:28).

In New Jersey, a series of legal decisions has led to dramatic outcomes through early childhood education in the state's thirty-one poorest school districts. In the *Abbott v. Burke* equity litigation, the state supreme court ordered high-quality preschool to be provided to all three- and four-year-olds in the state's poorest school districts and specified that the state and local districts meet the following standards of quality recommended by research: full-day, full school year programs; small class size; certified teachers and trained aides; developmentally appropriate curriculum linked to state K–12 academic standards; and adequate state funding to support delivery of high-quality early learning across the diverse program settings (Darling-Hammond et al. 2013). A key part of these decisions is the mandate that all lead teachers acquire a bachelor's degree and an early childhood credential. The number of early childhood teachers meeting these criteria went up from 15 percent to 90 percent in four years. As a result, the proportion of classrooms rated near the top of the scale on quality indicators doubled to 72 percent between 2003 and 2007, and evidence about student learning followed suit. The National Institute for Early Education Research assessed more than one thousand kindergarten students from Abbott districts in 2006 and found that those who had attended two years of preschool cut the "vocabulary gap" in half (Darling-Hammond et al. 2013:1).

Despite progress occurring in some states, early childhood education continues to be a "step-child" in the U.S. educational system in a number of ways. Not all early childhood education teachers are required to have bachelors' degrees, and post-secondary programs often "do a poor job of preparing teachers to work effectively with children in pre-K" (Guernsey et al. 2014:11). In addition, a study of elementary school principals reveals that they often place their most effective teachers in the upper grades. Additionally, early childhood teachers' pay lags way behind that of K–12 teachers, with a median salary of $25,700 being just barely above the poverty line for a family of four (Guernsey et al. 2014).

Elementary and Middle and High School

School-linked services exist at all public school levels from preschool through high school. Exemplary initiatives described throughout this book increasingly operate in a range of grades. However, their design and implementation differ depending upon the age group targeted. For example, family engagement is often easier at the elementary level because it is a time when parents need to be more involved with their children (Dryfoos 1994).

Although there are some innovative programs that are youth-led at the elementary level (e.g., see Blinn, Carpenter, & Mandel 2012), more youth-led initiatives occur at the middle and high school levels. Moreover, because middle and high school students and the programs serving them are more complex, issues arise at these levels that do not arise in elementary schools. For example, attendance is easier to measure in elementary schools, where students are in a single classroom; in higher grades, students might attend homeroom and then cut classes, thus requiring a more sophisticated approach to assessment and remediation of attendance challenges. Additionally, issues of confidentiality in service programs with older adolescents are also more complex. Service providers are sometimes bound to share information with parents of adolescents, and yet sometimes they are bound *not* to share information. Oakland, CA community schools have built school-based health centers with separate doors for students (accessed only through the school building) and the community (with an external entrance/exit) to assure students' confidentiality. As discussed earlier, confidentiality and information-sharing guidelines regarding utilization of physical and mental health services are complex and often dependent on state laws (Armbruster et al. 1999). Complications can arise depending on whether and when information is shared with or withheld from teenagers' families much more than is the case with elementary school students, about whom information-sharing is more commonly accepted. Another age-related issue, also more complicated in the older grades, comes from those with concerns that school-based health centers lead the way for schools to become "sex clinics" (Dryfoos 1994; Pacheco et al. 1991).

While it is critical for students to develop good attendance and academic habits in the early years, unfortunately they do not always do so. As a result, community schools operating in upper grades often focus their efforts on dropout prevention. Over 1.2 million American students drop out of high school each year, and half of these dropouts come from just 15 percent of high schools in our nation's high-poverty neighborhoods. Nearly a third of all first-year public high school students, including close to half of all African American, Hispanic, and Native American students, fail to graduate with their class (Axelroth 2009).

Many community schools at the high school level have had great success in improving graduation rates. For example, Cincinnati Public Schools, which set a goal in 2002 to make every school a community learning center, saw its district-wide graduation rate improve from 51 percent to 82 percent over a six-year period (Axelroth 2009). The successful dropout prevention programs in high schools in low-income communities across the United States are characterized by strong partnerships. Community agencies and educational institutions provide a range of activities and services depending on needs, including tutors and mentors from local colleges, college and career-related support, and culturally specific programming to support the needs of ethnically diverse students and families (Axelroth 2009). Communities in Schools, discussed earlier, addresses dropout prevention through a highly individualized, student-focused approach.

Because internships are often seen as valuable school-linked services, and because older students are more likely to seek them out, this is a service most applicable for students in the older grades. Securing opportunities for students in communities that may be reluctant to invite disenfranchised students into their work organizations may, however, be difficult. A principal at a Hartford, Connecticut, high school described his school's partnership with a law firm, noting that when he spoke to one of the partners about internships, the partner said, "'We have a really hard time accepting second- and third-year law students as interns. I have a hard time understanding what a sixteen-year-old high school student can do.' The principal responded by saying 'what we want [students] to do is be around it. We want them to breathe in the air. What does it look like to work in this kind of an organization? What does it look like to be part of a high-functioning team?'" A successful internship program was developed with this approach, as the law partner decided he also wanted to afford teenagers in his community the opportunities to learn and practice these skills (Pappano 2010:133).

• • •

As stated throughout this book, optimal linkages between schools and communities grow out of careful needs assessments. Issues raised in this chapter, including community setting (disenfranchised, low-income, and urban versus rural) and school setting (e.g., grade level) are critical variables to consider in planning and executing effective programs. While this book, thus far, has primarily emphasized an array of school-linked services including school-based health centers and community schools in the United States, the next chapter describes how these initiatives function in other places around the globe.

6

International Initiatives

THIS CHAPTER FOCUSES ON MODELS OF school-linked initiatives developed in countries outside of the United States. In doing so, we subscribe to the notion put forward by U.K. educators that supporting the well-being of children through culturally responsive education and needed health and social services supports families and communities as well (Cummings, Dyson, & Todd 2011). This is especially true for children living in poverty conditions where school attendance and completion rates are far below their country's norm. Aware that the definitions of school-linked services, community-school partnerships, and community schools vary among and within countries, we will attempt to articulate and maintain each country's definitions as we describe these initiatives.

We begin by citing the work of the International Center of Excellence for Community Schools (ICECS), founded with support from the Charles Stewart Mott Foundation. Its agenda calls for forming a network of people and organizations to research, fund, and implement community schools throughout the world (Children's Aid Society National Center for Community Schools, 2011; International Center of Excellence for Community Schools 2014). At this time, the center has identified a number of schools that have a community school model that is similar to that of the United States.

The rationale for developing school-linked services differs in various parts of the world depending on the needs of each region. For example, while many community-school partnerships are established to combat poverty, others are dedicated to supporting reconciliation in response to war, instilling democratic ideology, furthering civic engagement, advancing adult education, and/or encouraging social inclusion and cultural integrity. Clearly, political and economic resources differ throughout these geographical and cultural settings, and each group of community-partnership schools is thus unique and continually evolving. The following are standards that ICECS has put forth as components of internationally based community schools: leadership, partnership, social inclusion, services, volunteering, lifelong learning, community development, parent engagement, and school culture (International Center of Excellence for Community Schools 2014). There is no expectation that all schools with strong partnerships score high on all of these standards, but they do provide a framework for goal setting and attainment.

We begin by describing some of the community-partnership schools identified by ICECS and then continue on to add others that we find interesting based on their unique cultural and socioeconomic context. In doing so, we must add the following disclaimers: first, we could not possibly include all the schools listed by ICECS and therefore chose several based on their reputations for strong partnership models, as well as their geographic diversity. As with our discussion of policies (chapter 7) that impact partnerships in the United States, because the political environments of countries change (some more rapidly than others), we acknowledge that there may be information lags in our descriptions. We encourage our readers to conduct their own research for updates as the movement for integrated partnerships between schools and communities grows across the globe.

COMMUNITY-SCHOOL PARTNERSHIPS IN NORTHERN EUROPE

Community schools are prevalent in an array of northern European countries, with the United Kingdom (especially England, Scotland, and Wales) and the Netherlands providing clear models. They also exist in Scandinavian and Nordic countries, especially Finland, which is known for its excellent educational system and has social and health services available to all community members; Finnish schools, with their links to local providers, are all full-service (Dryfoos 1994; Hargreaves, Halasz, & Pont 2007; Sahlberg 2007). This is especially important, given that Finland is becoming a more heterogeneous society where as many as 50 percent of the children in some urban schools do not speak Finnish and increasing numbers of immigrant families are struggling economically (Sahlberg 2007; Tanner 2004). Below we share details of integrated school-community partnerships in the United Kingdom and the Netherlands.

The Community School Model in the United Kingdom

England has a strong commitment to community schools, which are known there as *extended schools*. Community links with schools began in the early twentieth century in rural parts of the country, where community members used school buildings when schools were not in session (Cummings, Dyson, & Todd 2011). As in the United States, England's extended schools today are predominantly located in economically disadvantaged urban areas where achievement levels have been traditionally low and where large numbers of students have dropped out of school and have few employment options. The motive for creating extended schools is to influence young people to stay in school and thereby have better economic opportunities. In addition to fighting generational poverty, these schools hope to lower criminal activity and discourage early pregnancies among students. Students are given access to physical and behavioral health, nutrition, and vocational counseling services (Cummings, Dyson, & Todd 2011). In addition to providing services, it has been suggested that schools must work to raise aspirations of young people; the connection in England between low aspirations and poverty is one that is thought to affect not only students, but also their families and communities (Blunkett 2000; Cummings, Dyson, & Todd 2011).

In addition to urban areas, small English villages also have community-school partnerships. There, they have developed naturally, unlike in urban areas, where they are intentionally created. Only primary schools exist in the villages; English children travel outside their local communities for secondary school. Because of their location and size, small village primary schools are often connected with their communities. Similar to rural schools in the United States, English village schools often employ local residents, and this economic relationship ties schools firmly to families and communities. A recent ethnographic study of two rural schools in English villages illustrated that the nature of the communities and of the school leadership are key factors in the quality of these partnerships. Thus, although there are variables that support these "natural" connections, some degree of intentionality is helpful to strengthen and sustain them (Bagley & Hillyard 2011).

Like those of the United States and England, Scotland's extended schools have been created to remedy the negative effects of poverty (which are sometimes connected with recent immigration) on educational opportunity and achievement. With urban conditions similar in many ways to England's, Scotland is attempting to implement legally mandated school-linked services to mediate the effects of poverty (Coburn & Wallace 2011; Organisation for Economic Cooperation and Development 2007). In both England and Scotland, extended schools are part of their respective central governments' social and economic policies, and local community members play an active part in interpreting policies and implementing programs through their participation in parent councils (Carnie 2006; Cummings, Dyson, & Todd 2011; Nixon, Walker, & Baron 2002). The parent councils—or parent forums—help increase schools' relevance for young people by reinforcing in the home what is learned in the classroom (Mackenzie, 2010).

Wales also has a government-mandated policy for establishing what are referred to there as *community focused schools*, which are designed to serve children and families and to connect them with services. These schools are often open on weekends for families and community members, with courses designed to improve academic skills and assist families in their ability to help their children with homework (Egan 2012).

It is important to note that the ways in which U.K. schools implement the school-community partnership model vary, even when the partnerships are mandated by their central governments. Much of this variability is due to differences in community resources, school leadership, and the local school council's commitment to the community-school partnership model (Currie & Lockett 2007; Cummings, Dyson, & Todd 2011; Egan 2012; Mackenzie 2010). U.K. governments support universal access to free health care and social services, and because of this, schools and communities do not have to seek funding for these supports as they need to do in the United States. Nonetheless, U.K. schools still seek out additional monies from communities and donors for services that are not government subsidized, such as special recreation or sports events.

Community Schools in the Netherlands

Community schools in the Netherlands were originally established for reasons similar to those in the United Kingdom: to provide better life opportunities to children living in poverty. As in the United Kingdom, low-income neighborhoods tend to have large numbers of recent immigrant families. Providing opportunities for these children to achieve in school and feel part of the larger society and for families to feel included in the country's way of life have been motivating factors for community schools in the Netherlands (Community Schools in the Netherlands 2010). More recently, the national government of the Netherlands has ceded most school policy decisions to localities, so there is no longer a national community school policy. While some schools must continue to devote most of their resources to educating children living in disadvantaged conditions, the goal of many others has moved beyond a compensatory role to offering a high level of education that includes active participation from families and others interested in partnerships (Community Schools in the Netherlands 2010). Despite its original goals for community-school partnerships, schools in the Netherlands are increasingly shifting their focus from supporting inclusion and combating the effects of poverty toward making quality educational improvements.

Health and social services are offered to all legal residents of the Netherlands, and families are free to choose the schools they want their children to attend. Community schools are the primary choice for disadvantaged students, and it may be that those who are not disadvantaged avoid these schools in order to protect their status and avoid stigma. The term *vensterscholen*, or "window schools," refers to schools that offer health and social services linkages. In addition to health and social services, some community schools in the Netherlands offer daycare for young children or help families access daycare in designated facilities (Studulski & Kloprogge 2006).

An important component of education in the Netherlands is the track system that begins when students enter secondary school at age twelve and includes the senior general secondary, the pre-university, and the pre-vocational tracks. In the city of Rotterdam, where there are many disadvantaged students and where there are many community schools, most students are in the pre-vocational track. Students who are part of this track participate in out-of-school internships that are coordinated with their schools.

There is evidence that community schools in Rotterdam have about the same dropout rate as non-community schools serving children in the prevocational track but that the education that children receive in community schools is perceived as more holistic and takes place in a more attractive learning environment (Heers et al. 2012).

EASTERN AND CENTRAL EUROPEAN COMMUNITY SCHOOLS

ICECS has focused on community schools in eastern and central Europe, with reports on schools in Ukraine, Bosnia and Herzegovina, the Czech Republic, Croatia, Kazakhstan, and Russia. These schools are as diverse in their structure as their countries. However, they all have one thing in common: the intentional connection with their surrounding community in service provision and resource sharing.

In Ukraine, for example, schools with integrated intentional community partnerships are funded by the central government and called *community active schools*. Because of Ukrainian financial difficulties, the government has closed smaller schools and consolidated them into larger "hubs," where education and other services are available to the larger surrounding communities. This makes the school an important central service organization as well as an educational facility (Ukrainian Step by Step Foundation 2004). In 2014 the Charles Stewart Mott Foundation awarded support to Ukrainian schools through the country's Step by Step Foundation to consolidate and sustain its community school program and to raise educational standards (Charles Stewart Mott Foundation 2014). Although there are about eight hundred community schools operating in Ukraine today, political instability is a threat to the country's educational system.

War-torn and religiously divided Bosnia and Herzegovina have struggled to create an education system that supports children of all religions. Schools devote teaching time to religious education, with the specific religious material taught being dependent on the ethnic composition of the schools. The proportions of the population of Bosnia and Herzegovina, by religion, are as follows: Muslim, 45 percent; Serb Orthodox Christian, 36 percent; Roman Catholic, 15 percent; Protestant, 1 percent. There is also a small number of Jewish families. For the most part, the religious groups live in separate parts of the country, but in many places they live side by side. For years, each religious group was taught to disrespect the others, and there was no cohesion in the schools. Some schools were divided into two or more parts by religion as per the "two schools under one roof policy" (Risher & Kabel 2010). The government is now attempting to change this situation and create opportunities for inclusion, where democratic principles and respect for other groups take hold. Community schools are part of this strategy and are considered a means of disseminating these ideals among students, families, and community members (Risher & Kabel 2010; U.S. Department of State n.d.).

Croatia, which is 86 percent Roman Catholic (U.S. Department of State 2012), is similar to Bosnia and Herzegovina in that recent wars and atrocities have created a tense atmosphere throughout the country. In response, nongovernmental organizations (NGOs) have promoted reconciliation and forgiveness programs for young people, sometimes through the schools (Kosic & Tauber 2010). The work of schools in this effort is slow but showing some progress. In Northern Croatia, the Open Schools Foundation funded a program managed by the Step by Step Foundation to help integrate Roma children into a school with Croatian children. Relying on school-community partnership principles, families and community members play an active role in this effort (Bowers 2013). ICECS includes Croatia on its list of countries where the school-community partnership model is advanced as a means for addressing challenging social issues (Schools for All 2014).

In the Czech Republic, Kazakhstan, and parts of Russia, school-community partnerships are also furthering democratization and social inclusion. Initially, three community schools in the Czech Republic were supported and partly funded by the Charles Stewart Mott Foundation and the Open Society Foundation. In 2006, additional schools were funded by New School, an NGO interested in supporting the Czech government's desire to help create schools that children from many ethnic backgrounds (including Roma children) could attend. Community schools are seen as a way to make this happen, and additional funding has been found in the European Union and the Czech state budget to further this work (Greger, Levinska, & Smetcatkova 2012).

Today, community schools in the Czech Republic continue to struggle with the perceived stigma of serving Roma children, which has led to decreased enrollment and educational quality in these schools. In 2013, the Association of Organization Development Consultants, an NGO, analyzed data from forty Czech schools that self-identified as community-linked and made policy recommendations in favor of supporting and maintaining these schools. Subsequently, the Ministry of Education created a national group interested in sustaining and growing school-community partnerships (International Standards for Community Schools 2013).

Kazakhstan's community active schools, funded by the Soros Foundation, are dedicated to extending education and services beyond schools and into communities. Schools cooperate with agencies to provide lifelong learning, community and family inclusion, leadership, and community development. Children in these schools, known as schools of proactive youth, or SAYs, decide on projects to undertake in collaboration with their local community association, such as teaching community members how to do budget analyses for their local government and helping community members petition the government for better street lighting. SAY schools have classes for community members of all ages, and it is hoped that the SAY model will expand from about seven schools to all schools in Kazakhstan (International Quality Standards for Community Schools 2014).

In 2011, a conference devoted to the development of community schools and funded by the C. S. Mott Foundation helped educators in Russia consolidate their views regarding creating and sustaining community schools. Since Russian community schools are focused on social inclusion as well as needs identified by community members, there are numerous examples of community-school partnerships. Among these are fifteen schools in rural parts of Murmansk, Tomsk, and Kursk, which were funded by the U.S. Agency for International Development and serve as hubs for youth activities. Teachers and principals are leaders in community projects, such as the demolition of abandoned buildings in the Murmansk region for the subsequent development of a playground. In Kursk, a small grant funded an outdoor sports facility, built with the help of the school and local government leaders (International Research and Exchanges Board (IREX), 2011). The Krasnoyarsk Centre for Community Partnerships (KCCP), formed in 1997 by teachers and leaders of NGOs from the United States and Siberia, has been an important promoter of community schools in the Siberian region (Krasnoyarsk Center 2012).

COMMUNITY-SCHOOL PARTNERSHIPS IN AFRICA

In most African countries, community schools and public schools are created and managed as two different systems. Community schools are typically set up by NGOs, and although their establishment is permitted by each country's ministry of education, there are often tensions due to differences in curriculum and accountability. Parker's (2010) report on community schools in Africa sponsored by ICECS explains that because community schools are developed as grassroots endeavors and are accountable to the local community, they have better recruitment and retention rates but a narrower curriculum. Another source of tension, according to Parker, is that community schools developed by NGOs are not part of the state and may represent agendas and political ideologies that differ from those supported by the state. Because state governments cannot always afford to sustain public schools, in many parts of Africa, especially in urban poor areas or in more isolated rural villages, NGOs step in and in many cases create schools that are viewed very positively by their communities, though not necessarily by the larger state constituencies.

Community schools in Kenya illustrate many of the issues these schools face in African nations (Onsomu et al. 2004). Kenya has public schools managed and funded by the government, private schools managed by NGOs, informal learning centers managed by communities, and community schools also managed by communities. Funding for community schools rests with communities and NGOs. Although theoretically education is free, there are fees for public schools that the poorest families cannot afford. These children either do not go to school, attend an NGO private school if available, or pay the much lower fees charged by the community schools.

The community schools in Kenya serve mostly poor families, but even so, many cannot afford to pay the monies needed for teachers' and social workers' salaries. Because money is tight, these salaries are low compared to those in the public schools, and because of this, most community school teachers and social workers do not meet the education standards required by the government for public schools. Additionally, services are limited. Some community schools have food for children, which is funded by NGOs or by some affiliation with the government, but many do not. Buildings are often substandard, and the schools often have limited sanitary and recreational facilities. Despite these drawbacks, the community schools benefit by stable enrollments with fewer dropouts than public schools, and in Kenya, children graduating from the community primary schools can sit for the national examinations to be admitted into public secondary schools. Further, their lower cost makes community schools more accessible to children from economically disadvantaged families, providing them with a wider range of opportunity (Onsomu et al. 2004).

COMMUNITY SCHOOLS IN CANADA

Individual Canadian provinces are largely responsible for funding, managing, and sustaining their public schools, and thus there are differences and disparities across the provinces. There are 1.4 million indigenous people living in Canada, including First Nation, Metis, and Inuits, many of whom need economic assistance (Government of Canada 2013). One way Canadian provinces such as Saskatchewan, Manitoba, and British Columbia support aboriginal communities is through school-linked services for children and families, utilizing schools for community activities including meetings and recreation. These schools are sometimes referred to as *hub schools*. Although not all schools that serve indigenous populations function as hub schools, some that are hub schools also serve non-indigenous Canadians (Clandfield 2010).

Saskatchewan has been committed to community involvement in education for over thirty-five years, during which time local communities have had different priorities. Today, the Community Schools Program in Saskatchewan aims to provide education for the large numbers of First Nation and Metis families, most of whom live in areas with very limited economic resources (Thomson 2008). The province, previously largely rural, has undergone a geographic transformation over the past ten years with a population shift to urban areas, which has left rural communities increasingly isolated. This change has created a greater need for educational innovations, especially among the less populated and more impoverished areas of the province. There, most hub schools are funded by donations from local businesses, families, and education associations. Today only one hub school receives a subsidy from the Ministry of Education. Nevertheless, the hub concept is considered an important part of the province's commitment to community involvement in education (Saskatchewan Ministry of Education 2012). Any school in the province may partner with community agencies and become a community or hub school, but only schools designated by the Ministry of Education receive extra funding for staff and programs (Graves 2011; Thompson 2008).

Where ministry funds are received, the hub services offered are partly determined by the provincial government rather than solely by communities. The degree to which community members have the power to choose services varies from school to school, and mutual benefits to schools and communities are not always realized in practice. Careful planning by the hub school coordinator is focused on managing scheduling so that interactions between educators and local residents are maximized (Clandfield & Martell 2010). Recently, the Saskatchewan Ministry of Education established a nutrition program for all schools with the goal of assuring that no child is deprived of learning due to hunger. The government's stated rationale for establishing this initiative is: "Comprehensive approaches are the most effective means to address the needs of the whole child and youth (i.e. physical, mental, emotional and spiritual) to support learning and well-being" (Saskatchewan Ministry of Education 2012:4). The nutrition program is part of the province's initiative to promote its Comprehensive School Community Health Program (CSCHP), in which ministry and local resources are joined together in the schools (Graves 2011).

Community schools in Manitoba and British Columbia follow many of the same principles as those in Saskatchewan, including limited government subsidies to hubs. Community schools are part of Manitoba's official Ministry of Education policy for education for all residents, although the focus is on those living in the northern regions, which are heavily populated by aboriginal groups (Manitoba Education, Citizenship, and Youth 2006). The Community Schools Partnership of Manitoba Initiative, launched in 2005, continues under the jurisdiction of the Manitoba Education, Citizenship, and Youth government office and "seeks to encourage families, organizations and schools to work together to improve students' success and strengthen communities. Thompson, Flin Flon, South Indian Lake, Lynn Lake, The Pas, and Grand Rapids are all participating in this initiative" (Government of Manitoba 2014). In addition to school-community partnerships, the province has initiated a program in which "Lighthouses" function as community recreation places for youth during out-of-school times. Community facilities are funded by the Department of Justice and serve as a means of integrating community services for school-age youth (Government of Manitoba 2014; Manitoba Education, Citizenship, and Youth, 2006).

In British Columbia, community schools are called *neighbourhood learning centers*. Schools and communities are encouraged to investigate how they can utilize their resources and gain new ways of funding to establish these centers (Province of British Columbia 2010). Learning centers are described as "an inviting place where everyone can access education, community services, recreation and culture" (Province of British Columbia 2010). Thus, for example, administrators at the Harwin Elementary School in Prince George have reached out to welcome urban aboriginal parents. They have met with parents outside of the schools and created a special gathering room in the school where they can access resources and services (Province of British Columbia 2010). At the Hesquiaht First Nation Place of Learning on Vancouver Island, a community school serving First Nation children and families, participation in cultural activities such as potlatch is encouraged, while the native language, Nlakapamux (also spelled Nlha.kAPmhh), is also taught along with traditional Canadian academic subjects. And then there is the 'Na aksa Gila Kyew Learning Centre for the Kitsumkalum First Nation, an adult education center started by the community school principal as a way to keep the community engaged (Government of Canada 2010).

Additional examples of community integration and development are in Newfoundland and Labrador, where programs functioning since the early 1990s began with the specific aim of developing of human capital. Encouraging students to learn a marketable skill, to engage in local entrepreneurial projects, and to remain in the provinces, schools employ staff to establish relationships with students, mentor them in community assets and opportunities, and provide afterschool programs for students and their families. This program, sponsored by the Community Education Network, complements the typical integration of social and health services found in hub schools (Barter 2007).

SCHOOL-COMMUNITY PARTNERSHIPS IN NEW ZEALAND

New Zealand has seen an increasingly diverse school population. Maori tribes, Pacific Islanders, and immigrants from a variety of countries bring cultural and language challenges to both the schools and the communities (Mutch & Collins 2012; New Zealand Demographics 2013). To integrate such diverse populations into the public education system, the concept of *whānau*, which involves a wider community-based network of caretakers being responsible for a child's well-being, has been especially useful. Even though *whānau* is a Maori concept, other cultural groups in the country have adopted it, as have many New Zealand schools. These schools, which are funded primarily by the Ministry of Education, but also receive financial and in-kind contributions from community members, focus on collaborations that invite parents, *whānau*, and community members into the schools (Mutch & Collins 2012). A variety of activities are planned by these collaborations and center on respecting diversity and encouraging inclusion. Examples include: evening programs for parents and *whānau*, community picnics, and cultural sharing events.

In addition to cultural engagement of diverse population groups in parts of New Zealand, some schools have developed community linkages with services, such as referrals to medical clinics (Mutch & Collins 2012). The ministry's recent decision to support the creation of what it calls *partnership schools*, or schools funded by both the government and businesses based on the charter for-profit school model, is an attempt to stem the tide of high dropout rates among Maori and Pacific Islanders. This may impact the future of the community school model that serves many children in these population groups (Education Review Office 2014; New Zealand Ministry of Education 2014).

SCHOOL SERVICES IN INDIA

It is estimated that almost 50 percent of children in India do not receive adequate nutrition (Baru 2008). To address this, all children in designated Indian public schools receive midday meals. Eating together as a group, they gain not only nutrition but also opportunities for socialization with children of different races, classes, and castes (Dreze & Goyal 2008). This meal is meant to constitute one-third of the calories children need for the day; however, it can be even more critical since many families are too poor to provide more than one meal (Baru 2008). In many cases there is sufficient food left over from the midday meal in school for children to take home to their families for the evening meal or as a supplement to it. In this way, the schools function as an important resource for community families not only by providing food, but also by saving time for food preparation, leaving families with more time for other tasks including longer work hours.

Importantly, the program has encouraged girls to attend schools. In many poor Indian families, girls have tended to be kept at home to help with household work, take part-time jobs, and contribute to the family's economic situation. But with the food supply coming in from each child in school, families have started to send more girls to school, so that they will be fed and have leftover food to bring home for the family (Dreze & Goyal 2008).

The midday meal program is managed either by India's federal government or by the provincial government, with little input from local communities. However, because community residents staff the schools, there is local influence on how the program is implemented (Ramachandran, Jandhyala, & Saihjee 2008). Moreover, community participation in the preparation of the midday meal program is essential to its functioning (Dreze & Goyal 2008).

In addition to the midday meal program, India passed the 2009 Right of Children to Free and Compulsory Education Act (RTE), setting up school management committees made up of family members, school professionals, and children to oversee the inclusion of all children in the schools. "For the first time in India's history, children will be guaranteed their right to quality elementary education by the state with the help of families and communities" (Right to Education Fact Sheet 2014). Another goal is to provide all schoolchildren with biannual screenings for growth, disease, and eye, ear, and dental health, as well as referrals for those needing treatment. Teams of doctors, specialists, and public health nurses are expected to carry out the screenings. However, many states in India are very poor, and school health screenings are not always a priority. These states ask for help from the central School Health Services Department, but resources are scarce and not always forthcoming. Consequently, screenings are often lax and require additional funding (Baru 2008).

SCHOOL SERVICES IN CUBA

School is free in Cuba, as are the uniforms that all children must wear (Legon 2012). Cuba is a country where health and social services are also free, and a system of neighborhood doctors and polyclinics provides health and mental health services to all children in their local communities (Feinsilver 2010). In addition, Cuba has a strong corps of teachers. According to the official government publication, the ratio of teachers to the population is one to every forty-two people, with over 400,000 teachers in the country (Legon 2012). In Havana, education, health, and social services are primarily delivered within neighborhoods where the school is the central point of contact for families with children.

Although there is a commitment to education and services, there are scarcities in food supplies, which Cuba continues to ration. Typically, people make up for the ration's limited supply of fresh produce through small gardens and farms. In Havana, for example, families share land for food production on urban farms. While there is agreement that the country needs to import food, there is not agreement about the amount of food that needs to be imported. Some say it is more than 80 percent, while others report 16 percent (Altieri & Funes-Monzote 2012). In response to food shortages, schools function as an important source of nutrition for Cuba's children by providing lunches. In a country where there is universal free education and children are required to attend school from ages six to at least fifteen, this is a major contribution to the country's nutritional needs. Children receive at least one meal a day out of the home, relieving the pressure on the family's monthly ration allotment (Classbase 2012). In addition, many schools have their own gardens, where children participate in food producing activities at school.

Cuba has an unusual way of supporting children with special needs in the community. Instead of special education classes at schools, teachers travel to homes and hospitals where children with cognitive and physical disabilities are educated. Another atypical practice relative to other countries is that Cuban children are required to provide services to their respective communities. While civic engagement is a common school-linked service in many countries, it is most often not a national requirement. In Cuba, however, students are expected to participate in community service projects during their school vacations (Classbase 2012). Civic engagement projects address a range of community issues, such as improving community health by ridding communities of mosquitoes and promoting health awareness campaigns. It is unclear at this time how changes in U.S.-Cuban relations will affect everyday life on the island. If, for example, food becomes more available, the role of the schools in feeding the country's children may become less important. It is also unclear whether new diplomatic relations with the

United States will in any way impact Cuba's practice of supporting children with special needs outside of schools or its requirement for civic engagement.

* * *

In this brief overview of school-community partnership configurations in select countries, it becomes clear that there is no singular model that prevails and that changes in policies over time impact the structures of these systems. As in the United States, most schools with strong community partnerships evolve in response to disadvantage, whether it be a lack of health and social services, food, etc. In all of these countries, schools typically serve as a place to bring opportunities and services to people who have little of both.

In some countries, like India and Cuba, universal services and programs support all children through the schools, especially by providing a meal for all students. Other countries, such as the United Kingdom and the Netherlands, have developed highly organized systems of services to address educational opportunity for disadvantaged groups, while in still others, the concern has been to bring minority children into the mainstream. The motivations are many, and the service models vary depending on the resources and culture of each location, but the centrality of the school as a place to improve lives of children, families, and communities is a common theme.

If any lesson is to be learned from the way each of these countries has adopted the school-community partnership model, it is that children are a vital resource and their well-being is crucial to future national development. Ideally, schools and the services they provide are a good fit with the various political and economic environments in which they exist. In the developed countries, the partnerships focus on children and families living in disadvantaged neighborhoods and on creating opportunities for workforce and civic participation, with the goal of reducing the official poverty numbers. In most countries we have discussed, with the exception of Cuba because of its history of extreme isolation, integrating minority children into the larger society can also be viewed as a strategy for encouraging national development. Schools bringing about opportunities for minority children help reinforce national stability and future economic growth, the latter being obtained largely by utilizing talent that otherwise would be unrecognized.

In countries suffering from recent ethnic warfare and in many cases atrocities, a national mission of encouraging peace and tolerance is supported in the schools. Bosnia and Herzegovina and Croatia are examples of countries that rely on schools to help bring about social stability, without which there is little hope for economic development. In other countries community civic participation is an important goal for maintenance of a stable population for future economic development. Parts of Africa, Russia, and Canada also depend on school-community partnerships to encourage educated children to remain in their communities.

These are just a few examples of schools that have community linkages and goals and outcomes that go beyond academic education for children. We included Cuba as an outlier, which has had a tight grip on its people with its restrictive travel and communication laws and yet has used its schools to engage children in projects that enhance public health and improve nutrition and thereby encourage patriotism.

In all countries that we have described, community-school partnerships are funded primarily by governments, although in some cases funds also come from government-sanctioned outside organizations. Therefore, it is safe to assume that the schools largely reflect current national policies. If and when policies change there are likely to be concurrent changes in the missions of partnership schools. The degree of such changes is as difficult to predict as the national policies.

In the next chapters we return to the United States and survey the policies, funding, and outcome measures used to support and assess school-linked services efforts.

7

Public Education, School-Linked Services, and Relevant Policies

PUBLIC SCHOOLS WITH STRONG COMMUNITY LINKAGES in the United States are governed by the general policies for U.S. public education, including the budgeting constraints that impact all public schools. In this context, there is a spectrum of funded education and adjunctive service programs that can be selectively and purposefully linked with schools including health, mental health, before- and afterschool programs, early childhood education, social services, etc. In this chapter the major policies that impact school-linked services and partnerships are reviewed. Because schools with strong community partnerships often aim at leveling the playing field for low-income students, policies that specifically address these students, their families, schools, and communities are a focus of this chapter. It is important to note that educational policies and programs can change frequently and rapidly based on economic and political conditions. What appears to remain is the dedication of those committed to community-school alliances.

For the most part, public education policies in the United States are the purview of the states. The federal government gets involved to ensure that civil rights, equal opportunity, and other laws are upheld. States may choose to ignore the bulk of federal policy initiatives, but in doing so, they risk losing large amounts of federal funding tied to these policies. Although most education funding comes from state and local resources, federal monies have increasingly become an important component of public school funding formulas. In some urban school systems, federal funding can contribute to between 30 and 40 percent of total school costs, which is considerably more than the typical contribution of less than 10 percent that most suburban districts receive (Federal Education Policy 2009). It is in this context that the federal, state, local, and district policies are reviewed, beginning with the ones emanating from Washington.

Sorting through the federal policies that support community-school partnerships and integrated programs is a complex task, given the numerous services that many of these schools offer. To facilitate a better understanding of the federal government's influence on communities and all pre-K–12 schools, it is helpful to review the major federal programs that support equity for children in schools and affect public (and some private) schools.

COMPENSATORY PROGRAMS

Compensatory programs in education became an important part of the mid-1960s War on Poverty, initiated by President Lyndon Johnson. The rationale for federal expenditures on these programs was to prepare children who were not succeeding in school with the knowledge and skills needed for graduation and employment. In 1965, Congress passed the Elementary and Secondary Education Act (ESEA), in which Title I provided compensatory funding for a variety of programs targeted at schools in economically disadvantaged neighborhoods based on their records of failures and dropouts. Congress authorized the Head Start Program during this same year with the goal of providing equal educational opportunity for all public school children (Vinovskis 2005). Both programs involved support for instruction, with the expectation that educational outcomes would be improved (Federal Education Policy 2009). In fact, educational outcomes did improve for many program recipients. According to the National Center for Education Statistics, achievement scores for African Americans in the 1970s and early 1980s showed improvement in both reading and math—gains attributed to increased resources given to poor urban school districts. In later years, as funding was reduced, many of these gains were unfortunately lost (Darling-Hammond 2010).

Additional compensatory programs have been created since the 1960s, reflecting both the economic need for an educated workforce and the belief that all children should have the opportunity to receive an adequate education. These programs include: bilingual classes for children whose first language is not English, special education and classes for handicapped students, youth employment programs, and monies for supporting mental health and health programs in schools. In this way, the original focus of compensatory services was extended over time to include educational equality for all children, including children with special needs. The Education for All Handicapped Children Act of 1975 provided "improved and equalized learning opportunities" for all children with disabilities. All schools receiving federal funding were obligated to educate all children ages six to seventeen regardless of ability. The act called for the establishment of individualized education plans for these children (IEPs) to be reviewed at least annually (Cengage Learning 2014).

Changes in funding policies in the early 1980s included the use of block grants, giving local governments the authority to distribute federal resources. This policy change yielded mixed results; in some cases localities consolidated programs or eliminated them in order to use the monies for other purposes. Bureaucratic rules, competing agendas for spending school-related funds, and a host of other types of squabbles over money sometimes sidelined resources intended for children. Large urban school systems such as those of Oakland and Chicago have been cited as examples where this occurred (Noguera 2003; Payne 2008), but they are not the only districts where this happened. In places where communities became involved in overseeing school policies, including compensatory programs, achievement scores increased—especially when families were engaged and specialized skills such as reading or math were targeted (Epstein 2011).

Despite gains in achievement for some minority sectors of the population, the Republicans who came to power in the 1980s were determined to decrease federal monies and even eliminate compensatory programs. Democrats held their ground, and even though funding was drastically reduced, most programs remained intact (Vinovskis 2005). *A Nation at Risk*, a 1983 report by an education commission initiated by President Reagan, showed the urgency of educational reform and called for a focus on student achievement rather than on supportive and supplementary programs that responded to children's needs. It advocated for high educational standards and for both the federal government and the states to set goals for raising standards and to hold educators and policymakers accountable if goals were not reached (Vinovskis 2005). It did not, however, specify how these higher standards were to be achieved. This report is often thought of as the beginning of prioritization of achievement outcomes over principles of equity in federal policymaking.

OUTCOME-BASED POLICIES

As federal programs and spending increased with the ESEA, the idea of using tests to monitor program effectiveness gained ground. The passage of the Hawkins-Stafford Amendment in 1988 required state achievement tests as a condition for states to receive federal funding. States could choose their own method of testing and the content of the tests, and no state was denied funding for any length of time. By the early 1990s, the Clinton administration was firmly in favor of testing learning outcomes, and federal policy tipped in favor of an achievement and outcomes focus over compensatory funding. Compensatory funding was not discontinued—program support continued through block grants to states—but the emphasis shifted to testing and results. The Improving America's Schools Act of 1994, a reauthorization of the ESEA under a new name, required states to use the same standardized tests for all students. Previously, states could use a separate set of tests for students in schools in economically distressed areas. Now, however, state statistics on educational outcomes had to include all students regardless of where they attended school, although states could still develop their own tests. The 1994 ESEA included support for teacher development, the delivery of software for standards-based instruction, and the Safe and Drug-Free Schools and Communities Acts. These additional programs were meant to assist school districts to meet the testing standards they set for all students (Federal Education Policy 2009).

The focus on standardized testing as part of education policy begun in the Clinton administration was taken on with greater zeal (but with fewer supports for its achievement) by the Bush administration that followed. The No Child Left Behind program (NCLB), the reauthorization of the ESEA in 2002, was created to underscore federal government policies that focused on school achievement. The act had three components:

1 By the year 2014, all students must be performing at the "proficient" level in reading, mathematics, and science;
2 In each school each year, students' "adequate yearly progress" (AYP) must increase at such a rate that 100 percent proficiency would be met by 2014; and

3 The annual rate of progress applies not only to the aggregate student enrollment of a school, district, or state but also to "disaggregated" groups of students according to income, race, gender, English-language ability, and special education status.

If any of the listed groups performed below expected progress rates, the entire school would be considered "failing" and in need of improvement, and sanctions would be applied (U.S. Department of Education 2002).

Sanctions were delineated for districts that received Title I monies but did not meet the state-defined adequacy standards. The process was as follows:

1 A Title I school that has not achieved AYP for two consecutive school years will be identified by the district (before the beginning of the following school year) as needing improvement. School officials will develop a two-year plan to turn around the school. The local education agency will ensure that the school receives needed technical assistance as it develops and implements its improvement plan. Students have the option of transferring to another public school in the district, which may include a public charter school that has not been identified as needing improvement.
2 If the school does not make AYP for a third consecutive year, it remains in school-improvement status, and the district must continue to offer public school choice to all students. In addition, students from low-income families are eligible to receive Title I–funded supplemental services, such as tutoring or remedial classes, from a state-approved public or private provider.
3 If the school fails to make adequate progress for a fourth year, the district must implement certain corrective actions to improve the school, such as replacing certain staff or implementing a new curriculum, while continuing to offer public school choice and supplemental educational services for low-income students.
4 If the school fails for a fifth year, the district must initiate plans for restructuring the school. This may include reopening the school as a charter school, replacing all or most of the school staff, or turning over school operations either to the state or to a private company with a demonstrated record of effectiveness (No Child Left Behind 2002).

In addition, No Child Left Behind required states to calculate AYP for whole districts and not for individual schools. An unspecified corrective action plan was prescribed for those districts that did not make AYP for two consecutive years. In other words, while districts were expected to correct the lack of adequate yearly progress, there was no federal plan in place specifying how to make this happen. States were still setting the yearly progress standards and constructing the tests. Furthermore, when a school or a district failed to meet standards and students could ask for a transfer, many districts allowed only within-district transfers, meaning students could move from one failing school to another.

The ESEA Flexibility Waiver Program

Under the Obama administration, the Department of Education authorized a School Improvement Waiver Program for the ESEA, No Child Left Behind regulations, which allowed states that did not attain 100 percent school proficiency to continue to receive federal funding for their Title I schools. Because of congressional opposition, the Obama administration had not been successful in rewriting the Bush administration version of the ESEA, which expired in 2007, and the ESEA waivers filled in for this inability to create a revised policy. The ESEA is still referred to as No Child Left Behind by policymakers, as many of its provisions remain in effect until the 2017–18 school year when the newest version of the ESEA, known as The Every Student Succeeds Act, (ESSA) takes its place (Every Student Succeeds Act 2015b).

Under the Waiver Program, announced in 2009, states could apply for ESEA waivers based on a set of four school improvement models and a separate list of turnaround principles. These models and principles created alternative plans for school improvement that were considered easier for school districts to comply with and retain ESEA funding. States were required to submit waiver plans directly to the Federal Department of Education and all states including the District of Columbia either applied or stated its intention to apply (Center for Education Policy 2014). As long as any of the four models were followed the turnaround principles were considered to be included in the state plans and waivers could be applied for (Turnaround principles 2014).

A brief summary of the 4 models:

1. A turnaround model, which replaces the principal and half the teachers and offers a new instructional program;
2. A restart model, which closes failing schools and replaces them with charter schools or an educational management system different from the previous system;
3. School closures, which shut down failing schools and sends students to high-achieving schools; and
4. A transformational model that addresses the following areas:

    a. increasing teacher effectiveness and replacing the principal;
    b. utilizing new teaching strategies;
    c. extending learning and teacher planning time;
    d. creating community-oriented schools; and
    e. providing operating flexibility and sustained support. (Pappano 2010).

The turnaround principles included meaningful interventions designed to improve the academic achievement of students in Title I priority schools along with provisions for school safety and family and community input:

1. Provide strong leadership by:

    a. reviewing the performance of the current principal;
    b. either replacing the principal if such a change is necessary to ensure strong and effective leadership, or demonstrating that the current principal has a track record in improving achievement and has the ability to lead the turnaround effort; and
    c. providing the principal with operational flexibility in the areas of scheduling, staff, curriculum, and budget.

2. Ensure that teachers are effective and able to improve instruction by:

    a. reviewing the quality of all staff and retaining only those who are determined to be effective and have the ability to be successful in the turnaround effort;
    b. preventing ineffective teachers from transferring to these schools; and
    c. providing job-embedded, ongoing professional development informed by the teacher evaluation and support systems and tied to teacher and student needs.

3 Redesign the school day, week, or year to include additional time for student learning and teacher collaboration;
4 Strengthen the school's instructional program based on student needs and ensure that the instructional program is research-based, rigorous, and aligned with state academic content standards;
5 Use data to inform instruction and for continuous improvement, and include time for collaboration on the use of data;
6 Establish a school environment that improves school safety and discipline and addresses other nonacademic factors that impact student achievement, such as students' social, emotional, and health needs; and
7 Provide ongoing mechanisms for family and community engagement (U.S. Department of Education 2012a:7–8).

The Every Student Succeeds Act (ESSA) and Full-Service Community Schools

In December 2015, President Obama signed into law what the New York Times (Carey 2015) referred to as the "biggest piece of federal education legislation in over a decade." Designed to replace No Child Left Behind (NCLB) and scheduled for implementation in the 2017–18 school year, the bill contains a huge win for school-linked services as part of Title IV of the legislation under the program, "Community Supports for Success" that includes funding for full-service community schools. The law lists numerous "pipeline services" that can be supported and which extend from early years to post-secondary and career attainment. They include high quality early childhood education, support for educational transitions, family and community engagement, health, nutrition and mental health services and supports. Spearheaded by Representative Hoyer in the House and Senators Brown and Manchin in the Senate, this bill presents a tremendous opportunity for community schools to expand, and therefore go further in leveling the playing field for American children from all economic backgrounds. The bill has been praised by an array of individual and organizational supporters of community schools including the Coalition for Community Schools, American Federation of Teachers, School Superintendents Association and United Way Worldwide, among many others (Coalition for Community Schools 2015).

In addition to Title IV, other reforms around struggling schools and testing that are relevant for addressing issues of equity are included in the ESSA legislation, outlined below.

ESSA and Other Reforms

With ESSA schools that are the lowest 5 percent of performers, where subgroups are struggling or where graduation rates are 67 percent or less, districts will structure an evidence-based plan for turning schools around and states will be responsible for monitoring the intervention's effects. If after 4 years the schools do not improve, the states will be required to take the schools over and provide a plan of its own. The plan could include a number of options including taking over the school, firing the principal or turning the school into a charter school. Students in low performing schools will be given the choice of moving into different schools in the same district. In schools with struggling students, there will need to be evidence-based plans for their academic improvement. Districts will be responsible to monitor these schools and could step in if improvement does not occur. A comprehensive improvement plan will be required for schools that continually have struggling subgroups of students. The School Improvement Grant Program will become an integral part of Title I increasing the monies delivered to the states for improving achievement for students living in poverty. States could set aside up to 7 percent of it's Title I ESSA funds for school improvement (Every Student Succeeds Act 2015).

Every Student Succeeds Act expressly states that states will continue to test students in reading and math in grades 3 through 8 and again one time in high school and report the data for whole schools and for subgroups including racial minorities, students living in poverty and those in special education. States would make up their own tests or opt to use standardized tests. At the high school level schools could use SAT's or ACT's with their state's permission.

Education standards have to be challenging and could include the Common Core Standards but need not. The Department of Education cannot force or even encourage states to adopt any specified set of standards including the Common Core (Every Student Succeeds Act 2015).

There are a host of additional changes in the new law related to funding and notably, teacher supports and evaluations. One big change is that teachers will not have to be evaluated using student achievement outcomes, as required by the No Child Left Behind and the Waivers, a very unpopular policy with many states and teachers' unions.

FEDERAL EDUCATION POLICY AND INEQUALITY

The main goal of federal education policy in the United States is to provide supplemental support for public education in neighborhoods where both financial and social capital resources are scarce. Federal education policy has always been concerned with creating skilled workers, reducing dependency on government supports, and encouraging economic growth. Indirectly, these policies have benefitted countless individuals and families by increasing opportunities for economic and social independence through education. Still there is a long way to go. States had been slow in providing plans for setting "college and career-ready expectations for all students under the ESEA Flexibility Waiver Programs (U.S. Department of Education 2012a). How the Every Student Succeeds Act will affect readiness for higher education remains to be seen. Without the benefits of education beyond the high school level, students are blocked from high-tech jobs that typically pay well and that the nation requires for its economic growth. This results in the nation having to offer this work to people who move from other countries to fill the demand for these jobs here, while many of our own high school graduates are steered into lower paying jobs or blocked out of employment completely. In 2008, 16 percent of the workforce holding a bachelors degree were immigrants, representing a 29 percent growth in the number of immigrants holding jobs in the United States between 1995 and 2008 (Kerr, Kerr, & Lincoln 2013). According to Kerr, Kerr, and Lincoln, "In occupations closely linked to innovation and technology commercialization, the share of immigrants is even higher at almost 24 percent" (2013:1). While the authors claim that by hiring these workers, employers are actually increasing employment opportunities (they state that Bill Gates has testified to Congress that for every visa worker hired, Microsoft hires four workers to support that employee), U.S. workers are not often hired at high levels or salaries. Proponents of school-linked services in communities in need argue that with adequate supports, more U.S. children can grow into adults with higher-level positions and salaries.

It seems clear that regardless of good intentions, federal policies cannot accomplish reducing inequalities with the current level of commitment and with the directions that policies have taken in the last several decades. Increased accountability among the states is clearly needed, but the means to assess accountability needs improvement. With states and localities supplying most educational funding through local property taxes, state aid, and state funds received from federal block grants, states and localities become largely responsible for reducing inequality. To its credit, the Obama administration stepped up accountability requirements that were reduced during the Reagan administration (Darling-Hammond 2010; U.S. Department of Education 2012a). Now, even with the allowance for the new ESSA law's flexibility, states will still have to supply data showing real accomplishments for students in specific categories, and not in aggregated formats.

Federal Policy Accomplishments

The biggest challenge that the American public education system continues to face is supporting academic success for children and families in poverty (Fuhrman et al. 2011; Steen & Noguera, 2010). The census statistics for 2012 show that 21.9 percent of children less than eighteen years of age are living in poverty in the United States—the equivalent of 16.1 million children (DeNavas-Walt, Proctor, & Smith 2013).

Title I funds were used by 56,000 public schools in 2009–10 (U.S. Department of Education 2015b), and 21 million children benefited from this program, of whom 59 percent were in grades K–5; 21 percent in grades 6–8; and 17 percent in grades 9–12. Only 3 percent of Title I funds supported preschool children. Children benefitting from Title I funding are likely to be living in families or circumstances that are considered below or near the U.S. poverty designation. These children are often attending underperforming schools. Title I funding alone is not sufficient to help children in poverty succeed in school at the level of their middle-class counterparts, but it is an important and effective program, moving us forward at least part of the way. Federal monies along with state and local resources must also be allocated for programs addressing the implications of poverty that impact academics such as access to adequate nutrition, health and mental health services, transportation, extended school hours, etc.

Federal Policy Challenges

Under the new ESSA Program beginning in 2017, the United States will have a stronger federal policy in support of community schools and other mechanisms for providing school-linked services. Under No Child Left Behind and the subsequent Waiver programs, the Department of Education funded Full Service Community School Grants, Promise Neighborhoods, and the 21st Century Community Learning Centers as ways to make up for not having these types of programs included in No Child Left Behind. The new version of the ESSA now has these programs included with additional funding as part of Title IV of the ESSA to be combined as Community Support for School Success (Every Student Succeeds Act 2015). This inclusion shores up their status making them, at least for now, appear more permanent and less subjected to political whims.

It has been suggested that the federal government makes best use of its funding for educational programs when it encourages new and innovative programs (Pappano 2010). School districts are often strapped for funds, and local educators often feel the need to spend on what they consider essential with few resources for new programs. Here is where the federal government makes its mark: through providing funding and grants that support services for children essential to their success in school. For all federally based grants, states and school districts need to take the initiative to apply, must be prepared to comply with federal regulations for eligibility, and must be equipped with personnel who are competent in writing grants. Grant writers may not be a viable choice for many smaller districts, especially those that most need the money. Additionally, in most cases, federal funding does not pay all the costs for suggested programs, and districts (and often community partners) are required to add their own monies and resources to federal grant programs (Pappano 2010).

A supportive federal policy for school-linked services is necessary, but not sufficient. For example, in Scotland, despite a national policy for integrated children's services, evidence shows that the policy does not always translate to the changes in teachers' practices that are necessary to support the utilization of an integrated services approach (Organisation for Economic Cooperation and Development 2007). While stronger federal policies are needed, also critical is a comprehensive approach that bridges policy at all levels of schools, districts, states, etc. and provides adequate supports for the translation of policy to practice.

School-Community Partnerships and Federal Policies

Public schools with strong community partnerships can accept Title I money, by virtue of their location in high-poverty neighborhoods. Because of their location, school-linked services in these schools typically support children who have not done well in school for a variety of reasons, such as social disorganization found in many poverty environments; poor access to health-related services; including adequate nutrition, medical and dental care, and mental health services; and, in many cases, speaking English as a second language.

Partnerships between schools and communities have a unique place within the bounds of federal school policy. In some ways, they are said to reflect the conclusions and intentions of ESEA and Title I policymakers. For example, parental involvement requirements were written into early versions of the ESEA, which directed that community advisory committees be established; however, due to a lack of fit between policy and practice, these committees had only a vague purpose and were often ignored by school personnel. As each new version of the ESEA was written, the inclusion of parental involvement in the schools became more central as a funding requirement. The No Child Left Behind version of the ESEA called for districts and schools to develop programs to encourage effective parental involvement (Epstein, 2011). The Every Student Succeeds Version includes family involvement as a priority. The vision of bringing parents into the schools to improve academic outcomes has thus become an important part of federal school policy. The establishment of schools integrated with community services and partnerships is a step toward more effective and intensive parental involvement in decisions affecting children's education.

Compensatory program monies described above have been available for out-of-school programs, including recreation, student development, arts and music enrichment, and drug and violence prevention. Since most schools with community linkages are eligible for these funds, Title I became an important source of federal support for them. Other federal programs were also useful and are utilized in a variety of ways. The Obama administration's Race to the Top program coming out of the American Recovery and Reinvestment Act of 2009, called for place-based competitive grants; school improvement grants (SIGs) are awarded to states' educational agencies, which then make sub-competitive grants to local educational agencies (LEAs) for districts demonstrating innovative programs to raise student achievement levels. Schools eligible for Title I monies that are implementing partnerships with their communities may apply. Funds from SIGs may be used to support community school coordinators, and 21st Century Learning Center Funds can be used to support expanded school time. There are other federal programs that schools may utilize in support of school-linked services and integrated initiatives. These programs that are now part of the new ESSA continue to support adjunctive services linked to schools.

It is important to note that the new ESSA calls for districts to conduct needs assessment for using monies for school supportive services, professional development funds to aid in teacher engagement of families and community resources, and the use of plans that account for school inequities in resources. Districts are also to examine and plan for emphasizing experimental and personal learning opportunities (Every Student Succeeds Act 2015).

STATE AND LOCAL POLICIES

The amount of federal government funding for schools varies greatly depending on the programs for which schools apply. As already noted, urban schools in disadvantaged neighborhoods that apply for federal programs can receive 30 to 40 percent of their budgets from these sources. On average, however, the federal government contributes only 8 to 13 percent of most school funding. Furthermore, federal programs are limited to those deemed to be creating equal opportunity or supporting civil rights. This leaves states and localities with a great deal of latitude when establishing education policy. Local policies support the majority of school funding that comes from property taxes and state block grants. Private donations are allowed, also based on state and local policies. There is no federal policy that prohibits private donors from contributing money to public schools, and local districts can initiate policies that allow individual schools to receive private funding. In California, school districts have begun to pool donations and redistribute them to their schools according to local policies. This is a way to provide less affluent communities with extra money for day-to-day expenses. The Santa Monica–Malibu, Manhattan Beach, and Palo Alto school districts have implemented policy to support redistribution (Yang Su 2012).

It is important to note that because of the complexities of and frequent changes in state and local policies *and* leadership, the actual supports for school-linked services can be erratic, especially when state budgets are tight. Personnel changes in the local district offices also affect commitment to integrated school-community partnerships. While there are many stable programs, some are influx due to local structural modifications. Without a strong state commitment, districts are often left to meet partnership-building challenges on their own, which can be difficult, especially in times of economic downturns or demographic changes.

State Policies That Support Community Schools and School-Linked Services

Several states stand out for policies that have increased the use of community involvement and services to support student learning. These states include California, Illinois, and New Mexico. More recently, Governor Andrew Cuomo of New York made support for community schools a prominent part of that state's education policy and allocated grants for new community schools. In addition, individual districts such as Chicago, Illinois, Cincinnati, Ohio, Oakland, California, Tulsa, Oklahoma, and Hartford, Connecticut, have strong systems of community schools, while the increase of such schools has become central to New York City's educational agenda.

California, Illinois, and New Mexico offer current examples of how state policies can make a difference in supporting partnerships between schools and communities. They also illustrate the importance of funding to support these policies.

California

California has a history of supporting school-linked services through its Healthy Start and School Restructuring initiatives. Since the late 1980s, California's State Department of Education has focused its mission of parent-school collaboration on offering support to districts to achieve this goal. Its official policy states: "Provide parents with skills to access community and support services that strengthen school programs, family practices, and student learning and development" (Epstein 2011:314). School budgets typically determine the extent to which that policy takes hold, and in California, recent inadequate education spending on the part of the state has led to large statewide educational inequities in school funding and student achievement. Darling-Hammond refers to the "incoherent funding and management" (2010:159) of California's system, where teacher training has been all but eliminated from the state's public universities, funding has been uneven and overly restrictive, and educational vision and commitment have been lacking. There has, however, been some indication that this state of educational affairs is improving and that the state's expectation for parent and community involvement will have increased meaning in the near future. Recent awards and policies supporting school-linked services in California include a federal school improvement grant in 2014 and the California Department of Education's emphasis on out-of-school programs for all schools linked with community services (California Department of Education 2014).

Illinois

Illinois has included community schools in its school code, and in so doing, legitimized community schools as a strategic model for inclusion in state funding and in efforts to seek funds beyond the state. With the influence of the state's active Federation of Community Schools membership, Public Act 96-0746 was passed in 2009, making Illinois the first state to codify school-community partnerships (Coalition for Community Schools, State Policy 2014). Both Chicago public schools and private donors funded 154 schools in 2010 as part of the Community Schools Initiative. In most schools today, services include tutoring, enrichment activities for children, programs for adults, and medical and dental services (Community Schools Initiative 2015).

New Mexico

In 2013, the state of New Mexico passed a Community School Act, which made full-service community schools a model for school turnaround and allowed the state to create full-service community schools. Elev8 (discussed in chapter 3) supported the legislative measure, and a small group of schools is gradually implementing the concept of full-service schools. While politics and budget cuts have taken their toll, the act has become part of state policy, and there are expectations that more full-service schools will be supported in the near future (Elev8 2013).

District Policies That Support Community Schools and School-Linked Services

Buffalo, New York, New York City, Middletown, Connecticut, and St. Paul, Minnesota, are examples of communities with policies that support school-family-community partnerships (Epstein 2011). Tulsa, Oklahoma, Oakland, California, Cincinnati, Ohio, Chicago, Illinois, Hartford, Connecticut, and other districts are committed to community schools and have led the way in developing and implementing policies supporting district-wide initiatives (see chapter 3 for discussion details of Tulsa and Hartford community schools).

In 2014, New York City received a $52 million grant from New York State to create forty community schools to be managed in partnership with the United Way of New York City. Partners in this initiative include professionals from foundations, businesses, schools and universities, the research community, health care, and nonprofit providers. At a press conference to announce the creation of the advisory board, Mayor de Blasio stated, "This is a critical pillar of our strategy to lift up students and schools across this city. Combined with pre-K for all and expanded after-school programs, Community Schools are going to be a vital tool of reaching thousands of children at risk of falling behind" (New York City, Office of the Mayor 2014a). New York City schools chancellor Carmen Farina echoes the mayor's commitment: "Community Schools serve a vital need for our students and families by providing academic enrichment in partnership with mental health and social services. This monumental expansion will partner schools with community-based organizations that bring a wealth of services to lift up students and parents and create a foundation for academic success, while supporting neighborhoods with high needs" (New York City, Office of the Mayor 2014a).

The city is slated to add more schools to the community schools initiative, with $150 million spread over two years designated for its most underachieving schools. The newly announced School Renewal Program will bring services to children and their families and assist in ensuring their increased mental and physical well-being, according to the Mayor's Office. In presenting the initiative, Mayor de Blasio was emphatic about using the term "community schools" and shoring up the city's commitment in support of this effort (New York City, Office of the Mayor 2014b). Of course, linking services to schools is not new in New York. The Children's Aid Society, the Beacons, and several initiatives taken on by the city's not-for-profit hospitals such as Columbia Presbyterian and Montefiore have offered programs to the city's public schools for a number of years. But the initiative made by the de Blasio administration does represent an official endorsement of large-scale comprehensive community school efforts.

Clearly, policy support for community-school linkages and integrated programs can come from federal, state, and local levels. Of course, a combination of policies at *all* levels is most likely to ensure success. Even with the fluidity of policies and programs, the basic commitment to public education in the United States has been historically stable and is expected to remain so. Nevertheless, the connection between policies and funding can bring about considerable controversy as will be discussed in the next two chapters on funding and outcomes.

ORGANIZATIONS DEDICATED TO THE ADVANCEMENT OF SCHOOL-LINKED SERVICES

A number of organizations focus on supporting policies to expand school-linked services. The Coalition for Community Schools, for instance, is a major organization devoted to promoting community schools through practice, policy, programs, and research. Founded in 1997 as part of the Institute for Educational Leadership (IEL), the coalition includes the following among its goals:

1. Sharing information about successful community school policies, programs, and practices;
2. Building broader public understanding and support for community schools;
3. Informing public- and private-sector policies in order to strengthen community schools; and
4. Developing sustainable sources of funding for community schools.

The coalition conducts research about community schools that demonstrates their effectiveness and explores the challenges involved in creating and sustaining community schools. It convenes national, regional, and local community school forums and partners meetings that help key stakeholders and their organizations move toward common ground. A website and an email newsletter are maintained as part of its effort to provide learning opportunities about community schools and funding resources. The coalition is involved in promoting a policy framework at the federal, state, and local levels to support community schools, the concept of full-service schools, and community school networks at the local and state levels. An important aspect of this mission is educating the public about the importance of community schools. The full mission statement and more information about the organization are available on its website, http://www.communityschools.org/about/mission.aspx.

Two other organizations that are policy leaders are profiled here: the Center for Health and Health Care in Schools (CHHCS) and the Broader Bolder Approach (BBA).

THE CENTER FOR HEALTH AND HEALTH CARE IN SCHOOLS, MILKEN INSTITUTE SCHOOL OF PUBLIC HEALTH, GEORGE WASHINGTON UNIVERSITY (Information provided by Olga Acosta Price, Director)

PROGRAM PURPOSE

While the value of accessible school-connected programs is increasingly recognized, less attention has been paid to the how-to of linking health and education services. Despite these challenges, CHHCS believes that using a school-based solution to achieve measurable gains in children's health and school success has the potential to effect long-term change. The CHHCS approach emphasizes the facilitation of communication among key stakeholders in the health and education sectors for building a mutual understanding of their programmatic, political, and funding priorities. Over time, CHHCS has built a network of allies, including researchers, practitioners, administrators, school and community leaders, funders, and policymakers who share a commitment to this work.

PROGRAM DEVELOPMENT

CHHCS has a twenty-five-year history of developing strategies that strengthen school-community and family partnerships to achieve better outcomes for children. CHHCS pursues this objective by linking educators, health professionals, families, and youth to the information essential to building effective school-connected health programs; testing new school-based and school-linked strategies; promoting awareness of successful new directions in school-focused approaches; and advancing policies that establish and sustain effective interventions integrated within school settings. School-connected health programs range from those that help students adopt healthy habits to those that foster a physically and emotionally healthy school environment. School-based health services include physical, mental, and oral health care, screenings and referrals to community resources, and services to support students with special health care needs.

COLLABORATIVE ACTIVITIES AND STRUCTURES

CHHCS employs partnership strategies in its work, beginning with its partnering with funders that share a commitment to collaboration, an essential foundation for sustainable community change. Building on the experience and skills of its staff members, CHHCS has undertaken a range of projects that include both short-term, single-site initiatives and multiyear, multisite demonstration programs. Because these projects involve schools that inevitably reflect the priorities of diverse groups, from elected officials to educators and parents and community leaders, CHHCS believes that all school-focused strategies must be built on functional, reciprocal partnerships.

CHHCS's collaborative work has taken many forms. For example, on behalf of the California Health Care Foundation, CHHCS developed a brief exploring key issues and challenges associated with the proposed launch of a school-based health center initiative. The analytical work involved in developing that report required consultation with state health department and finance agencies, community activists, school-based health center professionals, and members of the public health community and philanthropy. The report is available on the California HealthCare Foundation website, http://www.chcf.org/topics/view.cfm?itemID=133488 (Fall 2007).

CHHCS has also worked with the Nemours Foundation in Delaware and the Colorado Health Foundation. In both instances, CHHCS assisted the foundations in evaluating current school-based health center developments in their respective states, facilitated meetings to explore potential new directions, and created new products such as assessment tools, evaluation guides, and financing analyses to help support expansion of school-based health centers. Because both of these involved a sustained effort over a twelve-month period to prepare the ground for a new initiative, substantial time was invested in identifying who should join as decision-makers and influencers, as well as who else should be informed of the process and given opportunities to offer input.

In addition to its work with private philanthropy, the center has partnered with community organizations and public agencies to strengthen school-located services. For example, CHHCS collaborated with the Student Support Center (SSC) and the District of Columbia Department of Mental Health to assess the department's school mental health program. This program currently provides services in more than sixty schools across the District of Columbia. While this project involved a narrower target—improving school mental health programs in the district—the effort also required engaging not only the principal parties involved in paying for or delivering school-based services, but also tapping into the experiences of school officials and mental health leaders in the district and in other well-regarded programs across the United States. Resources developed as a result of these consulting engagements can be found on the CHHCS web site (The Center for Health and Health Care in Schools 2014) at http://www.healthinschools.org/consulting.aspx.

With support from a national foundation, CHHCS recently completed a multistate examination of the social, economic, and political factors that impact the development and sustainability of children's mental health prevention and intervention services. The analyses relied on a series of key informant interviews with state and local stakeholders from the education and mental health sectors, as well as child advocacy leaders, among others. Findings underscore the diversity of successful approaches and opportunities found across communities, as well as the challenges inherent in bringing together diverse individuals and organizations (despite a common interest).

TARGET POPULATIONS

The CHHCS strategy to strengthen the effectiveness of health services for children is to involve all parties in successful programs: funders, including private foundations and public payers such as insurance companies and Medicaid; policymakers at the local, state, and federal levels; program developers, including government health and education agencies, researchers, and nonprofit community agencies; program beneficiaries such as students, families, and teachers, among others.

FEATURED PROGRAM

On behalf of the Robert Wood Johnson Foundation (RWJF) the center managed a multisite grant initiative to assist children of immigrants and refugees in securing help for emotional and behavioral health problems. In support of this work, the center worked with local agencies to assess community needs, provided technical assistance to RWJF grantees, communicated with policymakers about program developments, and, during the four-year life of the program (2006–2010), facilitated inter-project learning through annual conferences. Information on this initiative is available on the center's website at http://www.healthinschools.org/Immigrant%20and%20Refugee%20Children.aspx.

Previously, the center and its predecessor offices assisted RWJF in implementing three multisite grant initiatives that piloted and replicated school-based health centers in sixteen states across the United States. These initiatives were: the School-Based Adolescent Health Care Program, 1986–1992; Making the Grade: State and Local Partnerships to Support School-Based Health Centers, 1993-2000; and Caring for Kids: Expanding Mental and Dental Health Services in School-Based Health Centers, 2001–2005.

FUNDING

CHHCS is funded primarily through grants from private foundations, particularly the Robert Wood Johnson Foundation. Other foundations that have supported its work include the California HealthCare Foundation, the Colorado Health Foundation, the Horning Family Fund, the Carbonell Family Foundation, the J. T. MacDonald Foundation, the Nemours Foundation, the Quantum Foundation, and the Vision Council of America. CHHCS has also received support from public sources, including the Bureau of Primary Health Care, Health Resources and Services Administration, the Department of Health and Human Services, the Agency for Health Research and Quality, the Prince Georges County Public Schools, and the Center for Student Support Services with the District of Columbia Department of Mental Health.

IMPLEMENTATION CHALLENGES

Collaborative approaches are challenging because they require patience and a willingness to share control. Working with multiple funders, building partnerships with diverse organizations, and, perhaps most complex, working collaboratively with two systems—health and education—can result in slow progress and frequent frustration. These systems have different funding structures, organizational imperatives, and political constituencies. These differences and the time commitment required to negotiate their intricacies are often barriers to implementation and sustainability.

POLICY RECOMMENDATIONS

In its work, CHHCS emphasizes the importance of linking schools with the multiple other systems that impact the well-being of vulnerable students, including primary care providers, hospital systems, government social services, and other community supports. Toward that end, CHHS offers the following policy recommendations for improving the health and health care for children and youth:

1 School-based interventions must make available a full continuum of supports that include health promotion, disease prevention, early intervention, and treatment services;

2 Schools must be invited to play a meaningful role in any system of care where young people are the focus, and educators must be treated as partners in essential prevention efforts, not just as stewards of convenient settings for care;
3 School-connected programs must include strategies for engaging diverse families at all levels of implementation to achieve success in education and to optimize health; and
4 Health and education policies, practices, and funding streams must be better integrated to improve the odds for achieving positive health and academic outcomes for youth.

FUTURE DIRECTIONS

CHHCS will continue to focus on three related areas to help improve child health and academic outcomes.

1 Financing and sustaining children's health initiatives: While school-connected care has many dimensions, CHHCS focuses on financing school-connected programs, policies, and systems that prioritize children's health and school success. Through field research and collaboration with public and private leaders in children's health, CHHCS will continue to identify revenue streams available to support these programs today and explore those potentially available in the future.
2 Building state and local partnerships for care: CHHCS works with system stakeholders to link and integrate the policies, strategies, and services that provide a system of care for children and adolescents. The vision is that all children should be supported by a system that begins with health promotion and disease prevention initiatives, and for those with specific needs, offers targeted, effective interventions to address behavioral, oral, and physical health.
3 Focusing on vulnerable populations: CHHCS is committed to supporting school-connected programs and policies that specifically help vulnerable children stay healthy and succeed academically. This work focuses on children from low-income, immigrant, and refugee families, as well as children who are physically or emotionally challenged. Progress in caring for the most vulnerable children requires that we continue to discover ways to engage schools and their community partners in order to effectively address children's unmet mental and physical health needs.

ADDITIONAL INFORMATION

CHHCS maintains an extensive website, www.healthinschools.org, making its resources available to regional, national and international audiences. Inquiries can be emailed to chhcs@gwu.edu.

BROADER BOLDER APPROACH TO EDUCATION (Information provided by Elaine Weiss, National Coordinator)

BRIEF OVERVIEW

The Broader Bolder Approach to Education (BBA) is a national campaign that acknowledges the impact of social and economic disadvantage on schools and students and proposes evidence-based policies to improve schools and remedy conditions that limit many children's readiness to learn.

OBJECTIVE

The purpose is to elevate the issue of child poverty and the range of impediments to learning associated with it in national, state, and local debates about education policy, and to spotlight the many evidence-based policies that can alleviate those problems.

PROCESS OF DEVELOPMENT

In 2007–2008, Economic Policy Institute president Larry Mishel and education economist Richard Rothstein began to assemble a group of scholars, practitioners, advocates, and policymakers who shared a concern that the standards-and-accountability education policy movement and No Child Left Behind could not substantially narrow our stubborn achievement gaps. Holding these as flagship policies could harm the low-income and minority students these policies purport to help. In collaboration with a high-profile task force, Mishel and Rothstein drafted and collected signatures for the BBA mission statement, which was launched in June 2008, with a full-page *New York Times* ad and extensive media coverage.

COLLABORATIVE ACTIVITIES/STRUCTURES

The Economic Policy Institute (EPI) is the founding and lead organization, but BBA was independently funded in its initial stages by the Nellie Mae Foundation and subsequently supported by the Atlantic Philanthropies, the Ford Foundation, the Annie E. Casey Foundation, the Schott Foundation, and others. BBA's policy positions are guided by its three co-chairs,

Helen Ladd, Pedro Noguera, and Thomas Payzant, and it is further supported by an advisory council comprised of leaders of allied organizations, universities, and other institutions.

TARGET POPULATION

BBA's activities are directed principally toward federal and state policymakers, as well as members of the media, advocates, and academics. Parent, teacher, and student organizers are increasingly important users of BBA materials and information, which are also intended for the general public's use and education.

FEATURED EFFORTS

BBA's advocacy activities fall broadly into three categories: early childhood education, comprehensive strategies, and school improvement. There is some overlap, and BBA works with allies both within and between categories.

BBA's major publications and products include:

1. Policy statements: "A Broader, Bolder Approach to Education: School Accountability"; "A Broader Bolder Approach to Education" and "Broader Bolder Early Childhood Education Framework: A Ten-Year Plan for Transformation";
2. Over a dozen one-page examples of BBA-oriented comprehensive educational strategies at the district level. Some of these are full-service community schools; others include the Harlem Children's Zone and Boston's City Connects;
3. BBA policy briefs: "Basics (Stop Waiting for Superman)"; "Turnaround Schools (The Inconvenient Truth About Turning Around Schools)"; and "Early Childhood Education (The ABCs of Achievement Gaps)";
4. A BBA bibliography with selected academic articles and books supporting the BBA policy framework, and including brief summaries and quotations;
5. A set of BBA "principles," or brief, policy-relevant BBA-oriented statements that are relevant to current education policy issues and can be shared via email, Facebook, or Twitter, with links to other resources;
6. A map of BBA-oriented, district-level efforts in states across the country, with contact information to connect BBA website visitors to activities of interest;
7. A major report on "Market-Oriented Reforms' Rhetoric Trumps Reality; The Impacts of Test-based Teacher Evaluations, School closures, and Increased Charter School Access on Student Outcomes in Chicago, New York City, and Washington, D.C." (April 2013);
8. A major report on "Mismatches in Race to the Top Limit Educational Improvement; Lack of Time, Resources, and Tools to Address Opportunity Gaps Puts Lofty State Goals Out of Reach" (September 2013);

9 Bill Moyers blog series, co-authored with educators, illustrating the many connections between poverty and education and strategies to weaken them; and
10 Film screening series illustrating connections between poverty and education and associated materials, including research and policy briefs and tool kits to host community screenings.

IMPLEMENTATION CHALLENGES

From the start, the biggest challenge facing BBA has been forming a well-funded education "reform" movement, driven at both the federal and advocacy/organizational/philanthropic levels and promoting a narrow set of market-oriented education policies. These policies are unproven, yet presented as evidence-based: test-based teacher and school evaluations, radical turnaround strategies (including school closures), and increased access to charter schools. With strong political and financial backing, these policies tend to absorb much of the education policy discussion and debate, making it difficult to obtain funding for BBA efforts and to present a different perspective.

FUTURE DIRECTIONS

BBA is developing mechanisms for teachers, parents, students, and others to share how schools can work to alleviate poverty-related barriers to learning through collaboration with teachers, filmmakers, and others. BBA also supports state and local-level organizing through partners and allies in order to establish more BBA efforts on the ground and inspire policy change.

• • •

Federal and state policies that impact public elementary and secondary education are complex and are in a continual state of change depending on the economy, demographics, politics, and fluctuating values. Federal policies are based on laws pertaining to equal opportunity and civil rights while states are responsible for maintaining their public schools. The federal government's education policies are meant to encourage economic growth by creating a skilled workforce. Compensatory education programs are an integral part of the ESEA and are meant to give children living in economically disadvantaged communities opportunities to attain economic independence through schooling. Additional federal programs and grants are aimed at reducing inequality by providing children with school-based social and health services.

State education agencies (SEAs) are responsible for everything that the federal government does not do, including setting education standards for all grades, determining teacher and principal eligibility, and funding schools. States may apply for federal programs to enhance state monies but they must comply with the policies associated with these programs.

Community schools and other schools with integrated school-linked services are typically situated in impoverished neighborhoods and are therefore eligible for federal compensatory programs. The ESSA and other federal programs include eligibility requirements for school-community engagement, but widespread school-linked services have yet to be included as a standard for school improvement, although schools may be able to make community engagement an accountability indicator under the new ESSA.

While this chapter focuses on policies relevant to school-linked services, chapter 8 focuses on public education funding and the controversies that surround its relationship to policy and measured outcomes, especially as funding impacts schools' abilities to partner with families and community resources.

8

Funding

FUNDING PROGRAMS THAT SUPPORT, foster, and provide school-linked services are complex and often involve a mix of public monies at the state, local, and federal levels, in addition to private dollars from local and national foundations, individual donors, and businesses. The funding streams include grant monies specifically designated for school-based health centers, full-service community schools, and additional funds available for both specific and general purposes. When such streams are well coordinated, resources can be aligned and brought to bear on the goal of supporting children.

As noted in chapter 7, the federal government through ESEA and other grants and programs typically contributes only 8 to 13 percent of all monies going to the states for public education. Although there will be a new ESEA known as ESSA beginning in 2017, this level of support is unlikely to change.

The remaining funding comes from local taxes and block, state, and local grants. Urban public schools in low-income neighborhoods (where many community schools and other schools with links to services are located) are eligible to apply for these federal programs and grants, and many Title I schools receive approximately 30 to 40 percent of their funds from a variety of federally sponsored programs and resources (Federal Education Policy 2009). Because some of these grants favor major metropolitan cities, these communities often are advantaged in the application process, leaving smaller cities and rural communities with fewer federal grant opportunities in which they can participate (Reeves 2003; Jimerson 2005). In addition, funds affiliated with federal and other grants are typically limited, so only a small percentage of eligible communities can benefit. Another 25 percent of funding for community-school partnerships comes from private sources such as businesses, foundations, individuals, and community-based nonprofit organizations. States and local districts contribute the rest, with school districts funding education mainly through property taxes (Blank et al. 2010).

It is important to note that public community schools, like other public schools, rely primarily on local resources; even their private monies come primarily from their local community and local contributors. While this makes their funding less controversial, it may also make such community schools financially insecure. Their sustainability is rooted in their popularity among families and communities, as well as their successes in boosting student achievement and other outcomes. However, financial vulnerability is always a concern, especially in times of economic instability. Now that charter schools can also be community schools, the trend complicates support for the more traditional community-based public schools. In education funding, change is always on the horizon, making fidelity to any single model a difficult challenge. Nevertheless, it is important for educators and others committed to serving children, families and communities to remain aware of the multiple funding sources that currently exist, as well as those proposed by advocates of school-linked services.

PUBLIC FINANCING: COMMUNITY-SCHOOL PARTNERSHIP FUNDING FROM FEDERAL SOURCES

Currently there are no large-scale federal funding programs with the expressed purpose of supporting ongoing, integrated school-linked services. Up until very recently, the Department of Education has offered an array of grant programs to support these schools. With the passage of the Every Student Succeeds Act (ESSA) many of these federally supported programs will continue under the auspice of the ESEA. It is too early to know exactly how this change will affect most school-linked services programs but for now it appears that there will be increased access to federal monies by way of grant applications. The extent to which the recommendations for financial support for community school partnerships set forth in the 2013 report from the Commission on Equity and Excellence in Education are now coming under the jurisdiction of the ESEA are discussed later in this chapter.

Under the NCLB and Waivers there are programs and grants that, when combined, could increase resources for school-linked services. Some of these programs and grants are meant for public schools serving children from economically poor families, while some can also be applied to all public school children regardless of economic status. Schools and their community partners can take advantage of programs such as those provided under various sections of the NCLB, Title I programs serving economically poor children, the 21st Century Community Learning Center Program (Title V of the ESEA) and school improvement grants (Title I of the ESEA). (Coalition for Community Schools 2014). A Full-Service Community School grant program funded a small number of grants in 2008, 2010, and again in 2014. The Coalition for Community Schools carefully tracks these funding programs and makes information available to schools wishing to take advantage of federal monies (see Coalition for Community Schools web page on federal funding).

Programs Related to the ESEA

When amended in 2002, the Elementary and Secondary Education Assistance Act (known as No Child Left Behind) included numerous programs to assist children in underperforming schools. Federal funding based on this act is subject to congressional budgetary processes, and programs listed are neither permanent nor consistently funded. Most of these programs have been functioning for the past decade and are considered relatively stable, at least for now, although it is important to keep in mind that public school policies and funding are always within the purview of the political arena, so changes are expected and dependent upon the interactions of political power and economic necessities. The new ESSA consolidates some of these grant programs into Title IV, Community Support for School Success with initial additional funding. It is also helpful to recall from chapter 7 that the federal government's main mission in funding public education is to create and sustain a workforce suitable for keeping the country competitive in the global economy. Descriptions of ESEA programs of special interest in funding community-school partnerships follow.

School Improvement Grants (SIGs)

These grants are targeted at the lowest performing schools that are in need of corrective action to comply with the ESEA. They will remain as part of Title I in the ESSA with increased priority for future funding.

Community-school partnerships can be included in a program for school improvement using evidence cited in chapter 9 and throughout this book, illustrating correlations between school-linked services and improvements in children's test scores. Although these grants were not considered a full-fledged improvement model for ESEA waivers, it is not clear how they will be viewed with regard to corrective action in the ESSA. Nevertheless, integrated models of linking schools and communities in need fit perfectly into SIG criteria. States supporting community-school models to address disadvantage can participate in this strategy to obtain funding for local districts.

21st Century Community Learning Centers

This program is a formula grant allocated to state education agencies (SEAs) for out-of-school learning programs that promote academic achievement. These learning centers can include enrichment programs in the arts, recreation, and drug and violence prevention. School districts can apply for these funds from their states.

Promise Neighborhood Grants

These grants seek to enhance educational opportunities by creating "great" schools that encourage developmental support for children from the earliest grades through high school. Promise Neighborhood grants are given to localities for planning and implementing programs that create neighborhoods where schools, agencies, and families work together to develop positive learning environments that are likely to improve school achievement. While the program supports the community schools model, all Title I schools are eligible for funding. The last Promise Neighborhood grants were awarded in 2012, due to limited funds but they will now be incorporated into the new ESSA as part of Title IV's Community Support for School Success, likely ensuring funding (Every Student Succeeds Act, 2015; U.S. Department of Education 2014e).

Additional Sources of Federal Funding

Race to the Top District Competition

Race to the Top, initiated in 2009 by the Obama administration, allowed states to propose innovative ways to "turn around" its lowest performing schools. States needed to show that these schools were adopting standards and assessments to prepare students for college, build a data system to manage and monitor success, recruit and retain effective teachers and principals, and demonstrate progress in turning around the lowest performing schools (U.S. Department of Education 2014b). Although funding for this program ended in 2015, community schools and other models of school-linked services benefited since the program encouraged the coordination of community resources and in-school and extended care for low-performing students (U.S. Department of Education 2015a).

Corporation for National and Community Service (CNCS)

Funding available from CNCS includes Volunteers in Service to America (VISTA), AmeriCorps, Senior Corps, and Experience Corps, all of which can provide support for a range of roles within community-school partnerships.

Nutrition Programs

These programs offer on-site or nearby programs easily accessible to students. The Food and Nutrition Program for After School Snacks, administered by the Department of Agriculture, provides food for children to take home, while the Summer Food Service Program provides snacks and meals for families and children. Both programs can be coordinated through the schools, and schools with strong community partnerships related to nutrition initiatives are often best able to manage the distribution of food to community members in need. More detail on federal nutrition programs as components of community schools is provided in chapter 3.

Health Programs

Below is a partial list of health-related programs and grants that schools can apply for to support health-related services linked with schools:

1 Healthy Tomorrows Partnerships for Children: Funded by the federal Maternal and Child Health Bureau with technical assistance from the American Academy of Pediatrics (AAP), this program provides grants for health services to pregnant women, infants, children, and youth. Schools can apply for five-year grants that involve direct health services. In years two through five of the grant, the government provides monies when there is a two to one match; the district or school provides twice the amount that it asks for, which can include in-kind services.

2 Medicaid/Children's Health Insurance Program (CHIP): In some states, Medicaid can be billed for school-based or linked health programs.
3 Safe Schools–Healthy Students grants (SS-HS): These grants were first made available to school districts in 1999 and funded collaboratively by the Departments of Education, Health and Human Services, and Justice. Five major foci have been:
   a Promoting early childhood social and emotional learning and development;
   b Promoting mental, emotional, and behavioral health;
   c Connecting youth, families, schools, and communities;
   d Preventing and reducing alcohol, tobacco, and other drug use; and
   e Preventing youth violence and bullying.

   In 2013, the Substance Abuse and Mental Health Services Administration (SAMHSA) made SS-HS grants to states to carry out this work. Title IV of the ESSA includes a provision for activities related to safe and healthy students. States receiving funding through the 21st Century Schools Program will be required to devote some of its monies to these activities.
4 "Now Is the Time" Healthy Transitions (NITT-HT) and Project Aware (NITT AWARE-LEA): Both funded by SAMHSA, these new initiatives began in 2014. "Now Is the Time" Healthy Transitions: Improving Life Trajectories for Youth and Young Adults with, or at Risk for, Serious Mental Health Conditions, or NITT-HT offers competitive grant funding to states for youth and young adults ages 16–25 at risk for serious mental health and/or substance abuse conditions. "Now Is the Time" Project AWARE awards monies to local educational agencies (LEAs) to train school personnel and community support staff to detect mental illness in school-age youth and encourage them and their families to seek treatment. As of September 2015, 20 states received funds from this initiative (Substance Abuse and Mental Health Services Administration 2015).
5 Full-Service Community Schools grants: While these grants, which are funded by the DOE, offer substantial support for very high-needs districts, they have been awarded only to approximately between 10–12 community-school partnership projects during each of the three years they have been available: 2008, 2010, and 2014. According to the DOE, the purpose of the

program is to improve the quality of education for children at the elementary and secondary school levels and to assist children in "meeting challenging academic content and academic achievement standards." The Full-Service Community Schools (FSCS) program encourages coordination of academic, social, and health services through partnerships among schools and community—based organizations (U.S. Department of Education 2014c). Full Service Community Schools Grants are now to be included in Title IV of the ESSA under Community Support for School Success.

6 Centers for Disease Control and Prevention funding: The Centers for Disease Control offer states competitive opportunities to apply for funding for health initiatives in schools and their communities. A recent example is funding for capacity building of the HIV prevention workforce that was awarded in 2014. Among the awardees were community organizations serving minority groups.

The Coalition for Community Schools advocates for the use of existing and future funding strategies to support new and existing community schools with health-related initiatives. Although community schools largely rely on community services that already exist, the coalition encourages targeted and strategic use of federal programs to enhance schools' programs and sustainability in creating linkages with health and social service agencies, as well as local businesses.

STATE AND LOCAL PUBLIC FUNDING

Even with the federal grants available, approximately 90 percent of school funding comes from the states and, to a lesser extent, from the local community. Although many states have encouraged community-school linkages through special programs and projects, these relationships and programs rely largely on state and district funding formulas, which are often complicated and subject to fluctuating economic and political climates. States acquire monies for public education from a variety of sources, but mostly from block grants from the federal government, state taxes, and special education funds, such as those from lotteries. Unfortunately, there are interstate differences in the amount of monies targeted for education. Many states leave most financial distribution decisions to local communities, rather than weighing the larger needs of low-income districts where resources are scarce.

Local districts acquire education funds from local taxes, mostly those based on property values, and in some areas, on local sales taxes and/or income taxes. Local funding of schools is often controversial, since poorer communities have a more difficult time keeping up with their wealthier counterparts. Disadvantaged communities cannot obtain substantial funding through real estate taxes. Their tax bases are very meager; that is the reason why so many lawsuits have been brought to try to change the property-based system. States can make up for these inequities by revamping their state education finance systems to ensure that state funds are heavily weighted to benefit low-income communities that cannot raise sufficient funds through local property taxes, but this does not always happen. For example, although studies have clearly shown the advantages of preschool (Darling-Hammond et al. 2013; Magnuson et al. 2004; Magnuson, Ruhm, & Waldfogel 2007), academic content in kindergarten (Claessens, Engel, & Curran 2014), and small class sizes (Nye, Hedges, & Konstantopoulos 2000) for academic achievement, funding for these proven programs and class size adjustments are often difficult to provide to children in economically poor communities, especially when these districts have to rely heavily on their own resources.

Most states have taken on the challenge of providing low-performing low-income students with more equitable funding by funneling monies to schools directly from state departments of education (Epstein 2011). In some states, this change in allocation of resources came after years of litigation challenging state education departments on the basis of educational adequacy. Litigation cases for more equitable funding have been brought in forty-five states; as of 2010, twenty-two states had won their cases, and eight were pending (Access 2011). However, as Darling-Hammond (2010) suggests, winning is a tedious process that often involves multiple appeals, and sometimes decade-long lags between enforcement times. Even when cases are won, revised funding formulas are not always fully implemented when state legislatures fail to fully fund the proposed changes. This has happened in several states, including New York. The organization New Yorkers for Students' Educational Rights filed a new lawsuit asserting that the state violated students' education rights by "neglecting its constitutional obligation to ensure that every school has sufficient funding to provide all students with a meaningful educational opportunity" (Campaign for Educational Equity 2014a). In other states such as Pennsylvania, equitable funding is dependent on changes in state politics, and funding formulas supportive of less advantaged communities have been reduced by subsequent legislative action. In both of these states, the situation may change in any given year (Baker 2012; Baker & Corcoran 2012).

THE 2013 COMMISSION ON EQUITY AND EXCELLENCE IN EDUCATION

The Commission on Equity and Excellence in Education, established by Congress and appointed by DOE secretary Arne Duncan, consisted of twenty-seven educators, legal experts in education, labor, and civil rights, and other citizens with relevant expertise. Issued in 2013, the commission's report focused on ways to improve public schools and offered five action strategies, two of which are critical to funding school-linked services to promote equity. Action Strategy One involves a restructuring of the finance systems that underlie every decision about schools, focusing on equitable resources and their cost-effective use; while Action Strategy Four focuses on increased parental engagement, access to health and social services, extended instructional time, and assistance for at-risk groups so that students in high-poverty communities can start strong and stay on track (U.S. Department of Education 2013). Each of these is discussed in greater detail below.

Action Strategy One: Restructuring the Finance System

The first reported concern was improving school finance and efficiency. This section begins with a bold statement: "Achieving equity and excellence requires sufficient resources that are distributed based on student need, not zip code, and that are efficiently used" (U.S. Department of Education 2013:17).

With approximately 40 percent of American public school children attending schools in high-poverty areas, the commission aimed its discussion at the inequities in funding public education. According to the report, the biggest problem in state funding is the continued use of property taxes as a major funding resource.

The disparities in property values between wealthy and poor districts create huge differences in spending per pupil, especially in states relying predominantly on property taxes for school funding, such as Illinois and Nevada, where 60 percent of school funding comes from local sources (as compared to New Mexico and Vermont, which rely on local taxes for only 30 percent and 15 percent, respectively). Litigation has played a role in several states changing their funding formulas, including New Jersey, New York, and California (Darling-Hammond 2010).

It is important to remember that state funding methods are not written in stone and that formulas are based on changing economies, political climates, and court orders. The commission's report points out inequities with the goal of increasing funding for the poorest districts and shows funding disparities among the states in terms of total dollars spent. For example, when adjustments are made for a number of variables, such as student poverty, regional wage variation, and district size and density, 2009 data show spending per pupil in Tennessee as $7,306, compared with $19,520 in Wyoming. Further differences within school districts show that schools with the poorest children often receive less funding than those with fewer children living in poverty. The commission cites a 2011 report from the DOE that found that more than one-third of schools with the highest level of poverty received less funding than more advantaged schools within the same district.

These data confirm inequitable funding strategies among and within the states, with the poorest schools suffering most. The commission made numerous recommendations for remedy, including:

1 Have states identify and report the actual costs of providing meaningful educational opportunities for all their students, including those living in poverty, non-English-speaking students, and students with disabilities, based on evidence of effective practice.
2 Adopt and implement a school finance system that will provide equitable and sufficient funding for all students to achieve state content and performance standards. Equitable funding may mean more funds for schools with the greatest number of students living in poverty, students with disabilities, English-language learners, and schools in remote areas. States should assure stable funding sources for public education.

3 Update and review performance evidence and financing systems to ensure that students have meaningful education opportunities and attain high academic achievement levels. The federal government should provide incentives for states to implement a stable and equitable financing system.
4 The federal government should allocate more funding to schools with high concentrations of low-income, minority, and low-performing students and monitor the effectiveness in terms of academic achievement.
5 The federal government must increase its commitment to enforcing, under civil rights law, the elimination of race-based educational inequality.
6 The federal government must eliminate any loopholes in the Title I legislation that allow states to contribute lower amounts of monies to Title I schools.
7 The federal government can assist states with accounting and data management to ensure equitable distribution of state and federal funds.

Action Strategy Four: Provide Funding for Engaging Parents and Ensuring Children's Access to Health and Social Services Through Schools

The commission noted the importance of parental engagement in children's schooling. It also is committed to providing all children with sufficient access to health and social services, including resources for children in danger of dropping out of school and/or becoming involved in the juvenile justice system. The following recommendations suggest funding for parent engagement and community-based services linked to schools:

1 Provide incentives to states for funding parental education to encourage family involvement in education;
2 Provide funding for crisis counseling and monies that support access to health and nutrition, childcare, and transportation;
3 Provide incentives for enhancing effective communication between families and schools;
4 Provide basic health services to schoolchildren at risk;
5 Enhance afterschool activities through increased federal funding and use incentives to encourage states to increase learning time;

6 Appoint full-time health coordinators in schools with large populations or higher concentrations of low-income students, and establish school-based health clinics in areas that lack easy access to hospitals or community health clinics; and
7 Employ dropout prevention and alternative education for children experiencing difficulty learning in traditional settings.

BUSINESS, FOUNDATION, AND UNIVERSITY SUPPORT

Since most endeavors benefit from a mix of public and private funds, community schools and community-school partnerships utilize funds from foundations, businesses, and other private sector entities to support their efforts. For example, the 2010 Children's Aid Society's community schools portfolio was comprised of two-thirds public and one-third private monies. Business and foundation leaders support school-linked services in a variety of ways depending on the community context. Ideally, decisions regarding involvement are made collaboratively by business, foundation, community, and school leaders at the local level.

The Coalition for Community Schools identifies five types of community school funders from businesses and foundations: general foundations, corporate foundations, community foundations, local foundations, and United Way chapters (Coalition for Community Schools n.d.).

General foundations that operate at both national and local levels and actively support school-linked services are typically interested in education, youth development, and community development. The Charles Stewart Mott Foundation has been a committed leader for the better part of a century, and its support is now on a global level. Over the past decade, the foundation has made community schools one of its featured initiatives, providing "broad-based support for policy and technical assistance at the national level, while demonstrating effective local practice with select sites in the two states in which it concentrates its funding, California and Washington" (Coalition for Community Schools n.d.:1). Other national foundations, including the Annie E. Casey, Wallace, and Danforth Foundations, have been strong supporters of school-linked services as well. The Robert Wood Johnson Foundation and the W. K. Kellogg Foundation have been important supporters of school-based health centers and other health-related initiatives linked with schools. Corporate foundations such as those of J. P. Morgan Chase and Citibank are another source of support for school-linked services.

Community foundations across the country are another important funding source for school-linked services and have a focus on giving at local and regional levels. The San Francisco Foundation has made community schools "a key component of their funding approach" (Coalition for Community Schools n.d.:2). One of the Greater Cincinnati Foundation's target initiatives is to support Cincinnati public schools' community school efforts. The Lincoln Community Foundation has been supporting local integrated school-community partnerships since 1999 (Coalition for Community Schools n.d.). Local foundations are similar to community foundations with their focus on specific local geographic areas. However, they do not typically solicit donations and are usually supported by an endowment. The Polk Brothers Foundation is an example of a local private foundation that has supported school-linked services since the 1990s and helped to establish Chicago's 154 community schools (Coalition for Community Schools n.d.).

The network of United Way organizations throughout the United States has also been a strong supporter of school-community partnerships, providing financial, organizational, and technical support. United Way of Greater Lehigh Valley began its support for school-linked services in 2005 with "a vision to identify, strengthen, and promote community-connected schools so that all Lehigh Valley students succeed and graduate from high school ready to lead meaningful and productive lives" (United Way of the Greater Lehigh Valley 2014). Similarly, United Way of the Greater New Orleans Area convenes over thirty nonprofit organizations that focus on "the integration and coordination of efforts at community school sites" (Coalition for Community Schools n.d.:3).

Universities also contribute money and resources to community schools and other school-linked services efforts. Philadelphia community schools have received help from the University of Pennsylvania's Netter Center for Community Partnerships, and schools in New York City's Harlem neighborhood have benefited from resources from Teachers College of Columbia University (Blank et al. 2010). The Netter Center (see chapter 4) leads support for other private and public universities as they adapt the university-assisted community schools model, so that universities across the country (and in some cases the globe) can bolster school-linked services with an array of resources including funding, expertise, and personnel.

Obtaining funds from private and nonprofit sources can begin with the creation of a collaborative infrastructure, as suggested by the Partnership for Children and Youth, an organization committed to fostering community-school collaborations. Its report stresses the need for local partnership organizations to serve as magnets for both public and private funding. An example is City 2020, an organization in Redwood City, California, comprised of county, city, school district, high school, and private community-based funders. Another successful example is Sacramento's Unified School District, which, with the help of community partners, established nineteen youth and family resource centers at elementary, middle, and high schools. Managed by the city's Integrated Support Services, the centers have attracted over three million dollars yearly from partners among community nonprofits, county and city agencies, and interns and volunteers. In-kind community partner services provide the bulk of these resources (Partnership for Children and Youth 2013).

Clearly, there are a host of options for school-community partnerships to acquire funding for needed services. Organizations like the Coalition for Community Schools, the National Center for Community Schools, the Children's Aid Society National Technical Assistance Center, and the Partnership for Children and Youth are helpful starting points for securing information on raising both public and private funds for school-community partnerships.

THE POLITICS OF FUNDING SCHOOL-LINKED SERVICES

It is reasonable to assume that most community schools focus on serving low-income children and their families. Most of these schools qualify for Title I funding alongside other supplemental federal funding programs. Community schools and other schools with important community partnerships compete with all public schools for state monies, and because they are most often situated in low-income neighborhoods, politicians may not always be willing to give these efforts their full support. Furthermore, there is a great deal of inequality in state education funding formulas so that Title I schools are often required to manage with inadequate state contributions (Baker & Corcoran 2012; Baker 2014).

These schools also face competition from charter schools for funding in many localities. Charter schools often receive funding from federal, state and local governments in addition to private sources such as the Gates Foundation, the Broad Foundation, and the Walton Family Foundation (Ravitch 2013). Moreover, depending on state regulations and private or public status, charter schools may employ a selective admissions process to increase their overall test scores. This is not always the case, and many charter schools are in the same position as other schools in low-income areas; they select students through lotteries and often report low student achievement. Some charter schools with integrated community partnerships actually prioritize admission for low-income students. More about charter schools and school-linked services is presented in chapter 3, but the fact is they remain competitors with public community schools in many urban neighborhoods.

Finally, we must not forget that most urban and many rural schools in low-income communities serve children and families belonging to minority groups. This implies that community leaders and school advocates are also often members of similar racial and ethnic groups. Unfortunately, it is likely that racial and ethnic prejudices exist among some state legislators, which in turn impacts funding formulas and allowances. Such prejudices and lack of understanding serve to exacerbate racial and other inequities that permeate classrooms and communities (Delpit 2006; Epstein 2011; Noguera & Klevan 2010).

THE ECONOMIC IMPACT OF SCHOOL-COMMUNITY-FUNDED INITIATIVES

A large-scale study funded by the Casey and Clark Foundations and Capital One (Economic Modeling Specialists, Inc. [EMSI] 2012) examined the long-term economic effects of the Communities in Schools model of linking schools with community services through a system of integrated student supports. Community in Schools, a nonprofit organization dedicated to keeping children in schools and emphasizing dropout prevention and the inclusion of community services in public schools (see chapter 3) highlights its successes, claiming that 99 percent of students in schools affiliated with its programs stay in school (Communities in Schools 2014). The EMSI report shows that investments in bringing services to the schools using their model pay off economically, with an 18.4 percent return on investment to society.

So what does this mean for individual students and for the economy as a whole?

From EMSI (2012) and other studies (Milliken 2007; Smink & Schargel 2004), it is clear that individual students earn more money by staying in school, as well as by obtaining additional higher education. This return on investment also benefits families, communities, and the larger economy by reducing smoking, crime, alcoholism, welfare, and unemployment—a projected savings of $154.5 million per year (Economic Modeling Specialists, Inc. 2012). In addition, Communities in Schools found that the high schools in their affiliated programs averaged forty-two additional on-time graduations per year and promotions of an additional ninety-nine students to the next grade level. This data covers high schools from a variety of geographic and economic settings, including Title I schools.

As we highlight throughout this book, funding significantly improves student outcomes. The Communities in Schools report notes the importance of investing in social capital, an investment that may not have immediate returns, but one that successfully ameliorates the economic and social lives of individuals, families, and communities.

The Children's Aid Society (CAS) also commissioned a study on the social return on investment (SROI), which includes both economic and social gains from investment in community schools. The method is based on a formula established by the New Economics Foundation that takes into account multiple indicators of investment return, including what it calls "dead weight"—returns that cannot be attributed to outside interventions, like the community schools (Martinez & Hayes 2013; New Economics Foundation 2008). Results revealed that for every dollar invested in the CAS community schools there is a major financial value outcome. For pre-K to grade 5, for every dollar invested the return was $10.30; and for grades 6–12, it was $14.80 (Martinez & Hayes 2013). These financial returns go directly to families and communities, which yield for them tremendous social benefits. Schools reap the benefits of supporting data that help them improve their full-service programs and enhance their reputation, the latter being helpful in recruiting and retaining excellent teachers.

THE PROCESS OF FUNDING COMMUNITY-SCHOOL LINKAGES AND PARTNERSHIPS

As stated before, throughout the country, schools and districts have widely varying levels of school-community partnerships with equally variable levels of funding. To build, nurture, and expand school-community partnership programs is a continuously engaging process. As far back as the late

1980s, school policy analysts were suggesting ways for schools to acquire funding for school-linked initiatives.

In addition to dollars and cents, there is a multitude of other "costs" to bear in mind. For example, principals and teachers must take into account time and space allocations in the schools, and agency administrators and personnel must consider how to operate in a host environment (Farrow & Joe 1992; Gomby & Larson 1992). Funding of community-school partnerships requires evaluations to ensure that allocated funds are making a difference and to support continued and future funding. But financial support for these efforts is not based on evaluations alone. The process of funding public school education in general is often political, and sometimes judicial. Funding school-community partnerships, in most cases, depends on the political climates of districts, localities, and states and on their available resources. Relationships between school personnel and staff from community agencies also need to be negotiated. Much of what is required in developing these productive relationships through collaboration is laid out in chapter 4.

While funding school-linked services is a good investment overall, the process is complicated when incorporating federal, state, and local requirements. Poirier and Osher (2013) suggest a three-tiered approach to consider needed services and subsequent assessment plans: what services can be used for all students; what can be done for students at a greater level of risk or need; and, what is required for students at the greatest level of risk or need.

Based on this assessment, schools ascertain what funding is available:

1 Is the district already receiving funds from sources for these services?
2 Is the district eligible for funds for these services?
3 Is the district already allocating funds, and if so, where are they going?
4 Are schools authorized to pursue funds independent of the district?

These considerations are the first steps. Schools need to understand the different methods of funding: they are *categorical*, meaning that funds are available for certain purposes with specific eligibility requirements, and *general revenue*, meaning that monies can be used for a variety of purposes. Schools may combine categorical programs, but must keep detailed spending records. General revenue streams are easier to manage and require less record-keeping on the part of the schools. Poirier and Osher (2013) point out that depending on the state, schools are required to keep records of various kinds and degrees of detail. Funding guidelines may change quickly, requiring school and partner administrators to keep up with the latest funding formulas in their states and districts, as well as in federal programs.

ROLES OF FAMILIES AND COMMUNITY MEMBERS IN FUNDING PARTNERSHIP EFFORTS

Where do families and community stakeholders and leaders fit into these complicated funding processes? To begin with, families and community stakeholders can serve as advocates for uncommitted funding pools. They can serve on community boards and school boards, join state advocacy organizations, and keep the pressure on for monies for school-linked services. They can also support and participate in evaluations of both economic and social outcomes of these partnerships. Participation may include: helping to design surveys, informing evaluators about whom to speak with, and encouraging community members to take an interest in outcome-related studies. Thus, families and agencies in local communities are essential partners in funding school-community partnerships.

THE FUNDING VERSUS OUTCOME CONTROVERSY IN ASSESSING ADEQUACY OF EDUCATION

Understanding the relative importance of funding in relation to outcomes is essential for overcoming underachievement in public schools. It is especially crucial in discussions of public education funding and the value of school-linked services and partnerships.

Should measured outcomes or funding levels be the key variable by which to judge educational adequacy? If measured outcome is considered the key factor, then states may continue to focus on closing underperforming schools and replacing them with charters without increasing funding. If, on the other hand, funding is considered the crucial factor, then there is a stronger argument for reassessing and revising state funding formulas to ensure equity and adequacy for public schools, especially those in low-income neighborhoods. There are advocates on both sides, each purporting to champion excellence in education for all students regardless of socioeconomic status.

The group leading the cause that places outcomes before funding is headed by Stanford University economist Eric Hanushek, who argues that a performance-based funding system will promote higher achievement for students and more effective school management by administrators and teachers (Hanushek & Lindseth 2009). The group disputes the idea that inadequate school funding is responsible for underachievement, arguing that "no empirical evidence indicates that our current schools, even those with ample resources, are able to systematically turn students at risk of academic failure into high achievers" (p. 131). Instead, the group suggests that funding should be linked to raising student achievement and not to sustaining a system that is not working. Thus, "The answer to improving our schools lies not in spending more, but in spending more effectively" (p. 287). Others such as Dobbie and Fryer (2011) have argued against communities' influence on achievement.

Most proponents of school-linked services take a different position, advocating for adequacy in public school funding as a way to ensure equal achievement opportunities. Educators such as Linda Darling-Hammond, Joyce Epstein, Pedro Noguera, Diane Ravitch, Michael Rebell, and Richard Rothstein support funding based on the needs of children and the communities in which they live (Darling-Hammond 2010; Epstein 2011; Noguera 2003; Ravitch 2013; Rebell 2009; Rothstein 2004). Darling-Hammond refutes the validity of Hanushek's arguments. She writes that those who think schools are failing to raise test scores ignore the fact that many more children (who would have been previously excluded from education due to discrimination and lack of local resources) are now in school taking tests. Even with a larger pool of test takers, including students living in poverty, new immigrants, and students with special education needs, scores on the National Assessment of Education Progress test and the SAT have risen. This is especially true for minority students whose SAT scores have continued to rise since the 1970s. When children have been provided with expanded educational opportunities, educational attainment and literacy rates have increased, thereby indicating the efficacy of educational investments (Darling-Hammond 2010).

Others who agree with the critical role of funding in student success cite school-linked services that have significantly raised achievement and graduation rates for low-income students. But the question of whether successful educational outcomes are tied to funding is only a portion of the argument about outcomes. Other reasons for adequate funding for school-linked services include providing children with access to services to maintain their health, nutrition, and safety, as well as to increase their opportunities to graduate and obtain skills to prepare them for the modern-day workforce.

Funding school-linked services to support student success presents additional variables to the consideration of resources; many of these costs are not reflected in traditional education budgets. Mixing education funding with health and social service funding complicates states' formulas for public schools. Still, this approach makes more sense than arguing the benefits of policies like "funding versus outcomes" as the basis for assessing adequacy, especially when outcomes are likely to be linked to a multitude of environmental factors outside of schools (Rothstein 2004).

Rothstein (2004) points out that spending more money on the health of children and their parents (especially in the early years of schooling) would likely ultimately decrease costs in special education, now an expensive part of schools' budgets. He further makes a case for another cost-saver—namely, linking health care with schools—and suggests that doing so would probably lessen the need to decrease class size. If children and their families are well cared for and in good health, they will likely do well even in larger classes. He suggests that an extra expenditure of $2,500 per child in schools serving children from low-income families would pay for establishing health and social services in schools. The cost of a smaller innovation, such as vision and dental clinics, would cost only about $400 per pupil but could both save funds elsewhere and boost test scores for children who have visual deficits or are suffering from dental pain and missing school.

Still, it is difficult to argue that measured outcomes are not important. What can be a topic for debate, however, is research methodology and specific implications for achievement (Ravitch 2014). To rely on testing as the sole or primary means to determine funding in schools without supports makes little sense when it is clear that neither schools nor individual teachers are solely (or even primarily) responsible for achievement levels. Even advocates of this agenda point to environmental factors that influence academic achievement (Hanushek & Lindseth 2009). We leave the rest of this discussion for chapter 9.

Very few believe that environments do not influence children's schoolwork. Community schools and other school-linked services partnerships exist precisely because of the tremendous impact of community context in educational achievement. A multitude of studies cited in this book show that school success is dependent on community and family involvement, as well as economic and immigration status, quality of teaching and teacher experience, and overall child well-being, which includes physical and mental health and other critical contextual variables (Bryk et al. 2010; Epstein 2011; Rothstein 2004). Funding for these supports is a prerequisite for academic achievement for many students in low-income communities.

THE PLACE OF THE COURTS IN EQUITABLE SCHOOL FUNDING

When we consider the place of the courts in issues involving funding public education, we must look at the recent history of judicial decisions and the schools. No one can deny the impact of the *Brown v. Board of Education* case, which called for desegregation of public schools in 1954, based on the simple but profound proposition that separate was not equal. When we look back on this case today, the reality is that desegregation has not been fully implemented, yet this does not negate its relevance to fundamental social policy.

Similarly, court cases regarding educational adequacy are often won in state courts, but practices struggle to keep up with court decisions. Since 1989, plaintiffs in educational adequacy cases have won almost 70 percent of final decisions, forcing states to devote more funds to schools in low-income districts in needs of resources (Rebell 2009). As Baker and Corcoran (2014) point out, even though many of these court victories have yet to be fully implemented, educational adequacy has become an important part of state education law. Funding formulas change each year, but laws are far more stable and educational adequacy has become firmly entrenched in educational terminology through these successful court cases. Even with partially implemented rulings, states direct more money to low-income districts, and the weighted distribution of state funds in favor of disadvantaged schools is an accepted practice.

How do court cases that garner increased funding matter? Does increased funding lead to better education for children living in low-income neighborhoods? If so, how? These are difficult questions to address using standardized data that are usually limited to test scores and graduation rates. Increases and decreases in test scores are not always stable; these are affected by test takers, allotted test time, the NCLB standard, changes in tests and testing procedures over the years, and, unfortunately, occasional cheating by teachers and principals.

For example, between 1994 and 1998 scores on the Texas Assessment of Academic Skills exam rose, and the pass rate for success was outstanding, going from 52 percent to 72 percent. It turned out that the increased scores could mostly be attributed to transferring children into special education classes and allowing dropouts to leave schools prior to the testing (Haney 2000; Rebell 2009). In Atlanta, test scores were raised when teachers erased wrong answers and substituted correct ones (Winerip 2013). Relying solely on test scores as assessments of the impact of funding is not always accurate and can promote stresses for school personnel, which in most extreme cases leads to unethical behavior.

As for graduation rates, they too can be manipulated. Hanushek & Linseth (2004) call attention to New Jersey, which has reported high rates of graduation since its state funding formula has been revised as a result of years of litigation. Again we see a problem with the data. New Jersey, as well as other states have included students who failed to graduate but later earned their diplomas by taking the GED test or by earning alternative types of diplomas. In some states, only students who graduated in four years are included in the data, while in others students who took as many as seven years to graduate are part of state reports (Rebell 2009). This mixed use of data and reporting among the states makes it difficult to use graduation rates as a basis for school performance assessment.

Therefore, in order to profit from measures like standardized tests and graduation rates, we need statistical clarity and transparent, consistent methodology. All schools need to articulate the process of securing these data when they report them. This includes schools with school-linked services programs, among which are community schools that rely on these data as indicators of their efforts and as ways to increase funding and reputation.

Increased funding, garnered through court cases or other methods, means that programs can be available for children who are likely to have few similar resources either from their schools, families, or communities. Afterschool tutoring, sports, arts, and community fellowship and service are examples of activities that many children in moderate- or high-income districts enjoy by virtue of their families' and communities' economic status. Children in low-income communities gain equal footing when these kinds of enrichment and extended day programs are funded so that they can be linked with and/or based at schools and be accessible to all children.

THE CAMPAIGNS FOR FISCAL EQUITY AND EDUCATIONAL EQUITY

The Campaign for Fiscal Equity began in 1993 when concerned parents challenged the way New York State was allocating educational funding. They sued the state, claiming that New York City children were being discriminated against due to inequitable funding of their public schools. The ruling favored the children and the court defined "sound basic education" in terms of providing students with a "meaningful high school education" that will prepare them to "function productively as civic participants" (*Campaign for Fiscal Equity, Inc., v. State of New York* 2003; Rebell 2012:52). The legal process continued with a lawsuit filed in 2014 demanding that New York State sufficiently fund all its schools so that children may have educational opportunities (Campaign for Educational Equity 2014a; Education Law Center 2015). As noted above, states do not always follow the rulings of courts in educational funding matters, often by claiming fiscal challenges (Baker & Corcoran 2014). An example of this occurred in New York State, where the state legislature passed the Education Budget and Reform Act of 2007, which called for the distribution of funding based on both student needs and the ability of localities to pay with local revenues. The recession of 2008 caused New York State to renege on its commitment to schools; funding was cut and has not yet been restored to the amount promised by the 2007 act. This prompted the renewal of legal challenges by New Yorkers for Students' Educational Rights and the court filing of 2014 (Campaign for Educational Equity 2014a; Education Law Center 2015).

Michael Rebell, JD, was an early proponent of fiscal equity and continues to be a leader of the effort. Upon joining the faculty of Teachers College at Columbia University, he founded the Campaign for Educational Equity, a nonprofit research and policy center housed at Teachers College. Its purpose is to assure that all children have meaningful educational opportunities and that schools receive the resources they need to provide supports and services to disadvantaged children (Campaign for Educational Equity 2014b). A profile of the work of the Campaign for Educational Equity follows.

CAMPAIGN FOR EDUCATIONAL EQUITY (Information provided by Michael Rebell, JD)

BRIEF OVERVIEW

The Campaign for Educational Equity came out of my initial work with the Campaign for Fiscal Equity, which was successful in convincing the court that New York State needed to more equitably distribute funds to low-income district schools, primarily in New York City. The state's defense was that poor academic achievement was a result of low socioeconomic status, and not inadequate funding of schools. It argued that by the time kids are five years old, the die is cast and that their life situation precludes them from making much progress in school. Although we won, I thought that there was some validity to that position. So when the case was over, and I came to Teachers College, I started the Campaign for Educational Equity. First our focus was fiscal equity, and now my colleagues and I focus on educational dimensions and find out how much impact socioeconomic status makes, and what we can do about it.

The first thing we did was commission a large range of papers from Teachers College and other places to review the literature and analyze the relationship between early childhood experiences and academic achievement, as well as better health services, family engagement, and more time in school. The research strongly substantiates the fact that having these services does make a huge difference, especially cumulatively. Afterschool services on their own did not show a huge gain but when you combined it with health services, and pre-K, the evidence is overwhelming. I engaged Richard Rothstein in this work, and he came up with numbers that showed that New York City is already spending a lot of money on these services but not as coordinated or efficiently as they might be. The bottom line is that it would cost between $4,000 and $5,000 per child above what we are now spending for education to provide the full range of services in a quality manner. That is without taking into account some of the greater efficiencies you could get if you linked these kinds of services in a better manner. These numbers are from a few years ago, but we had a start.

For example, the Say Yes program in Syracuse linked the summer school recreation program to the city's Parks Department, which in turn worked it into its summer programming. This linkage saved the schools a lot of money in that they did not have to pay for recreational personnel. This is the kind of thing we are trying to look at more closely. We are also studying ways to reconsider various laws and regulations. For instance in the health area, I think you could have an enormous expansion of health services if you could deal with the irrational impediments that Medicaid puts in the way of schools' operating school-based health clinics. If schools could get a per capita guarantee of reimbursement for services provided to children, many more schools would open such clinics, which make a huge difference in the availability and actual use of health services by students from disadvantaged backgrounds. We are also trying to show that this would result in a net savings to Medicaid. Those services can be provided much more efficiently at the school level, and for less money. In essence our project has moved from doing the basic research for understanding the problems to laying out a direction for implementation of some of these programs in this current fiscal climate.

Teacher's College is now working with a public school in which we are creating a community school of sorts. We are starting with the first grade, and we expect it to eventually run as preschool through high school. We are committing our students and faculty to work on creating a school that is based on children's needs. We also have partnerships with other schools in Harlem, where we are working towards creating a comprehensive model. We are intent on bringing as many services as possible to kids by integrating services with the schools. We organized a task force consisting of people from different groups, including the Harlem Children's Zone and Say Yes. We have been looking at dozens of community school models, and we see strengths and problems with all of them. Our basic position is that it is essential that schools find ways to provide comprehensive services to kids, but they need to be appropriate to the context. For example, a model like the Harlem Children's Zone is wonderful, but it is very expensive. Cincinnati's model has a much bigger impact, and it is less expensive, but services are less intense.

When you get to the implementation stage, there are tremendous challenges. First of all, there should be an assessment of what kids in that particular school or area really need in priority order, and that is easier said than done. For example, you have to sell the idea to teachers and parents and convince them that this is important and that they should put time and effort into it. With teachers and administrators, you have to understand that they need to put their educational responsibilities first and that it is not easy for them to find time to work on facilitating a different model. Ideas for change sound great in the abstract, but like anything else, actually implementing them is a major challenge.

My thinking is that the Campaign for Educational Equity will become more involved in the application of school-based services on a large scale. For example, in the area of health, we are looking into social impact funds and other ways to bring the concept of school-linked services beyond demonstration projects to large-scale implementation.

• • •

There are currently no large-scale federal funding programs dedicated to community-school partnerships, school-linked services, or full service community schools. Instead, there are a number of grant programs with limited awards. Aside from the Title I ESEA funds, schools interested in developing and expanding their school-linked services, family, and community partnerships have to apply for state and federal grants, a process that requires considerable expertise, time, and effort. Additionally, on the state level, schools in need face competition from other public schools including charter schools. Nevertheless, aided by dedicated activists, selective political support, the Coalition for Community Schools and other organizations profiled in this chapter and preceding ones, many schools have succeeded in procuring needed funds.

Evidence points to funding as an important propellant of student outcomes, and although there is controversy surrounding this concept, most educators and the courts have, in large part, agreed. This discussion will be continued in the following chapter, which focuses on educational outcomes.

9

Assessing Outcomes

FOR ALL SCHOOLS—THOSE with and without strong family and community partnerships—the educational "outcomes" most discussed by the media are standardized test results, spurred on by the No Child Left Behind (NCLB) legislation of 2002 and the U.S. Department of Education's (DOE) policies since then. But there are additional ways to measure educational achievement, including attendance, graduation rates, grades, college acceptance, and citizenship preparation—the last being gauged by community service behaviors. Other measures have been suggested and are often assessed as well, including utilization of services, development of positive self-image, and creativity.

Despite the multiple assessment measures available, standardized test scores have become central in measuring school success. The use of standardized test scores as a primary means of determining academic achievement and funding is controversial, though, with a growing number of educators, parents, and politicians voicing opposition. Nevertheless, supporters of standardized tests remain convinced that testing learning outcome is the most accurate and efficient way of measuring individual achievement as well as the efficacy of the schools. We begin with a discussion of standardized tests and the controversy surrounding their use and move on to additional ways of measuring learning.

THE STANDARDIZED TEST CONTROVERSY

The NCLB legislation of 2002 made it clear that schools, not individual children, would be held responsible for students' achievement, which would be measured quantitatively by scores on reading and mathematics tests. While penalties were laid out for schools that were deemed "failing," the states remained responsible for testing their students based on their state-developed curricula and tests. The same tests had to be given to all schools; there could be no differentiation between high- and low-achieving schools or differences in curricula. As already noted, this arrangement was based on the idea that education is in the hands of the states and not the federal government. Most public education funding does come from the state legislatures, but originates from federal block grants and state and local taxes. The federal government's direct contribution to education primarily focuses on schools in economically poor districts, special education, and a number of specific programs.

In the past forty years, federal funds have consistently comprised approximately 8–13 percent of state education budgets. The fact that each state takes on the bulk of both funding and implementing public education creates significant differences across the fifty states. For example, Vermont, followed by New York and New Jersey, spent the most money per student on K–12 education in 2012–13 (National Education Association 2014). With decisions on expenditures for public education remaining at the states' discretion, varying standards in academic achievement across states became a problem for federal policymakers. How could the DOE differentiate the NCLB's so-called failing schools from one state to another with fifty different standards for funding and assessing failing schools?

To promote some across-state consistency, educators moved forward with the state-initiated development of the Common Core Standards, which were followed by a system of associated tests. The Common Core Standards were developed by the state governors, the National Governor's Association (NGA), and the Council of Chief State School Officers (CCSSO) with funding from private concerns—chiefly the Bill and Melinda Gates Foundation (Ravitch 2013).

The Common Core Standards have two parts: reading and mathematics in the K–12 grades, and readiness for entry into higher education.

For the states, the motive for the development of the Common Core and continued monitoring by the Governors Association was to assure that students graduating from high school had a standard level of competence. Students would thus be better able to succeed in the increasingly competitive economy, and businesses would have workers who met their needs and expectations.

Initially, the Common Core consisted only of standards, and states were expected to develop their own assessments, which was very similar to what they had been doing all along. In 2010 the federal government (via the DOE) provided two consortia of states that had adopted the standards with a total of $330 million to create an assessment system to be used by all adoptee states by 2014. Some educators criticized federal funding for test development, believing that DOE had overstepped its authority (Ravitch 2014). DOE paid for but was not otherwise involved in the writing of the tests, although it did provide substantial technical and organizational assistance to the consortia for this purpose.

Further controversy arose regarding assessment of the Common Core. In 2009, when Race to the Top competitive monies were first awarded, states had to agree to a system of standardized learning goals and tests, even when these goals and tests had yet to be developed. Later, states receiving Race to the Top funding had to adopt the Common Core standards and agree to use the tests, providing further incentives (or pressures) for states to adopt these standardized assessment measures.

Forty-six states plus the District of Columbia adopted the Common Core Standards, but some states subsequently bailed out. Alaska, Nebraska, Texas, and Virginia never adopted the Common Core Standards and instead continued to use their own state-developed standards and testing. By the end of 2014 other states that had initially adopted the Common Core Standards had withdrawn. These states opted to use their own standards and tests, which included many, but not all, aspects of the Common Core to determine academic achievement and readiness for graduation. This group included Florida, Georgia, Indiana, Iowa, Michigan, Minnesota, New Hampshire, Oklahoma, and South Carolina and others. States unwilling to adopt Common Core in the first place were primarily reacting to the general perception that the federal government should stay out of the states' jurisdiction on determining public school standards (Common Core Issues 2014). Additionally, there have been districts within states that have dropped the Common Core. Recently, some families have also decided to "opt out" (Associated Press 2014). States opting out or never adopting the national standards and tests remained eligible for federal programs through the waiver process for ESEA and other DOE funding.

It is clear from observing Common Core State Standards and testing that outcome measures, funding, and policy are closely connected. As noted in chapter 8, some educators think that funding should be based solely on outcomes and that policy should support whatever works to increase overall student achievement. They criticize the close connection between funding and policy, arguing that it inhibits innovations and provides monies to support the status quo (Hanushek & Lindseth 2009). Others disagree. They view outcome results as only one aspect of our national policies supporting inclusion and equal opportunities and believe funding needs to be equitable across districts in order for all students to be able to achieve quality outcomes (Darling-Hammond 2010). Additionally, politics comes to bear on the controversy. State legislatures have been deeply divided on the use of the Common Core State Standards and testing, and their use is being challenged even in states where they have been adopted. In some cases these challenges are bipartisan and in others they follow political party affiliation, making the future of the standards less than assured.

In general, standardized testing is not without its staunch defenders and equally passionate debunkers. Other than school desegregation, standardized testing has likely been the most prominent educational issue taken up by educators and media alike over the past fifty years. Standardized testing is not a new concept. New York State, for example, has been using standardized tests, known as its Regents exams, since the late nineteenth century. These tests created a multiple tier system whereby college-bound students who passed the Regents examination received Regents diplomas and those who did not were granted local district diplomas. New York State still uses Regents exams, but they are now infused with the Common Core State Standards. In addition, the state no longer awards local diplomas; instead, it awards only Regents diplomas, at two levels—the Regents diploma and the Regents diploma with advanced designation.

New York State is but one example of the long-term use of state-developed testing in secondary schools. Most states had their own systems that were similar and did not result in major controversy, largely because students who did not pass the tests could graduate on the basis of alternative tests, waivers from taking any tests, and alternative types of diplomas (Rebell 2009). Regardless of whether the Common Core State Standards and its tests prevail, federal funding requirements remain closely connected to standardized testing, though not necessarily the Common Core. The newly revised ESSA calls for states to decide on the standards and tests they wish to use. States can now create their own standards and tests without pressure or penalties from the DOE. States may remain with the Common Core Standards and tests, but the DOE is expressly prohibited from either insisting or encouraging them to do so (Every Student Succeeds Act, 2015).

Arguments in Favor of and Opposed to the Common Core State Standards Initiative

Proponents of the Common Core see it as a way of raising national education standards so that the United States can become more globally competitive, especially in commerce, which increasingly requires high-level technical skills. Much has been made of the fact that the United States has lagged behind in international rankings in reading, math, and science education, according to the Organization for Economic Cooperation and Development (OECD). In tests given in 2012 to participating countries by the OECD (often referred to as the PISA tests), the United States ranked seventeenth in reading, twenty-sixth in math, and twenty-first in science. These approximate ratings (from tests given every three years) have held true for the past decade.

During that time frame, other countries made progress in their scores, including Poland, Germany, Ireland, and Vietnam. The lack of movement in the United States' rankings has concerned many educators, including Education Secretary Arne Duncan. The educational stagnation he perceived contrasted with President Obama's view, expressed in a 2009 speech, that the United States possessed "the best-educated, most competitive workforce in the world" (Obama 2009; Resmovits 2014).

Common Core does not mandate curriculum. Rather, it creates standards for evaluation, which are meant to include the skills and knowledge arguably needed for success in the global economy. Districts and teachers determine how to teach and what materials to use in the classroom. Since the Common Core State Standards include only language arts and mathematics, they do not address the remainder of what is taught in school. Their supporting organizations have included the U.S. Army, the American Federation of Teachers (AFT), the College Board, the Council of Great City Schools, the National Association of Secondary School Principals, and the national Parent Teacher Association, to name just a few (The Common Core 2014).

Although polls show that about 75 percent of educators continue to support the Common Core Standards, there is increasing opposition largely based on implementation concerns, including insufficient support and funding from the state and federal governments (Obrien 2014; Williams 2014). At the time of this writing, neither the Coalition for Community Schools nor the Federation for Community Schools has taken a public stance regarding the Common Core State Standards Initiative.

The National Education Association (NEA), which was initially a supporter, has voiced strong concern about the viability of the initiative, especially in terms of what its president, Dennis Van Roekel, sees as poor implementation and insufficient input from teachers (National Education Association 2014). Educator and historian Diane Ravitch is a leading spokesperson expressing concerns about the Common Core's emphasis on testing. In a speech to the Modern Language Association, Dr. Ravitch stated that she supports the concept of learning standards, but favors more flexibility within standards and does not support the current testing regimen, which she predicts will lead to failure for so many young people: "I fear that the Common Core plan of standards and testing will establish a test-based meritocracy that will harm our democracy by parceling out opportunity, by ranking and rating every student in relation to their test scores." She goes on to say that each and every one of us should have "the opportunity to learn, the resources needed to learn, and the chance to have a good and decent life, regardless of one's test scores" (Ravitch 2014:18).

Another prominent educator with concerns is Tom Loveless, a senior fellow at the Brown Center on Educational Policy and the Brookings Institute. He has written that implementation is crucial, and because there is very little evidence about which curriculum materials are superior to others, it is likely that teachers and school curricula specialists will chose materials that are closely related to the Common Core tests. He worries this will result in teaching to the tests, as opposed to teaching to the children (Loveless 2014).

Where Community Schools Stand in This Controversy

Public community schools and public schools with school-linked services are subject to the same set of standards as other public schools in their states. Depending on where they are situated, they may be required to use

Common Core State Standards and testing. This means that in the states remaining with the Common Core, most schools with school-linked services are required to adopt them as well. The dilemma is that since the majority of these schools serve children and families in low-income districts with large numbers of minority students and recent immigrant families, Common Core tests could very well raise failure rates to unacceptable levels, despite increased supportive services to students who may still be making progress according to other measures.

A recent experience in New York State illustrates this dilemma. There, when state tests reflecting the Common Core State Standards were given in 2013, one year prior to the actual rollout of the official Common Core tests, 31 percent of students in grades 3–8 passed math and English tests, compared to previous years where 65 percent passed in math and 55 percent passed in English using the easier state-developed tests. The data are even worse for New York State minority children, of whom only 16.1 percent of African American and 17.7 percent of Hispanic students in grades 3–8 passed the English test in 2013 (Crotty 2013). These high failure rates were due in part to a state-mandated increase in the passing grade from the traditional 65 to 75, and then again to 80. Students in all parts of the state had difficulty passing, but children from unstable homes and those living in poverty had lower chances of success—especially when their schools lacked strong community partnerships for services and programs to level the playing field.

Data from schools with integrated community supports have shown that test scores increase upon involving families in the educational process and providing health and behavioral health services to children at school (Epstein 2011). The Coalition for Community Schools keeps track of community school successes in increasing test scores and notes several schools that have made important gains. The Tulsa Area School Community Initiatives Program published a 2010 report comparing achievement scores of eighteen community schools and eighteen non-community schools in the Tulsa area and showing that students in the community schools who were economically disadvantaged and received mentoring and other services scored higher than economically disadvantaged students in the traditional schools. The report indicates that community schools give an extra boost to students who may have few home and neighborhood resources, a phenomenon often reflected in standardized test scores (Adams 2010).

The Roosevelt Community School in Allentown, Pennsylvania, is an example of a United Way–sponsored community school program, known as COMPASS, which has shown very positive results in raising test scores in reading and mathematics. According to the Coalition, the school advanced its proficiency in reading scores from 33.8 percent in 2006 to 46 percent in 2010. School scores moved in proficiency in mathematics from 50.9 percent in 2006 to 65 percent in 2010 (Coalition for Community Schools 2014).

These are but a few examples of community schools raising achievement scores for children from neighborhoods in need of resources. Other examples are cited in the exemplars and research provided throughout this book. Despite the centrality of standardized tests used in educational assessment today, most educators concerned with equity and supportive of school-linked services acknowledge the importance of assessing educational success through a range of measures. Before we highlight the many ways schools with integrated community partnerships and services measure success beyond standardized test scores, we outline the standards and testing provisions of the Every Student Succeeds Act.

The Every Student Succeeds Act and Education Standards and Standardized Tests

Under the new ESSA, states will be responsible for creating "challenging standards" for their public schools as they did prior to the development of the Common Core State Standards Program. They may also choose the Common Core State Standards. States receiving monies from the ESSA will be required to submit to the DOE an accountability plan describing how they will be measuring student achievement based on their selected standards. Proficiency on state tests or Common Core tests in English and Math, with a 95 percent participation rate and a reporting system showing scores for both whole schools and sub-groups will determine if achievement levels are within a satisfactory range. A small number of states could ask the DOE for permission to use local tests; an approved plan for reporting results would need to be in place. States and districts will have to manage accountability when there is a less than 95 percent participation rate in test taking.

Outcome measures will also include data on additional indicators such as English language proficiency and at least one additional academic factor such as growth in state test results. States will need to include at least one non-academic indicator examples of which are school climate, teacher or student engagement, post- secondary readiness, or whatever the state chooses (Every Student Succeeds Act 2015).

Clearly there are details to be worked out for the acceptance of accountability plans under the new ESSA and no doubt there will be revisions and possibly waivers so that all states can access federal funds for their schools in poverty areas. There are no time-lines in this version of the ESEA, an important change from NCLB and as already noted states will not be required to evaluate teachers on the basis of student test scores.

BEYOND STANDARDIZED TESTS: OTHER WAYS TO ASSESS OUTCOMES

Tests are but one method used to assess educational achievement. Community schools and schools integrating services as supports often look to a wider cluster of indicators, believing that school success is made up of a complex set of factors, and that standardized testing can lead to "teaching to a test," where the test and not individual students become the focus of education. Researchers recently compiled an annotated bibliography of research published between 2001 and 2013 on the link between behavioral and emotional health interventions and student academic performance (Center for Health and Health Care in Schools 2014). Most of the twenty-eight studies (out of the 157) that fit the rigorous methodological criteria for inclusion relied on a range of indicators and outcomes related to academic success, where an academic outcome was defined *both* in terms of a measure of achievement (e.g., test scores, grades) and in terms of indicators that were "less proximal but still related to academic success" (Center for Health and Health Care in Schools 2014:3), such as absenteeism.

Overall, the studies revealed that school-based behavioral health interventions were associated not only with improved academic achievement, but also with a range of behaviors that influence academic success, including:

1 Increased on-task learning behavior;
2 Improved time management;
3 Stronger goal setting and problem solving;
4 Decreased absenteeism and suspensions;

5 Increased academic motivations;
6 Self-efficacy, commitment to school, and stability during grade-level transitions; and
7 Decreased violence, bullying, and other problem behaviors (Center for Health and Health Care in Schools 2014).

Below we highlight indicators often examined to assess effectiveness of school-community partnerships. These include: graduation rates; grades; attendance; student, family, school, and community engagement; college admissions; service utilization; and, behavior related to good citizenship.

While these are addressed separately or with other variables with which they are intrinsically related, it is important to note that achievement is defined in a variety of ways and is therefore a complicated construct to measure. As a result, all of these measures are in some ways connected with the others.

Graduation Rates

A technologically skilled workforce is an important asset to all countries in our global economy. Although not every child in the United States is interested in attending college, the federal government has made it clear that its primary interest in public education is to encourage a highly skilled workforce that can compete with other nations. Over the years, federal legislation funding education has been based on this premise, as well as on the goal of promoting equality of opportunity. Taken together, these goals allow the federal government to intervene in public education, a domain that otherwise belongs to the individual states.

Although an abundance of evidence suggests that linking schools and communities contributes to an increase in graduation rates, it should be noted that these rates are subject to fluctuations and this may be especially true for children in the economically disadvantaged communities where these rates have been historically depressed. Nevertheless, the Coalition for Community Schools, together with the National Association of Secondary School Principals, issued a 2009 report on eight community schools that experienced important increases in graduation rates (Axelroth 2009). According to the report, demographic similarities across these eight schools include: a preponderance of children from low-income families (60 percent qualify for free school lunches), large numbers of English language learners, and an ethnically diverse population. Typically, these students would not be expected to achieve high graduation rates. The report shows the eight community schools exhibited extremely high rates of graduation, with the rate of college–bound students in many of these schools scoring in the eightieth percentile. One school had a 100 percent graduation rate.

These are highly encouraging statistics, considering that national four-year graduation rates in 2010–11 were 67 percent for African American children and 71 percent for Hispanics (National Center for Education Statistics 2014a). A notable community school, Oyler School, serving K–12 in Cincinnati, had fewer than 20 percent of its students reaching tenth grade in the late 1990s; after implementing a community schools model in 2010, 82 percent of students graduated high school (Jacobson, Hodges, & Blank 2011).

The advantage of graduating from high school cannot be overstated, even when students do not go on to college. Studies have shown that staying in high school and graduating is a stronger indication of economic success than test scores alone (Rothstein 2004). The Census Bureau currently estimates that young people who drop out of school are twice as likely to live in poverty as graduates (National Center for Education Statistics 2011); even getting a GED does not match the economic value of graduating from high school. The reason is a bit elusive, but there is an indication that a diploma is perceived to reflect a person's perseverance and commitment. Even the U.S. Army much prefers to induct high school graduates over those with GEDs, and no armed services today will consider someone without either. These facts make high school graduation crucial for young people; schools assisting in this endeavor are serving not only individual students, but also their current and future families. Without the diploma, the lifetime economic situation for these students is not promising. Lowering dropout rates alone can reduce poverty rates and increase young people's economic opportunities (National Center for Education Statistics 2011). For a more detailed discussion of dropout prevention, see chapter 3, including the exemplar focused on Communities in Schools.

Grades and Attendance Rates

Numerous studies, including a Child Trends report on the impact of integrated student supports (ISS) for academic and nonacademic barriers to achievement, show a correlation between grades and school attendance, which stands in statistical relationship with the rate of high school completion (Anderson Moore & Emig 2014). The ISS approach, even when only partially implemented, is proven to increase academic achievement. This is especially true in math scores, as well as in improving overall attitudes toward school, as reflected by increasing attendance rates (Anderson Moore & Emig 2014; Little, Wimer, & Weiss 2008; Vandell, Reisner, & Pierce 2007).

Interview data suggest that poor grades and erratic attendance impact a young person's decision to drop out of school. According to Bridgeland, Dilulio, and Morison (2006), 35 percent of students who dropped out stated that failing in school was a significant reason for leaving, and 43 percent attributed their decision to drop out to their poor attendance. Attendance Works (http://www.attendanceworks.org/about/), discussed earlier, has initiated some of the most creative and successful work concerned with strategies to increase attendance. Schools with strong integrated supports and services that can improve achievement and attendance are in a good position to reduce dropout rates (see also chapter 3).

Student, Family, School, and Community Engagement

Engagement among students, families, schools, and communities is complex. While many of us believe that these relationships are enhanced by diversity, these relationships grow in complexity as we become a more diverse society. Results from the 2011 National School Climate Survey show that students' feelings that school is not a safe place negatively affect their school attendance. This is especially the case for LGBT youth (Kosciw et al. 2012). Poverty and unsafe neighborhoods designate schools as safe havens, and students' ability to feel safe in school not only impacts attendance but affects achievement as well (Bryk et al. 2010). Bryk and colleagues state: "We found that schools with robust ties to parents and the local community benefited . . . as they . . . create a safer and more orderly environment that would enhance students' participation in schooling" (2010:134).

According to an extensive review of the literature on school climate, feelings of school connectedness or engagement are also impacted by attitudes about how race and ethnicity are managed in the schools (Thapa et al. 2013). Bullying is a notably pervasive topic of concern for all schools, and it directly affects attendance. It is estimated that as many as 160,000 children stay away from school each day for fear of being bullied (Nansel et al. 2001). Not surprisingly, a positive school climate has been found to reduce bullying behavior (Thapa et al. 2013; Meyer-Adams & Conner 2008). The federal Safe Schools–Healthy Students program initiated in 1999 has provided grants to schools and their communities to implement projects aimed at reducing school violence and bullying behaviors (U.S. Department of Education 2014d) and has shown a range of successes in schools implementing evidence-based antibullying programs (e.g., Olweus) across the country. Although the program was not funded in 2014, a school safety program is included in the new ESEA.

Thapa et al. underscore the need for more attention to be paid to the multiple effects of school climate, finding that "sustained positive school climate is associated with positive child and youth development, effective risk prevention and health promotion efforts, student learning and academic achievement, increased student graduation rates and teacher retention" (2013:369). In addition to student engagement with schools, engagement with community is a proven factor in fostering preparation for citizenship in democratic societies (Flanagan et al. 2007). Melaville, Berg, and Blank (2006), writing for the Coalition for Community Schools, describe community-based learning strategies to enhance student connectedness with local communities as well as the larger social environment.

Family engagement is both an indicator and an outcome of a positive school environment. Parent outreach programs, as described by numerous researchers (e.g., Blitz et al. 2013; Noguera 2003), are confirmed to empower families, especially poor and minority parents who see schools as a means for alleviating inequality and marginalization. Bryk et al. report from their research on Chicago public schools that parent involvement in schools predicts "value added to learning" (2010:251) and is a supportive factor that helps create positive change. Epstein's (2011) research emphasizes family engagement in the schools as a key component of increasing children's success. Stormshak et al. (2011) showed that involving families and children in a program that provided school adaption intervention strategies for middle school children attending public schools produced positive results by reducing antisocial behavior and substance abuse.

A meta-analysis of fifty-one studies of family engagement programs in elementary and secondary schools found correlations with higher academic achievement (Jeynes 2012). Researchers at the Harvard Family Research

Project (2014) have identified family engagement in the schools as a priority for further studies. Altogether, research shows that student, family, school, and community engagement are important measures of effective schools.

College Attendance Rates

College attendance rates have increased to almost 70 percent of all high school graduates (U.S. Department of Labor 2013). Those completing college with a bachelor's degree are somewhat lower, at about 59 percent (National Center for Education Statistics 2014b). Yet the data for college completion rates for minorities show that blacks' and Hispanics' graduation rates are noticeably lower. In 2011, the proportion of whites completing a bachelor's degree within six years was 62.1 percent; for Hispanics it was 51 percent, and for blacks, 39.9 percent (Yeado 2013). This disparity is often attributed to college readiness. The growth of remedial courses in college indicates that many students, although motivated, may not be graduating from high school with the skills needed to successfully earn a bachelor's degree (Hanuschek & Lindseth 2009).

Schools with strong service linkages, like other public and private schools today, are in tune with the need not only to improve graduation rates, but to graduate college-ready students. There are no national community school statistics on college admission rates. Instead, we have information collected by the Coalition for Community Schools on individual school successes. Here, the numbers of college acceptances for students in community schools remain encouraging for children living in some of the most difficult circumstances, characterized by family instability, poverty, and neighborhood crime (for details of these data on college admission, see Axelroth 2009).

Utilization of Services

Another way to assess outcomes of community-school partnerships is to examine the actual use of services that these schools offer. When Dryfoos (1997) addressed service utilization in full-service schools, she focused on family planning services utilization. At that time, she reported aggregated statistics of only 10 to 20 percent of students actually utilizing family planning clinics in the schools. However, for the users of these services, contraception use increased, and attitudes toward pregnancy changed so that it was considered less of a viable option.

More recent studies have shown an increase in use of all school-based health services clinics (SBHSC). One large-scale study of urban and rural schools grades K–8 found that about 57.2 percent of children were enrolled in SBHCs, and of this group, 59.3 percent actually used the clinics. Clinic services were used at an average of about three times per person. Urban children were more likely to use these clinics, as were African American children. The clinics reported that asthma and ADHD were the most common reasons for utilization (Wade et al. 2008). The Children's Aid Society has found that in the five schools that it operates as full-service community schools with SBHCs, 83 percent of the students are enrolled in the clinics. Its SBHCs were utilized 28,000 times in 2010–2011; in addition, over 40 percent of children in the schools have utilized school-based dental services (Children's Aid Society 2012). Advocacy and outreach regarding the availability of school-linked services significantly increases use, but much more research is needed to better support increased utilization.

Behavior Related to Good Citizenship

One purpose of the public school system is to foster educated citizens who can successfully participate in our democratic system, follow our laws, and contribute to the well-being of local communities. The effectiveness of good citizenship education is difficult to measure, but one way is to look at youth participation in community service projects. Community-based learning, an approach advocated by the Coalition for Community Schools (Melaville, Berg, & Blank 2006), it involves several domains: academically based community service, civic education, environmental education, place-based learning, service learning, and work-based learning. (Darling-Hammond 2010), (Pappano 2010), and (Rothstein 2004) argue that community-based learning promotes good citizenship and enhances students' fit into the world of organizations, work, and the larger society. Below, we discuss these different types of community-based learning made possible by community partnerships; assessing their impacts is a critical factor for their expansion.

Academically based community service (ABCS) capitalizes on partnership projects between universities and public schools. College students work with public school children on a wide range of community projects and offer their skills and knowledge to their younger partners. At the same time, college students learn about and contribute to the community, school, and their peers. Secondary school students may join college classes or college events to learn about college through first-hand experiences.

The University of Pennsylvania's Netter Center has advanced the practice of ABCS and assessed its significance through its pioneering university-assisted community schools, and other universities around the country have followed. "Students from the University of Pennsylvania and from local public schools of West Philadelphia work and learn together in the context of courses. Teams of Penn and West Philadelphia student leaders have collaborated with one another to bring about positive change in the community" (Barbara and Edward Netter Center for Community Partnerships 2012). Chapter 4 includes details about outcomes for public school students and schools associated with the Netter Center's ABCS programs.

Civic education occurs when students have the opportunity to participate in local government services and activities. It is meant to promote an understanding of how governments function and to support a positive attitude toward participating in civic projects. An example of a civic project is having students work in a local soup kitchen or homeless shelter. The Maryland Department of Education notes a variety of successful civic projects (Maryland Department of Education 2003).

Environmental education occurs when students determine the needs of the environment of their school or community, and it is participatory in that students decide on projects and envision what they would like to accomplish and learn in the process. The U.S. Environmental Protection Agency has suggestions for environmental projects for school-age children (U.S. Environmental Protection Agency 2014).

Place-based education occurs through the process of being situated in a place such as a nursing home, a housing project office, or any place in the community where students can learn from personnel at the site. Workers at these sites guide students in learning about the needs of their clientele and how they attempt to satisfy those needs.

Service learning combines on-site experiences with academic understanding of the role of service providers. For example, students might learn in school about the importance of early childhood learning centers and then be placed in a center, where they see first-hand how the center functions and understand the children's and family members' experiences of the services provided.

Work-based learning occurs when students have the opportunity to spend time in a place of work so that they can learn what is required of a particular job. The work sites can vary from small businesses, to professional offices, to large-scale corporations. When information gained from work-based learning informs school curricula, the learning process becomes interactive (Melaville, Berg, & Blank 2006). As part of its community schools efforts, Hartford, Connecticut, has built a range of partnerships with local businesses to provide work-based experience for public school students (see chapter 3).

Each of these community-based learning opportunities has an important place in schools with strong community partnerships because of the relationships they foster among the school, family, and community. For many students, community learning can raise self-esteem, especially for those who are not high academic achievers. Instead of viewing community-based learning as an alternative form of education, it is best to see it as an integral part of the learning process that complements children's academic experience.

Many colleges today expect community service from their applicants, seeing such service as a way to discern character and maturity. A 2008 study coming out of the Harvard Family Research Project found that in addition to its impact on citizenship, consistent attendance in high-quality community-based programs resulted in better attitudes toward school and higher education, better attendance and fewer disciplinary actions, lower dropout rates, better grades, and overall improved engagement in learning (Little, Wimer, & Weiss 2008). A 2005 study (Billig, Root, & Jesse 2005) of the impact of community-based learning on high school students' civic engagement utilized a national sample of classrooms of students who participated in community-based learning matched with classrooms of students of similar demographic and achievement backgrounds who did not participate in these opportunities. The following results were found:

1. Student outcomes improved when community-based learning programs lasted longer, although year-long programs often had slightly less benefit than semester-long programs.
2. Teacher characteristics were related to outcomes. Number of years of teaching experience was significantly related to some student outcomes

(valuing school, enjoying math and science, civic skills, and civic dispositions). Longer experience using community-based learning was associated with higher civic knowledge, civic dispositions, and efficacy scores.

3 The type of community-based learning project was related to the outcomes. Students who engaged in direct service (e.g., tutoring or visiting seniors) were most attached to their communities. Students who engaged in indirect service (e.g., fundraising or research) showed the highest levels of academic engagement. Students who engaged in political or civic action (e.g., circulating a petition or organizing a community forum) scored highest on civic knowledge and civic dispositions.

While there is some evidence of a link between participation in substantive community-based activities and later civic behavior, there is a need for more research on the effects of these activities on long-term civic and other behaviors and attitudes (Rothstein 2004). One potential measure that lends itself to evaluation is performance-based assessment, which presents results in narrative and other formats in a portfolio to be assessed by faculty. According to Darling-Hammond (2010), this is sometimes called the *portfolio system*, and is a way of describing the finished capstone project. These projects are examples of the educational concept of *authentic achievement* (Newmann, Marks, & Gamoran 1995); proponents claim they promote inquiry, analysis, and communication and presentation skills. In addition to their use as assessment tools, they may also promote creativity and enhance a sense of achievement, especially for students in need of additional encouragement.

THE NATIONAL RESULTS AND EQUITY COLLABORATIVE

In May 2014, the National Results and Equity Collaborative (NREC) was announced as a new player in the field of educational assessment. This consortium includes the Coalition for Community Schools with its mission to help vulnerable children succeed academically. The group was established to "(1) accelerate positive results for vulnerable children throughout the country by creating a national network to align results-based technical assistance, measures, effective strategies and solutions across multiple national and local initiatives; and, in so doing, (2) promote consistency and greater impact in the use of results-based methodologies at the federal, state and local levels" (National Results and Equity Collaborative 2014). A summary of a conversation with Nina Sazer O'Donnell, director of NREC, is provided below.

National Results and Equity Collaborative (NREC)

INTERVIEWER: *What led to the founding of your organization?*

NINA SAZER O'DONNELL: In August 2012, several leaders of national organizations, all working on improving educational outcomes for the most vulnerable children, came together to explore how to align their work, given that in many communities, the same local constituents were working on several initiatives with similar but slightly different goals, definitions, measures, and often redundant technical assistance. These leaders then decided that the time was right to create tools and processes to build greater alignment, hypothesizing that doing so would help accelerate results and enable communities to improve conditions that help young people at greater scale.

INTERVIEWER: *How is your organization funded?*

NSO: We were not funded for the first one and a half years of development, with partners all contributing time, talent, and treasure to the effort. In January 2014, the Annie E. Casey Foundation joined the partnership and provided a planning grant, which is funding current efforts. The group also agreed not to start a new organization, but to function as a collaborative, staffed by a consultant (me). The Center for the Study of Social Policy acts as fiscal agent.

INTERVIEWER: *In your mission statement online you address the importance of community-school partnerships: "a shared commitment to building community capacity, allowing multiple initiatives to generate evidence about how community capacities contribute to results." Are there any additional ideas you would like to add to your organization's commitment to enhancing community supports for children in need of the resources to succeed in school?*

NSO: The whole effort is focused on multiple local strategies, broad grass tops and grass roots engagement, and aimed at improving community conditions for helping the most vulnerable kids and families (from cradle to career) succeed.

INTERVIEWER: *What do you see your organization accomplishing in the next five years?*

NSO: Ultimately our goal is national adoption of aligned measures and strategies for multisector local and state collaboratives aimed at improving school and life outcomes for the most vulnerable children and youth.

INTERVIEWER: *Are there specific goals that are being set for schools and/or students?*

NSO: Yes—the first set are really for many players in communities, including schools and students, and relates to improving young children's success (birth–eight). They are: (1) families are strong and supportive; (2) births are healthy and well timed; (3) children are safe, healthy, and developing on track; (4) children are emotionally, socially, and cognitively ready for school; and (5) children perform on grade level (literacy and numeracy).

INTERVIEWER: *Are there specific indicators such as test scores, graduation rates, college admissions, etc., that will be used to judge your successes?*

NSO: Yes, we are working on shared goals and measures, starting with a first set focused on results for children from birth to age eight. Next, we'll tackle similar tools for older children and youth. We are also establishing a curated resource library of technical assistance (TA) tools and resources to help communities succeed.

INTERVIEWER: *Who will be conducting evaluations, determining indicators, etc.?*

NSO: At this point, communities will be, but we hope to find future funding to evaluate various strategies and progress overall.

INTERVIEWER: *Can you identify any social policy or funding obstacle that needs to be addressed in order for your mission to succeed?*

NSO: The biggest one is the lack of coordination among various public and private funders—they often work and fund work in parallel, rather that helping communities leverage multiple resources to more powerful and aligned results. Various public and private sector funders also often fail to build the capacity of local communities to produce results using strategic planning disciplines that can add up to more than individual initiatives. It could also really help if there were ways for public education, housing, transportation, economic development, nutrition, social services, child welfare, health care, and other dollars (from pre-K to higher education) to be braided more flexibly to fund aligned and focused results-based local work.

• • •

Since schools with strong community partnerships operate within the same policy context as all schools, in this chapter we attempted to provide an overview of the policies and legislation that govern evaluation of all schools in the United States. Given that these assessment tools are often used to argue the value of schools with strong community partnerships, such schools need to consider them even if they are flawed.

In addition to traditional means of assessment through standardized testing, many schools with strong community linkages also assess student success according to a wider array of outcomes, including graduation, grades, college acceptance, attendance, civic service, and service utilization. Ultimately, the true test of the value of school-community linkages comes when looking at their ability to cut across economic realms such that students in low-income communities succeed at a level equivalent to those in middle-class communities. Then, the public school system will be characterized by equity and have a goal of breaking the cycle of poverty—the primary objective of linking schools and communities.

Epilogue

CREATING A SUCCESSFUL SCHOOL-COMMUNITY PARTNERSHIP FOR SCHOOL-LINKED SERVICES

WE HOPE THIS BOOK has adequately delineated the critical variables to consider, engage, and implement in building and sustaining partnerships between schools and communities to support success for all children. *But where do you start?* It is not a simple process, because to build genuinely integrated systems requires structural change at all levels. Adelman and Taylor (2000) argue that policies and programs are necessary, but not sufficient, for systemic change. Also needed is a redeployment of a multitude of resources, including finances, personnel, time, space, and equipment. This requires change in governance structures, a sophisticated planning process, coordination and integration of people and programs, daily leadership, and communication and information management.

Ferro (1998) delineates specific steps in moving forward. A first step involves identifying roles and key players. This includes designating leadership; identifying other core participants in decision-making and responsibilities; and obtaining buy-in. Buy-in is important at all levels, from superintendents, to boards of education, to all types of school staff (e.g., teachers, counselors, bus drivers, cafeteria staff, etc.), to youth, families, community members, and leaders.

The most comprehensive integrated initiatives require the most buy-in because they are the most far-reaching and benefit from support from community leaders, including local politicians. Once key partners are identified and committed, an assessment process occurs that involves mapping resources (activities, resources, and policies) and needs in the school and community. As an assessment is finalized, a plan can be developed and funding sources identified to support the plan. As discussed in chapter 8, these efforts are almost always supported through a blend of funding from public and private sectors.

Ruglis and Freudenberg (2012) outline roles for professionals and constituents in the process of building what they call "healthy schools." These include roles impacting policies that guide the work of schools, human services, and communities. For example, there are roles for professionals and constituents in joining, creating, and/or leading community councils, coalitions, and forums. Documenting and evaluating the impact of current programs are also critical in moving forward, in addition to summarizing and synthesizing existing research findings for policymakers. It is also critical to support the work and voice of *all* constituents (families, communities, and youth) in both program development and planning, as well as in advocating for increased funding and supportive policies. Ruglis and Freudenberg emphasize the importance of strengthening youth voice and youths' roles in leadership development, service delivery, policy advocacy, and research and evaluation efforts. Additionally, they address the importance of training and educating professionals who work across systems. This is where universities and colleges can be useful partners both in providing continuing education for school and community staff and faculty and in educating the next generation of professionals in the classrooms and through internships.

McKenzie & Richmond (1998) outline three steps to educational reform brought about by linking schools with supports for students' health and well-being:

1 A customized plan: each school and community needs a plan that fits its specific needs, resources, problems, financial capabilities, demographics, and location.
2 Teamwork and constituent involvement: since linkages between schools and communities are based on principles of partnership, teamwork and collaboration need to occur among all constituents—different agencies, professionals, support staff, community members, families, and youth.
3 Commitment to continuing improvement: "systemic changes in schools require a long-term, steady commitment" (1998:11). It also requires continuing education for all school staff, professional development in colleges and universities, and continuous improvement through ongoing research and evaluation.

Taking an approach that is consistent with the guidelines above, the Children's Aid Society National Center for Community Schools (2011) has laid out a detailed needs assessment process to develop a "customized plan" for getting started. This includes:

1 Identifying the team to collect the data;
2 Conducting a resource inventory of existing programs and services;
3 Reviewing archival data to identify patterns and gaps and areas to explore;
4 Conducting surveys with key constituent groups to identify strengths and needs;
5 Interviewing key stakeholders for their interpretation of the data and their suggestions for its implications;
6 Facilitating focus groups of stakeholders;
7 Analyzing the data to develop priorities and an action plan; and
8 Sharing findings and recommendations with stakeholders.

Once a plan emerges from the assessment, a team can come together to carry the work forward. Critical team partners include:

1 A lead partner agency or a district-employed site coordinator;
2 School leaders and other key staff from *all* components of the school;
3 Additional community-based agency partners (e.g., child welfare, local hospital, library, university, law enforcement, local businesses);
4 Parents and other community members;
5 Students;
6 Public and private funders; and
7 Community leaders and elected officials to "champion" the endeavor (Childrens Aid Society, 2011).

After an initial assessment is complete and a team is assembled, the Children's Aid Society (2011) encourages building a supportive infrastructure to support the effort by:

1 Assessing the assets and contributions of all partners, starting off with small efforts and programs and building gradually;
2 Planning short- and long-term programs and negotiating locations;
3 Developing a plan and implementing staff development, paying attention to relationship-building and group problem-solving; and
4 Assessing results.

Once school-community partnerships are in place and programs, services, and structures are operative, all results need to be communicated and marketed to all constituents, funders, and community members (Children's Aid Society 2011) by a variety of means, including websites, emails, and local media.

Because needs and resources are always changing, continuous assessment and flexibility are critical. Below we highlight resources that are available as you move forward on the exciting adventure of linking schools and communities to maximize success.

Resources for Getting Started

Children's Aid Society National Center for Community Schools. 2011. Building community schools: A guide for action. New York: Author.

Coordinated School Health Publications and Resources http://www.cdc.gov/healthyyouth/cshp/publications.htm

How Schools Can Implement Coordinated School Health http://www.cdc.gov/healthyyouth/cshp/schools.htm

Scaling up School and Community Partnerships http://www.communityschools.org/ScalingUp/

The purpose of this book is to demonstrate the advantages of an ongoing trend for public schools in economically challenged neighborhoods to partner with their communities and add services in order to enhance academic achievement and community life. The evidence presented in this book points to the many potential advantages inherent in providing children with supportive services such as health and social service programs. There is further evidence that widespread community and family involvement also increases achievement. With staying in school and moving beyond secondary education having been shown to increase chances of economic gain and avoiding poverty, schooling is a crucial factor for both the well-being of the nation and that of individuals in our country. The social and economic costs of poor educational outcomes are so debilitating that public education issues need to be brought to the forefront of social policy, and legislation needs to respond to the evidence of what is necessary to enhance success for all children.

As some educational activists note, integrated community-school partnerships have evolved into a "social movement." Time will tell if this label holds up, but there is no doubt that the idea is catching on and becoming more and more popular throughout the country. Yet there are challenges, and those with other ideas. Some view charter schools as the way to increase achievement. Others believe that schools should not be addressing issues "outside of the classroom". Some believe that federal policy has no business supporting integrated services for students, and yet others believe the focus should be on evaluating and "changing" teaching, as opposed to assessing and alleviating students' barriers to success. We hope this book has made the case that services and supports for children are critical to combat the impacts of poverty.

There are two additional points to make. First, starting small, with just a few partnerships can lead to larger changes later on. What is vital is that the partnerships are thoughtful, strategic, integrated into the fabric of the school, and match the needs of the children, schools, and communities where they are implemented. The materials presented in this book may seem overwhelming to schools just at the beginning stages, but they are meant to describe what is available and to show how schools have made use of these resources. Second, while this book has not addressed internal conflicts, they are likely to emerge in any change project. Conflicting ideas should be expected and addressed as partnerships form. The bottom line is that not everyone will agree to every change, but school leaders may want to get the assistance of consultants, perhaps from a local college or university, to help mediate controversies. The chapter on collaboration addresses some of the challenges in partnerships; we hope it is also persuasive in terms of their benefits.

There are entire books and websites dedicated to the process of forming and implementing school-community partnerships, and we have featured the voices of many of their leaders. What we offer here is a compendium of what has been achieved and a view of the available resources. For the serious reader, we suggest further research, since, as we have learned, there is no status quo in education. We know that if you are reading this book, you care deeply about children, families, and communities. We wish you the best in your own journey for equity for all.

REFERENCES

100 years of community school history. web.utk.edu/~fss/minutes/history.doc.

Access. 2011. *Litigation.* http://www.schoolfunding.info/litigation/litigation .php3.

Adams, C. 2010. *The community school effect: Evidence from an evaluation of the Tulsa Area Community School Initiative.* Tulsa, OK: Oklahoma Center for Educational Policy.

Adelman, H. 1998. School counseling, psychological and social services. In *Health is academic: A guide to coordinated school health programs,* ed. E. Marx, S. F. Wooley, & D. Northrop, 142–168. New York: Teachers College Press.

Adelman, H. 1996. Restructuring education support services and integrating community resources: Beyond the full service school model. *School Psychology Review* 25 (4): 431–445.

Adelman, H., & L. Taylor. 2000. Promoting mental health in schools in the midst of school reform. *Journal of School Health* 70 (5): 171–175.

Adelman, H. S., V. Lusk, N. R. Alvarez, & K. Acosta. 1985. Competence of minors to understand, evaluate, and communicate about their psychoeducational problems. *Professional Psychology: Research and Practice* 16 (3): 426–434.

Adolescent and School Health. Coordinated school health FAQS. http://www .cdc.gov/healthyyouth/cshp/faq.htm.

Agatston Urban Nutrition Initiative. Netter Center for Community Partnerships. https://www.nettercenter.upenn.edu/programs/auni.

Alderson, J. 1972. Models of school social work practice. In *The school in the community,* ed. R. Sarri & F. Maple, 151–160. Washington, DC: National Association of Social Work Press.

Alexander, K., D. Entwisle, & L. Olson. 2007. Lasting consequences of the summer learning gap. *American Sociological Review* 72 (2): 167–180.

Allan, J. 2012. Emergent spaces: Looking for the civic and the civil in initial professional education. In *The transformation of children's services: Examining and *debating the complexities of interprofessional working*, ed. J. Forbes & C. Watson, 141–153. New York: Routledge.

Allison, M., L. Crane, B. Beaty, A. Davidson, P. Melkinovich, & A. Kempe. 2007. School-based health centers: Improving access and quality of care for low income adolescents. *Pediatrics* 120: 887–894.

Altieri, M., & F. R. Funes-Monzote. 2012. The paradox of Cuban agriculture. *Monthly Review*, January 63 (8). http://monthlyreview.org/2012/01/01/the-paradox-of-cuban-agriculture/.

American Bar Association. 2013. The Uninterrupted Scholars Act: How do recent changes to FERPA help child welfare agencies get access to school records? *Foster Care and Education*. http://www.fostercareandeducation.org/portals/0/dmx/2013/02/file_20130211_145758_xjnFqt_0.pdf.

American Bar Association. 2014. *Mandatory reporting*. http://www.americanbar.org/content/dam/aba/administrative/domestic_violence1/Resources/PracticeArea/mandatoryreporting/Minors_and_Mandatory_Reporting_Flow_Chart.authcheckdam.pdf.

American Bar Association and Casey Family Programs. 2014. Special education decision making: The role of educators. *Special Education Series*. http://www.americanbar.org/content/dam/aba/publications/center_on_children_and_the_law/education/special_ed_series_dm_educators.authcheckdam.pdf.

Anderson-Butcher, D., & D. Ashton. 2004. Innovative models of collaboration to serve children, youths, families and communities. *Children and Schools* 25: 39–53.

Anderson-Butcher, D., H. A. Lawson, J. Bean, P. Flaspohler, B. Boone, & A. Kwiatkowski, A. 2008. Community collaboration to improve schools: Introducing a new model from Ohio. *Children & Schools* 30: 161–172.

Anderson-Butcher, D., & L. Paluta. 2015. Evaluation of the Canyons Community Schools Initiative: Findings after two-year post-adoption and implementation. Columbus, OH: College of Social Work. Ohio State University.

Anderson Moore, K., & C. Emig. 2014. Integrated service support. *Child Trends*. http://www.childtrends.org/wp-content/uploads/2014/02/2014–05ISSWhitePaper1.pdf.

Armbruster, P., E. Andrews, J. Couenhoven, & G. Blau. 1999. Collision or collaboration? School-based health services meet managed care. *Clinical Psychology Review* 19 (2): 221–237.

Associated Press. 2014. 50-state look at how Common Core playing out in U.S. *Huffington Post*, September 2. http://www.huffingtonpost.com/2014/09/02/50-states-common-core_n_5751864.html.

Attendance Works. n.d. Advancing student success by reducing chronic absence. http://www.attendanceworks.org/about/.

Axelroth, R. 2009. *The community schools approach: Raising graduation and college going rates—Community high school case studies.* Washington, DC: Coalition for Community Schools, Institute for Educational Leadership.

Baker, B. D. 2014. America's most financially disadvantaged school districts and how they got that way. Center for American Progress. https://cdn.americanprogress.org/wp-content/uploads/2014/07/BakerSchoolDistricts.pdf.

Baker, B. D. 2012. *Revisiting the age-old question: Does money matter in education?* Washington, DC: Albert Shanker Institute. http://files.eric.ed.gov/fulltext/ED528632.pdf.

Baker, B. D., & S. P. Corcoran. 2012. The stealth inequities of school funding: How state and local finance systems perpetuate inequitable student spending. Center for American Progress, September 19. http://www.americanprogress.org/issues/education/report/2012/09/19/38189/the-stealth-inequities-of-school-funding/.

Bagley, C., & S. Hillyard. 2011. Village schools in England: At the heart of their community. *Australian Journal of Social Work* 55 (1): 37–49.

Barbara and Edward Netter Center for Community Partnerships. 2012. *Universities-communities-schools partners for change.* https://www.nettercenter.upenn.edu/abcs-courses/faq.

Barter, B. 2007. Communities in schools: A Newfoundland school and community outreach in need of stability. *The Alberta Journal of Educational Research* 53 (4): 359–372.

Baru, R. V. 2008. School health services in India: An overview. In *School health services in India*, ed. R. V. Baru, 142–154. Los Angeles: Sage.

Basch, C. E. 2010. *Healthier students are better learners: A missing link in school reforms to close the achievement gap.* New York: Columbia University Press.

Baskind, F. R., & K. Briar-Lawson. 2005. Advancing social work with older adults. *Families in Society* 86 (3): 424–431.

Benson, L., I. Harkavy, & J. Puckett. 2007. *Dewey's Dream: Universities and democracies in an age of education reform.* Philadelphia: Temple University Press.

Benson, L., I. Harkavy, M. Johenek, & J. Puckett. 2009. The enduring appeal of community schools. *American Educator* 33 (2): 22–29, 47.

Berg, A. C., A. Melaville, & M. J. Blank. 2006. *Community and family engagement: Principals share what works.* Washington, DC: Coalition for Community Schools.

Berman-Rossi, T., & P. Rossi. 1990. Confidentiality and informed consent in school social work. *Social Work in Education* 12 (3): 195–207.

Berzin, S. C., K. H. M. O'Brien, A. Frey, M. S. Kelly, M. E. Alvarez, & G. L. Shaffer. 2011. Meeting the social and behavioral health needs of students: Rethinking the relationship between teachers and school social workers. *Journal of School Health* 81 (8): 493–501.

Billig, S., S. Root, & D. Jesse. 2005. *The impact of participation in service- learning on high school students' civic engagement.* CIRCLE Working Paper 33. Denver, CO: RMC Research Corporation.

Blank, M. 2003. *Making the difference: Research and practice in community schools.* Washington, DC: Coalition for Community Schools.

Blank, M. J., R. Jacobson, A. Melaville, & S. S. Pearson. 2010. *Financing community schools: Leveraging resources to support student success.* Washington, DC: Coalition for Community Schools. http://www.communityschools.org/assets/1/assetmanager/finance-paper.pdf.

Blinn, A. M., N. W. Carpenter, & L. A. Mandel. 2012. A newfound voice: Elementary-age student engagement. In *School-based health care: Advancing educational success and public health,* ed. T. D. Wright & J. W. Richardson, 261–267. Washington, DC: American Public Health Association.

Blitz, L., L. Kida, M. Gresham, & L. R. Bronstein. 2013. Prevention through collaboration: Family engagement with rural schools and families living in poverty. *Families in Society* 94 (3): 157–165.

Blunkett, D. 2000. Raising aspirations for the 21st Century. Speech to the North of England Education Conference (January 6). London: DfEE.

Bowers, J. 2013. *Roma inclusion: What we can learn from Croatia.* Open Societies Foundations. http://www.opensocietyfoundations.org/voices/roma-inclusion-what-we-can-learn-croatia.

Brener, N. D., M. Weist, H. Adelman, L. Taylor, & M. Vernon-Smiley. 2007. Mental health and social services: Results from the School Health Policies and Programs Study 2006. *Journal of School Health* 77: 486–499.

Briar-Lawson, K., & J. L. Zlotnik, eds. 2003. *Charting the impacts of university–child welfare collaboration.* Binghamton, NY: Haworth Press.

Bridgeland, J., J. Dilulio, & K. B. Morison. March 2006. *The silent epidemic: Perspectives of high school dropouts.* Washington, DC: Civic Enterprises.

Brimfield, W., A. Ammerman, & L. Juszczak. 2012. Making the business case for school-based health centers. In *School-based health care: Advancing educational success and public health,* ed. T. D. Wright & J. W. Richardson, 417–431. Washington, DC: American Public Health Association.

Bringle, R. B., & J. A. Hatcher. 1996. Implementing service learning in higher education. *Journal of Higher Education* 67 (2): 221–239.

Bronstein, L. R. 2002. Index of interdisciplinary collaboration. *Social Work Research* 26 (2): 113–126.

Bronstein, L. R. 2003. A model for interdisciplinary collaboration. *Social Work* 48 (3): 297–306.

Bronstein, L. R., & J. S. Abramson. 2003. Understanding socialization of teachers and social workers: Groundwork for collaboration in the schools. *Families in Society* 84 (3): 323–330.

Bronstein, L. R., & T. B. Kelly. 1998. A multidimensional approach to evaluating school-linked services: A school of social work and county public school partnership. *Social Work in Education* 20 (3): 152–164.

Bronstein, L. R., A. Ball, E. Mellin, R. Wade-Mdivanian, & D. Anderson-Butcher. 2011. Advancing collaboration between school- and agency-employed school-based social workers: A mixed methods comparison of competencies and preparedness. *Children and Schools* 33 (2): 83–95.

Bronstein, L.R., E. Anderson, S. Terwilliger, & K. Sager. 2012. Evaluating a model of school-based health and social services: An interdisciplinary community-university collaboration. *Children and Schools,* 34 (3), 155–165.

Bronstein, L. R., & S. Terwilliger. 2007. Collaboration in rural school health. In *Conversations in the disciplines: Sustaining rural populations,* ed. L. L. Morgan & P. Fahs-Beck, 13–29. Binghamton, NY: Global Academic Publishing.

Bruner, C. 1991. *Ten questions and answers to help policy makers improve children's services.* Washington DC: Education and Human Services Consortium.

Bryan, J., & L. Henry. 2012. A model for building school-family-community partnerships: Principles and process. *Journal of Counseling & Development* 90: 408–420.

Bryk, A. S., P. B. Sebring, E. Allensworth, S. Luppescu, & J. Easton. 2010. *Organizing schools for improvement: Lessons from Chicago.* Chicago: University of Chicago Press.

Burns, B. J., S. Phillips, H. R. Wagner, R. P. Barth, D. J. Kolko, Y. Campbell, & J. Landsverk. 2004. Mental health need and access to mental health services by youths involved with child welfare: A national survey. *Journal of the Academy of Child and Adolescent Psychiatry* 43 (8): 960–970. doi:10.1097/01.chi.0000127590.95585.65.

Cahill, M. 1997. *Youth development and community development: Promises and challenges of convergence.* Community and Youth Development Series, vol. 2. Takoma Park, MD: Forum for Youth Investment, International Youth Foundation.

Caldwell, D., M. Nestle, & W. Rogers. 1998. School nutrition services. In *Health is academic: A guide to coordinated school health programs*, ed. E. Marx, S. F. Wooley, & D. Northrop, 195–223. New York: Teachers College Press.

California Department of Education. 2014. http://www.cde.ca.gov/.

Campaign for Educational Equity. 2014a. http://www.tc.columbia.edu/equity campaign/?Id=Home&Info=all.

Campaign for Educational Equity. 2014b. Campaign staff. http://www.tc.columbia .edu/equitycampaign/index.asp?Id=ABOUT&Info=Campaign+Staff.

Campaign for Fiscal Equity, Inc., v. State of New York. 2003.100 N.Y. 2d 893.

Campbell-Allen, R., M. P. A. Shah, R. Sullender, & R. Zazove. 2009. *Full-service schools: Policy review and recommendations*. Cambridge, MA: Harvard Graduate School of Education. http://a100educationalpolicy.pbworks.com/f/Full +Service+Schools+complete+paperZ.pdf.

Carey, K. 2015. Federal intervention in schools? It happens less than critics think. *New York Times, Education*, August 20. Electronic version. http://www.nytimes .com/2015/08/21/upshot/federal-meddling-in-schools-it-happens-less-than -critics-think.html?_r=0.

Carlyon, P., W. Carlyon, & A. R. McCarthy. 1998. Family and community involvement in school health. In *Health is academic: A guide to coordinated school health programs*, ed. E. Marx, S. F. Wooley, & D. Northrop, 67–95. New York: Teachers College Press.

Carnie, F. 2006. *Setting up parent councils: Case studies*. UK: Human Scale Education and the Department for Education and Skills. http://webarchive .nationalarchives.gov.uk/20130401151715/http://www.education.gov.uk /publications/eOrderingDownload/RW58.pdf.

Carr, W. G. 1945. *Only by understanding, education, and international organization*. New York: Foreign Policy Association.

Carter, J. L. 1992. Taking a family-centered approach. In *Ensuring student success through collaboration*, 37–45. Washington, DC: Council of Chief State School Officers (CCSSO).

Caruso, N. 2000. Lessons learned in a city-school social services partnership. *Children & Schools* 22 (2): 108–115.

Casto, R. M., M. C. Julia, L. J. Platt, G. L. Harbaugh, W. R. Waugaman, A. Thompson, T. S. Jost, E. T. Bope, T. Williams, & D. B. Lee. 1994. *Interprofessional care and collaborative practice*. Pacific Grove, CA: Brooks/Cole.

Cengage Learning. 2014. The Education for All Handicapped Children Act (PL 94–142) 1975. http://college.cengage.com/education/resources/res_prof/students /spec_ed/legislation/pl_94–142.html.

Center for Health and Health Care in Schools. 2014. *The impact of school-connected behavioral and emotional health interventions on student academic performance: An annotated bibliography of research literature.* Washington, DC: Center for Health and Health Care in Schools. http://www.healthinschools.org/School-Based-Mental-Health/Revised-Annotated-Bibliography.aspx.

Center on Educational Policy. 2014. *Federal Educational Programs. NCLB/ESEA Waivers.* http://www.cep-dc.org/index.cfm?DocumentSubTopicID=48.

Centers for Disease Control and Prevention (CDC). 2010. *School health programs: Improving the health of our nation's youth.* Atlanta, GA: CDC.

Centers for Disease Control and Prevention (CDC). 2013. *Parent engagement: Strategies for involving parents in school health.* Atlanta, GA: CDC.

Centers for Disease Control and Prevention (CDC). 2014. *PS14–1403, Capacity Building Assistance Awards, PS14–1403 Capacity Building Assistance for High-Impact HIV Prevention.* http://www.cdc.gov/hiv/pdf/policies_funding_PS14–1403_CBA_Awardees.pdf.

Centers for Disease Control and Prevention (CDC). n.d. *Building competencies for managers and staff of coordinated school health programs.* Atlanta, GA: CDC. http://www.cdc.gov/healthyyouth/cshp/faq.htm.

Chang, H., & M. Romero. 2008. *Present, engaged and accounted for: The critical importance of addressing chronic absence in the early grades.* New York: National Center for Children in Poverty.

Chang, T., & C. Lawyer. 2012. *Lightening the load: A look at four ways that community schools can support effective teaching.* Washington, DC: Center for American Progress.

Charles Stewart Mott Foundation. 2014. *Community Development in Ukraine through Community School Programs.* Step by Step Foundation. http://www.mott.org/sitecore/content/Globals/Grants/2013/20020318_06_Community%20Development%20in%20Ukraine%20Through%20Community%20School%20Programs.aspx.

Children's Aid Society. 2012. School-based health centers. http://www.childrensaidsociety.org/files/upload-docs/SBHC%20DASHBOARD_2012_1.pdf.

Children's Aid Society National Center for Community Schools. 2011. *Building community schools: A guide for action.* New York: Children's Aid Society.

Child Welfare Information Gateway. https://www.childwelfare.gov/preventing/programs/types/familyresource.cfm.

Christopher, G. 2012. Foreword. In *School-based health care: Advancing educational success and public health,* ed. T. D. Wright, & J. W. Richardson. Washington, DC: American Public Health Association.

Cincinnati Public Schools. http://www.cps-k12.org/.

City Connects. 2011. *City Connects: The lasting impact of optimized student support*. Chestnut Hill, MA: Boston College.

Claessens, A., M. Engel, & F. C. Curran. 2014. Academic content, student learning and the persistence of preschool effects. *American Educational Research Journal* 51 (2): 403–434. doi:10.3102/0002831213513634.

Clandfield, D. 2010. The school as community hub: A public alternative to the neo-liberal threat to Ontario schools. In *The school as community hub: Beyond education's iron cage*, ed. D. Clandfield & G. Martell, 1–74. *Our Schools/Our Selves. Special Issue.* Canadian Centre for Policy Alternatives.

Clandfield, D., & G. Martell, eds. 2010. The school as community hub: Beyond education's iron cage. *Our Schools/Our Selves* 19 (4). Canadian Centre for Policy Alternatives.

Clark, H., & C. Grimaldi. 2005. Evaluation of CAS Community Schools. In *Community schools in action*, ed. J. Dryfoos, J. Quinn, & C. Barkin, 166–184. New York: Oxford University Press.

Classbase. 2012. *Education system in Cuba*. Education Data Base. http://www.classbase.com/Countries/Cuba/Education-System.

Clayton, S., T. Chin, S. Blackburn, & C. Echeverria. 2012. Different setting, different care: Integrating prevention and clinical care in school-based health centers. In *School-based health care: Advancing educational success and public health*, ed. T. D. Wright & J. W. Richardson, 17–24. Washington, DC: American Public Health Association.

Coalition for Community Schools. 2012. Guide to Race to the Top District Competition. Community Schools Approach to the Race to the Top Competition. http://www.communityschools.org/assets/1/AssetManager/RTTD%20Guide%20on%20Final%20Guidance.pdf.

Coalition for Community Schools. 2014. Community school results. http://www.communityschools.org/results/results.aspx.

Coalition for Community Schools. n.d. *Role of business and foundation leaders in supporting community schools.* http://www.communityschools.org/assets/1/AssetManager/Role%20of%20Business%20and%20Foundation%20Leaders%20in%20Supporting%20Community%20Schools.pdf.

Coalition for Community Schools, Federal Legislation. 2014. http://www.communityschools.org/policy_advocacy/federal_legislation.aspx.

Coalition for Community Schools, State Policy. 2014. http://www.communityschools.org/policy_advocacy/state.aspx.

Coalition for Community Schools. 2015. News Article. New federal education law boosts community schools. http://www.communityschools.org/new_federal_education_law_boosts_community_schools/.

Coburn, A., & D. Wallace. 2011. *Youth work in communities and schools*. Edinburgh: Dunedin.

Comer, J. P., & C. Emmons. 2006. The research program of the Yale Child Study Center School Development Program. *Journal of Negro Education* 75 (3): 353–372.

Common Core. 2014. *The Common Core State Standards Initiative: Statements of support*. http://www.corestandards.org/other-resources/statements-of-support/.

Common Core Issues. 2014. How is the federal government involved in the Common Core? http://www.hslda.org/commoncore/topic3.aspx.

Communities in Schools. 2012. *The economic impact of communities in schools*. http://www.communitiesinschools.org/media/uploads/attachments/CIS_2.pdf.

Communities in Schools. 2014. When it comes to making sure children get exactly what they need to succeed in school and in life, we never give up. http://www.communitiesinschools.org.

Community Schools Initiatives. 2015. Chicago Public Schools. http://cps.edu/Programs/DistrictInitiatives/Pages/CommunitySchoolsInitiative.aspx.

Community Schools in the Netherlands. 2010. Fact sheet. http://www.eunec.eu/sites/www.eunec.eu/files/event/attachments/development_of_community_schools_in_the_netherlands.pdf.

Connell, J. 1992. *The importance of learning about and building on the policies, programs and effects of voluntary youth-serving organizations*. Philadelphia: Public/Private Ventures.

Cooper, C. E., & R. Crosnoe. 2007. The engagement in schooling of economically disadvantaged parents and children. *Youth & Society* 38 (3): 372–391.

Crotty, J. M. 2013. A broken windows approach to education reform. *Forbes*, August 30. http://www.forbes.com/sites/jamesmarshallcrotty/2013/08/30/a-broken-windows-approach-to-education-reform/.

Cummings, C., A. Dyson, & L. Todd. 2011. *Beyond the school gates: Can full service and extended schools overcome disadvantage?* New York: Routledge.

Cummings, J., P. Harrison, M. Dawson, R. Short, S. Gorin, & R. Palomares. 2003. The 2002 conference on the future of school psychology: Implications for consultation, intervention and prevention services. *Journal of Educational and Psychological Consultation* 15 (3–4): 239–256.

Currie, G., & A. Lockett. 2007. A critique of transformational leadership: Moral, professional and contingent dimensions of leadership within public services organizations. *Human Relations* 60 (2): 341–370. doi:10.1177/0018726707075884.

Dallago, L., F. Cristini, D. Perkins, M. Nation, & M. Santinello. 2013. The adolescents, life context, and school project: Youth voice and civic participation. *Journal of Prevention & Intervention in the Community* 26: 41–54.

Darling-Hammond, L. 2010. *The flat world and education: How America's commitment to equity will determine our future.* New York: Teachers College Press.

Darling-Hammond, L., S. D. Glenn, R. Martire, M. Morial, M. A. Rebell, D. G. Sciarra, R. Weingarten & D. Van Roekel. 2013. *Early learning as a path to equity: The case of New Jersey.* Washington, DC: Equity and Excellence Commission.

Delpit, L. 2006. *Other people's children: Cultural conflict in the classroom.* New York: New Press.

DeMarrais, K. B., & M. D. LeCompte. 1999. *The way schools work*, 3rd ed. New York: Addison Wesley Longman.

DeNavas-Walt, C., B. D. Proctor, & J. C. Smith. 2013. *Income, poverty and health insurance coverage in the United States: 2012.* Washington, DC: U.S. Census Bureau. http://www.census.gov/prod/2013pubs/p60–245.pdf.

Dobbie, W., & R. G. Fryer, Jr. 2011. Are high-quality schools enough to increase achievement among the poor? Evidence from the Harlem Children's Zone. American Economics Journal. *Applied Economics* 3 (3): 158–187. http://www2.econ.iastate.edu/classes/econ321/orazem/Fryer_high_quality_schools.pdf.

Dreze, J., & A. Goyal. 2008. The future of mid-day meals. In *School health services in India*, ed. R. V. Baru, 46–78. Los Angeles: Sage.

Dryfoos, J. (1991). School-based social and health services for at-risk students. *Urban Education* 26 (1): 118–137.

Dryfoos, J. 1994. *Full-service schools.* San Francisco: Jossey-Bass.

Dryfoos, J. 1997. The prevalence of problem behaviors: Implications for programs. In *Healthy children 2010: Enhancing children's wellness*, ed. R. P. Weissberg. T. P. Gullotta, R. L. Hampton, B. S. Ryan, & G. R. Adams, 17–26. Thousand Oaks, CA: Sage.

Dryfoos, J., & J. Quinn. 2005. Looking to the future. In *Community schools in action*, ed. J. Dryfoos, J. Quinn, & C. Barkin, 259–263. New York: Oxford University Press.

Dryfoos, J., J. Quinn, & C. Barkin, eds. 2005. *Community Schools in action.* New York: Oxford University Press.

Duncan, A. 2009. Economic security and a 21st century education: Secretary Arne Duncan's Remarks at the U.S. Chamber of Commerce's Education and Workforce Summit, January 9. https://www2.ed.gov/news/speeches/2009/11/11092009.html.

Duncan, A. 2012. Fighting the Wrong Education Battles—Remarks of Secretary Duncan at the Askwith Forum. Cambridge, MA: Harvard Graduate School of Education, February 7. http://www.ed.gov/news/speeches/fighting-wrong-education-battles.

Economic Modeling Specialists, Inc. (EMSI). 2012. The economic impact of communities in schools. http://www.communitiesinschools.org/media/uploads/attachments/CIS_2.pdf.

Education Law Center. 2015. New York: ELC Advocacy for Education Rights http://www.edlawcenter.org/initiatives/new-york-elc-advocacy-for-education-rights.html.

Education Review Office. 2014. *ERO reviews*. http://ero.govt.nz/.

Egan, D. 2012. *Communities, families and schools together: A route to reducing the impact of poverty on educational achievement in schools across Wales*. Research report commissioned by Save the Children Wales. https://www.savethechildren.org.uk/sites/default/files/images/Communities-families-and-schools-together-report.pdf.

Elev8. 2013. *Youth Development Incorporated New Mexico*. http://www.ydinm.org/index.php/component/k2/itemlist/category/52-elev8.

Epstein, J. L. 1995. School/family/community partnerships: Caring for the children we share. *Phi Delta Kappan* 76: 701–712.

Epstein, J. L. 2011. *School, family, and community partnerships*. Boulder, CO: Westview Press.

Every Student Succeeds Act. 2015. Reauthorization of Elementary and Secondary Education Act of 1965. Congress.Gov. https://www.congress.gov/bill/114th-congress/senate-bill/1177/text.

Fagen, M., Y. Asada, S. Welch, R. Dombrowski, K. Gilmet, C. Welter, L. Stern, G. Barnett, & M. Mason. 2014. Policy, systems, and environmentally oriented school-based obesity prevention: Opportunities and challenges. *Journal of Prevention & Intervention in the Community* 42: 95–111.

Farrow, F., & T. Joe. 1992. Financing school-linked integrated services. *Future of Children* 2 (1): 56–67.

Federal Education Policy. 2009. *Federal Education Policy and the States, 1945–2005*. States Impact of Federal Education Project. Albany: New York State

Archives. http://www.archives.nysed.gov/edpolicy/altformats/ed_background_overview_essay.pdf.

Federal Register. 5/6/2014:6188.

Feinsilver, J. 2010. Overview of the Cuban health system. In *Community Health Care in Cuba*, ed. S. E. Mason, D. L. Strug, & J. Beder, 24–38. Chicago: Lyceum.

Ferro, J. 1998. Implementing coordinated school health programs in local schools. In *Health is academic: A guide to coordinated school health programs*, ed. E. Marx, S. F. Wooley, & D. Northrop, 15–42. New York: Teachers College Press.

Flaherty, L. T., E. G. Garrison, R. Waxman, P. F. Uris, S. G. Keys, M. Glass-Siegel, & M. Weist. 1998. Mental health services in schools: The challenge of locating psychotherapy service for troubled adolescent pupils in mainstream and special schools. *Journal of School Health* 68 (10): 420–424.

Flaherty, L. T., M. D. Weist, & B. S. Warner. 1996. School-based mental health services in the United States: History, current models and needs. *Community Mental Health Journal* 32: 314–352.

Flanagan, C., P. Cumsille, S. Gill, S., & L. Gallay. 2007. School and community climates and civic commitments: Processes for ethnic minority and majority students. *Journal of Educational Psychology* 99 (2): 421–431.

Flores v. Arizona. 2008. 516 F. 3d 1140—Court of Appeals, 9th Circuit.

Food and Nutrition Service. 2014. *Farm to School.* http://www.fns.usda.gov/farmtoschool/farm-school.

Forbes, J., & E. McCartney, E. 2015. Educating child practitioners: A (re)turn to the university disciplines. *Discourse: Studies in the Cultural Politics of Education*, 36, 1, 144–159. doi:10.1080/01596306.2013.871235.

Forbes, J., & C. Watson, eds. 2009. *Service integration in schools: Research and policy discourses, practices and future prospects.* Rotterdam, the Netherlands: Sense Publishers.

Franklin, C., J. Kim, T. Ryan, M. S. Kelly, & K. L. Montgomery. 2012. Teacher involvement in school mental health interventions: A systematic review. *Children and Youth Services Review* 34: 973–982.

Freeman, E. M. 1995. School social work overview. In *Encyclopedia of Social Work*, ed. R. Edwards, 19th ed. (CD-ROM). Rec. No. 34325–34511. Annapolis Junction, MD: National Association of Social Work Press.

Friedman, L. N., & M. A. Schmitt-Carey. 2013. Schools are trapped in the past. Timesunion.com, January 24. http://www.timesunion.com/opinion/article/Schools-are-trapped-in-the-past-4221901.php.

Fuhrman, S. H., M. A. Rebell, J. B. King, Jr., M. A. Schmitt-Carey, D. Wakelyn, & R. Weingarten. 2011. *Achievable and affordable: Providing comprehensive educational opportunity to low-income students.* New York: Columbia University, Teachers College. http://www.youtube.com/watch?v=-5k2fuZ_STc&feature=youtu.be&noredirect=1.

Full-Service Community Schools Act of 2014. H.R. 1568. 2014. https://www.congress.gov/bill/113th-congress/house-bill/5168.

Galobardes, B., J. Lynch, & G. Smith. 2004. Childhood socioeconomic circumstances and cause-specific mortality in adulthood: Systematic review and interpretation. *Epidemiologic Reviews* 26 (1): 7–21.

Gardner, S. 1993. Afterword. In L. Adler & S. Gardner, *The politics of linking schools and social services.* Washington, DC: Falmer Press.

Glisson, C., & P. Green. 2006. The effects of organizational culture on the access to mental health care in child welfare and juvenile justice systems. *Administration and Policy in Mental Health and Mental Health Services Research* 33 (4): 433–448. doi:10.1007/s10488–005–0016–0.

Gomby, D. S., & C. S. Larson. 1992. Evaluation of school-linked services. *Future of Children* 2 (1): 68–84.

Government of Canada. 2010. *Community stories: Aboriginal successes in British Columbia.* Indian and Northern Affairs, Canada. https://www.aadnc-aandc.gc.ca/DAM/DAM-INTER-BC/STAGING/texte-text/cmstry10_1100100021664_eng.pdf.

Government of Canada. 2013. Aboriginal people and communities. Aboriginal affairs and Northern development Canada. http://www.aadnc-aandc.gc.ca/eng/1100100013785/1304467449155.

Government of Manitoba. 2014. Community schools partnership initiative. Education and advanced learning. https://www.edu.gov.mb.ca/cspi/.

Graves, D. 2011. *Exploring schools as community hubs. Investigating application of the community hub model in context of the closure of Athabasca School, Regina, Saskatchewan, Canada and other small schools.* Regina, Saskatchewan: University of Regina, Community Research Unit.. http://ourspace.uregina.ca/bitstream/handle/10294/3397/Community%20Hub%20Final%20Report.pdf?sequence=3.

Green, Y. 2005. Promoting community and economic development. In *Community schools in action*, ed. J. Dryfoos, J. Quinn, & C. Barkin, 114–124. New York: Oxford University Press.

Greenberg, M., & J. Levy, with R. Palaich, R. Veatch, L. Rubinstein, S. Kaplan, & N. Berla. 1992. *Confidentiality and collaboration: Information sharing in interagency efforts*. Denver, CO: Joining Forces, American Public Welfare Association, Center for Law and Social Policy, Council of Chief State School Officers, & Education Commission of the States.

Greger, D., M. Levinska, & I. Smetcatkova. 2012. Priority education policies in the Czech Republic: Redesigning equity policies in the post-communist transformation. In *Education policies and inequalities in Europe*, ed. M. Demeuse, D. Frandji, D. Greger, & J.-Y. Rochex, 191–222. London: Palgrave-Macmillan.

Guernsey, L., L. Bornfreund, C. McCann, & C. Williams. 2014. *Subprime learning: Early education in America since the Great Recession*. New America Education Policy Program. www.newamerica.org.

Guo, J. J., T. J. Wade, W. Pan, & K. N. Keller. 2012. School-based health centers: Cost-benefit analysis and impact on health care disparities. In *School-based health care: Advancing educational success and public health*, ed. T. D. Wright & J. W. Richardson, 397–414. Washington, DC: American Public Health Association.

Haney, W. 2000. The myth of the Texas miracle in education. *Education Policy Analysis Archives* 8 (41). ERIC Number: EJ617247. http://www.communityschools.org/policy_advocacy/federal_funding.aspx#Infrastructure.

Hanushek, E. A., & A. A. Lindseth. 2009. *Schoolhouses, courthouses, and statehouses: Solving the funding-achievement puzzle in America's public schools*. Princeton, NJ: Princeton University Press.

Hare, I. 1995. School-linked services. In *Encyclopedia of social work*, ed. R. Edwards, 19th ed. (CD-ROM). Rec. No. 34520–34689. Annapolis Junction, MD: NASW Press.

Hargreaves, A., G. Halasz, & B. Pont. 2007. *School leadership for systemic improvement in Finland: A case study report for the OECD activity improving school leadership*. http://www.oecd.org/education/school/39928629.pdf.

Harkavy, I., M. Hartley, R. Hodges, & J. Weeks. 2013. The promise of university-assisted community schools to transform American schooling: A report from the field, 1985–2012. *Peabody Journal of Education* 88: 525–540.

Harkavy, I., & J. L. Puckett. 1991. The role of mediating structures in university and community revitalization: The University of Pennsylvania and West Philadelphia as a case study. *Journal of Research and Development in Education* 25: 10–20.

Harkavy, I., & J. L. Puckett. 1994. Lessons from Hull House for the contemporary urban university. *The Social Service Review* 68 (3), 299–321.

Harvard Family Research Project. 2014. Family involvement. www.hfrp.org/family-involvement.

Heers, M., C. van Klaveren, W. Groot, & H. Maassen van den Brink. 2012. The impact of community schools on student dropout in pre-vocational education. TIER Working Paper Series. http://www.tierweb.nl/assets/files/UM/TIER_WP%2012–08.pdf.

Hernandez Jozefowicz, D. M., P. Allen-Meares, M. A. Piro-Lupinacci, & R. Fisher. 2002. School social work in the United States: A holistic approach. In *School social work world-wide*, ed. M. Huxtable and E. Blyth, 33–56. Washington, DC: National Association of Social Work Press.

Holmes, D. 2012. School-based health centers: Adapting to health care reform and the utilization of health information technology. In *School-based health care: Advancing educational success and public health*, ed. T. D. Wright & J. W. Richardson, 433–446. Washington, DC: American Public Health Association.

Hood, R. 2014. Complexity and integrated working in children's services. *British Journal of Social Work* 44: 27–43.

Horwath, J., & T. Morrison. 2007. Collaboration, integration and change in children's services: Critical issues and key ingredients. *Child Abuse & Neglect* 31: 55–69.

Huxtable, M., & E. Blyth, eds. 2002. *School social work worldwide*. Washington, DC: National Association of Social Work Press.

International Center of Excellence for Community Schools. ICECS. 2014. http://www.icecsweb.org; http://www.icecsweb.org/international-quality-standards.

International Quality Standards for Community Schools. 2014. Kazakhstan. Life-long learning education. http://www.schools-for-all.org/page/International+Quality+Standards+for+Community+Schools.

International Research and Exchanges Board (IREX). 2011. *Community schools*. Youth Development Competency Program. http://www.irex.org/system/files/YDCP%20Community%20School%20Brochure.pdf.

International Standards for Community Schools. 2013. Association of Organization Development Consultants. Czech Republic. http://csstandards.org/index.php/partners/12-the-association-of-organization-development-s-consultants-chezh-republic.

International Standards for Community Schools. 2014. NGO—Life learning education Kazakhstan. http://csstandards.org/index.php/partners/13-ngo-life-long-learning-education-kazakhstan.

Ishimaru, A. 2013. From heroes to organizers: Principals and education organizing in urban school reform. *Educational Administration Quarterly* 49 (1): 3–51.

Jacobson, R., R. Hodges, & M. Blank, M. 2011. Mutual support: The community schools strategy. *Principal Leadership,* October.

Jeynes, W. 2012. A meta-analysis of the efficacy of different types of parental involvement programs for urban students. *Urban Education* 47 (4): 706–742. doi:10.1177/0042085912445643.

Jimerson, L. 2005. Placism in NCLB—How rural children are left behind. *Equity & Excellence in Education* 38: 211–213. doi:10.1080/10665680591002588.

Jonson-Reid, M. 2000. Understanding confidentiality in school-based interagency projects. *Social Work in Education* 22 (1): 33–44.

Jozefowich-Simbeni, D., and P. Allen-Meares. 2002. Poverty and schools: Intervention and resource building through school-linked services. *Children & Schools* 24 (2): 123–136.

Kagan, S. 1992. Collaborating to meet the readiness agenda: Dimensions and dilemmas. In *Ensuring student success through collaboration*, 57–66. Washington, DC: Council of Chief State School Officers (CCSSO).

Kagan, S., S. Goffin, S. Golub, & E. Pritchard. 1995. *Toward systemic reform: Service integration for young children and their families.* Des Moines, IA: National Center for Service Integration.

Kahn, A. J., & S. B. Kamerman. 1992. *Integrating services integration: An overview of initiatives, issues, and possibilities.* New York: National Center for Children in Poverty.

Kalafat, J. 2004. Enabling and empowering practices of Kentucky's school-based family resource centers. *Evaluation and Program Planning* 27 (1): 65–78.

Kania, J., & M. Kramer. 2011. Collective impact. *Stanford Social Innovation Review* 9 (1): 36–41.

Kelley, C., & J. Kahne. 1995. Designing effective school-linked services programs: Lessons from collaborative programs for children with disabilities. *Journal of School Leadership* 5 (3): 163–182.

Kelly, M. S., S. C. Berzin, A. Frey, M. Alvarez, G. Shaffer, & K. O'Brien. 2010. The state of school social work: Findings from the national school social work survey. *School Mental Health* 2: 132–141.

Kenning, C. 2011. Cincinnati's Oyler Elementary finds winning formula to fight poverty. *Courier-Journal,* April 23. www.courier-journal.com.

Kerr, S. P., W. R. Kerr, & W. F. Lincoln. 2013. *Skilled immigration and the employment structure of U.S. firms.* Working Paper 14–040, November 15. Harvard Business School. http://www.personal.umich.edu/~wlincoln/KerrKerrLincoln2013.pdf.

Kezar, A. & R. A. Rhoads. 2001. The dynamic tensions of service learning in higher education: A philosophical perspective. *The Journal of Higher Education* 72 (2): 148–171.

Khalifa, M. 2012. A Re-New-ed paradigm in successful urban school leadership: Principal as community leader. *Educational Administration Quarterly* 48 (3): 424–467.

Klein, A. 2014. SIG program gets makeover in newly passed budget. *Education Week*, January 28. http://www.edweek.org/ew/articles/2014/01/29/19budget-sig.h33.html.

Kline, P. M., & M. M. Brabeck. 1999. Ethics and collaborative practice in public schools. In *Collaborative practice: School and human service partnerships*, ed. R. W. C. Tourse & J. F. Mooney, 285–297. Westport, CT: Praeger.

Kosciw, J. G., E. A. Greytak, M. J. Bartkiewicz, M. J. Boesen, & N. A. Palmer. 2012. *The 2011 National School Climate Survey*. http://files.eric.ed.gov/fulltext/ED535177.pdf.

Kosic, A., & C. D. Tauber. 2010. The perspectives of reconciliation and healing among young people in Vukovar (Croatia). *International Journal of Peace Studies* 15 (1): 45–70.

Krasnoyarsk Center. 2012. *Center for community partnerships. Community education*. http://www.kccp.ru/index.php?option=com_k2&view=item&layout=item&id=50&Itemid=66&lang=en.

LaCour, J. A. 1982. Interagency agreement: A rational response to an irrational system. *Exceptional Children* 49: 265–267.

Ladd, H. F. 2012. Education and poverty: Confronting the evidence. *Journal of Policy Analysis and Management* 31 (2): 203–277.

Larson, K., and N. Halfon. 2009. Family income gradients in the health and health care access of U.S. children. *Maternal and Child Health Journal* 14 (3): 332–342.

Larson, K., S. A. Russ, J. J. Crall, & N. Halfon. 2008. Influence of multiple social risks on children's health. *Pediatrics* 121 (2): 337–344.

Lawson, M., & T. Alameda-Lawson. 2012. A case study of school-linked collective parent engagement. *American Research Educational Journal*, 49 (4): 651–684.

Learning First Alliance. 2009. Principles for measuring the performance of Turnaround Schools. http://www.learningfirst.org/sites/default/files/assets/LFAPrinciplesMeasuringTurnaroundSuccess.pdf.

Legon, E. D. 2012. Cuban education, a state responsibility. *Havana Times*, September 7. http://www.havanatimes.org/?p=78108.

Lewis, T. L. 2004. Service learning for social change? Lessons from a liberal arts college. *Teaching Sociology* 32 (1): 94–108.

Little, P., C. Wimer, & H. Weiss. 2008. After school programs in the 21st century: Their potential and what it takes to achieve it. *Harvard Family Research Project* 10: 1–12.

Loveless, T. 2014. Implementing the Common Core: A look at curriculum. The Brown Center Chalkboard, Brookings. http://www.brookings.edu/blogs/brown-center-chalkboard/posts/2014/05/15-implementing-common-core-curriculum.

Mackenzie, J. 2010. *Family learning: Engaging with parents*. Edinburgh: Dunedin Academic Press.

Magnuson, K., M. Meyers, C. Ruhm, & J. Waldfogel. 2004. Inequality in preschool education and school readiness. *American Educational Research Journal* 41: 115–157.

Magnuson, K., C. Ruhm, and J. Waldfogel. 2007. Does prekindergarten improve school preparation and performance? *Economics of Education Review* 26: 33–51.

Manitoba Education, Citizenship, and Youth. 2006. *Community schools: A support document for partners in the community schools partnership initiative.* http://www.edu.gov.mb.ca/cspi/documents/support_doc.pdf.

Martinez, L. & C. Hayes. 2013. *Measuring school return on investment for community schools, a case study.* http://www.childrensaidsociety.org/files/CASE%20STUDY%20final.pdf.

Marx, E., S. F. Wooley, & D. Northrop. 1998. *Health is academic: A guide to coordinated school health programs.* New York: Teachers College Press.

Maryland Department of Education. 2003. Programs. Civic engagement. www.marylandpublicschools.org/MSDE/programs/servicelearning/civic_engagement.html.

McClanahan, W.S., J. Gio, F. Sanders. July 2013. Out-of-school time in Elev8 community schools: A first look at participation and its unique contribution to students' experiences in school. Research for Action & McClanahan Associates, Inc.

McInnis-Dittrich, K., O. J. Neisler, & R. W. C. Tourse. 1999. Socioeducational realities of the 21st century: A need for change. In *Collaborative practice: School and human service partnerships,* ed. R. W. C. Tourse & J. F. Mooney, 3–32. Westport, CT: Praeger.

McKenzie, F. D., & J. B. Richmond. 1998. Linking health and learning: An overview of coordinated school health programs. In *Health is academic: A guide to coordinated school health programs,* ed. E. Marx, S. F. Wooley, & D. Northrop, 1–14. New York: Teachers College Press.

McNall, M. A., L. F. Lichty, & B. Mavis. 2012. The impact of school-based health centers on the health outcomes of middle school and high school students. In *School-based health care: Advancing educational success and public health,* ed. T. D. Wright & J. W. Richardson, 47–64. Washington, DC: American Public Health Association.

Melaville, A., A. C. Berg, & M. J. Blank. 2006. *Community based learning: Engaging students for success and citizenship.* Coalition for Community Schools. http://files.eric.ed.gov/fulltext/ED491639.pdf.

Melaville, A., & M. Blank. 1991. *What it takes: Structuring interagency partnerships to connect children and families with comprehensive services.* Washington, DC: Education and Human Services Consortium.

Mellin, E., D. Anderson-Butcher, & L. R. Bronstein. 2011. Strengthening interprofessional team collaboration: Potential roles for school mental health professionals. *Advances in School Mental Health Promotion* 4 (2): 51–61.

Mellin, E., L. R. Bronstein, D. Anderson-Butcher, A. Amrose, J. Green, & A. Ball. 2010. Measuring interprofessional team collaboration in expanded school mental health: Model refinement and scale development. *Journal of Interprofessional Care* 24 (5): 514–523.

Mellin, E., & M. Weist. 2011. Exploring school mental health collaboration in an urban community: A social capital perspective. *School Mental Health* 3: 81–92.

Meyer-Adams, N., & B. T. Conner. 2008. School violence: Bullying behaviors and the psychosocial school environment in middle schools. *Children and Schools* 30 (4): 211–221. doi:10.1093/cs/30.4.211.

Milliken, B. 2007. *The last dropout: Stop the epidemic!* Carlsbad, CA: Hay House.

Mooney, J. F., P. M. Kline, & J. C. Davoren. 1999. Collaborative interventions: Promoting psychosocial competence and academic achievement. In *Collaborative practice: School and human service partnerships,* ed. R. W. C. Tourse & J. F. Mooney, 105–135. Westport, CT: Praeger.

Mutch, C., & S. Collins. 2012. Partners in learning: Schools' engagement with parents, families, and communities in New Zealand. *School Community Journal* 22 (1): 167–187.

Nansel, T. R., M. Overpeck, R. S. Pilla, W. J. Ruan, B. Simons-Morton, & P. Scheidt. 2001. Bullying behaviors among U.S. youth: Prevalence and association with psychosocial adjustment. *Journal of the American Medical Association* 285, no. 16, April 25: 2094–2100.

National After, School Association. http://naaweb.org/about-us.

National Assembly of School Based Health Centers. 2010–2011 Annual Report. Washington, DC.

National Center for Education Statistics. 2011. *Youth indicators 2011. America's youth: Transitions to adulthood.* U.S. Department of Education, Institute of Educational Statistics. http://nces.ed.gov/pubs2012/2012026/.

National Center for Education Statistics. 2014a. *Public high school four-year on-time graduation rates and event dropout rates: School years 2010–11 and 2011–12.* U.S. Department of Education, Institute of Education Sciences. http://nces.ed.gov/pubs2014/2014391/findings.asp.

National Center for Education Statistics. 2014b. Graduation rates. *Fast Facts.* U.S. Department of Education, Institute of Education Sciences. http://nces.ed.gov/fastfacts/display.asp?id=40.

National Education Association. 2008. *Parent, family, community involvement in education.* An NEA policy brief. Washington, DC.

National Education Association. 2014. *Rankings and estimates. Rankings of the states, 2013, and estimates of school statistics, 2014.* http://www.nea.org/assets/docs/NEA-Rankings-and-Estimates-2013–2014.pdf.

National Results and Equity Collaborative. 2014. About NREC. http://resultsandequity.org/about/.

Neisler, O. J., K. McInnis-Dittrich, & J. F. Mooney. 1999. Interprofessional collaboration in the process of assessment. In *Collaborative practice: School and human service partnerships*, ed. R. W. C. Tourse & J. F. Mooney, 79–104. Westport, CT: Praeger.

New Economics Foundation. 2008. *Measuring value: A guide to social return on investment,* 2nd ed. London: New Economics Foundation.

Newmann, F. M., H. M. Marks, & A. Gamoran. 1995. Authentic pedagogy: Standards that boost performance. *American Journal of Education* 104 (4): 280–312.

New York City Administration for Children's Services. 2014. *High school goal weekend.* http://www.nyc.gov/html/acs/html/home/home.shtml.

New York City, Office of the Mayor. 2014a. *De Blasio announces $52 million investment to launch community schools.* http://www1.nyc.gov/office-of-the-mayor/news/292–14/de-blasio-administration-52-million-investment-launch-community-schools.

New York City, Office of the Mayor. 2014b. *Pledging stronger public schools, Mayor de Blasio announces "School Renewal Program."* http://www1.nyc.gov

/office-of-the-mayor/news/904–14/pledging-stronger-public-schools-mayor-de-blasio-school-renewal-program.

New New York Education Reform Commission. 2013. *Education Action Plan: Preliminary results.* http://www.governor.ny.gov/assets/documents/education-reform-commission-report.pdf.

New York State Afterschool Network & Hunger Solutions New York. 2010. http://www.nysan.org/content/document/detail/3066/.

New Zealand Demographics. 2013. *Population*. http://www.indexmundi.com/new_zealand/demographics_profile.html.

New Zealand Ministry of Education. 2014. *NZ education*. http://www.minedu.govt.nz/.

Nixon, J., M. Walker, & S. Baron. 2002. The cultural mediation of state policy: The democratic potential of new community schooling in Scotland. *Journal of Education Policy* 17 (4): 407–421.

Noam, G. G. 2001. *Program in afterschool education and research and Harvard Afterschool Initiative.* Urban Seminar Series on Children's Mental Health and Safety: After-School Time. Cambridge, MA: Kennedy School of Government.

Noddings, N. 2005. What does it mean to educate the whole child? *Educational Leadership* 63 (1): 8–13.

Noguera, P. 2003. *City schools and the American dream: Reclaiming the promise of public education*. New York: Teachers College Press.

Noguera, P. 2011. A broader and bolder approach uses education to break the cycle of poverty. *Phi Delta Kappan*, 93(3): 8–14.

Noguera, P., & S. L. Klevan. 2010. In pursuit of our common interests: A framework for building school-university partnerships to improve urban schools and teaching. ERIC Number: EJ917614. *Teacher Education and Practice* 23 (3): 350–354.

North, S. W., & C. Kjolhede. 2012. Rural school-based health centers: Enhancing access to care by eliminating barriers. In *School-based health care: Advancing educational success and public health*, ed. T. D. Wright & J. W. Richardson, 359–368. Washington, DC: American Public Health Association.

Nursing History and Healthcare. *American nursing: An introduction to the past.* Philadelphia: University of Pennsylvania. http://www.nursing.upenn.edu/nhhc/Welcome%20Page%20Content/American%20Nursing.pdf.

Nye, B., L. V. Hedges, & S. Konstantopoulos. 2000. The effects of small classes on academic achievement: The results of the Tennessee class size experiment. *American Educational Research Journal* 37 (1): 123–151. doi:10.3102/00028312037001123.

Obama, B. 2009. *Remarks by the President on higher education.* The White House, Office of the Press Secretary, April 24. http://www.whitehouse.gov/the_press_office/Remarks-by-the-President-on-Higher-Education.

Obrien, A. 2014. Recent polls: Do educators support the Common Core? *Education Trends.* http://www.edutopia.org/blog/recent-polls-common-core-teachers-in-favor-anne-obrien.

Olivos, E. M., & M. Mendoza. 2010. Immigration and educational inequality: Examining Latino immigrant parents' engagement in U.S. public schools. *Journal of Immigrant & Refugee Studies* 8: 339–357.

OMG Center for Collaborative Learning. 2011. *Hartford community schools evaluation: Findings from year 2.* Hartford, CT: OMG Center for Collaborative Learning.

Onsomu, E. N., J. N. Mungai, D. Oulai, J. Sankale, & J. Mujidi. 2004. *Community schools in Kenya: Case study on community participation in funding and managing schools.* International Institute for Educational Planning/UNESCO. Paris: UNESCO.

Oppenheimer, J. 1925. *The visiting teacher movement with special reference to administrative relationships*, 2nd ed. New York: Joint Committee on Methods of Preventing Delinquency.

Organisation for Economic Cooperation and Development (OECD). 2007. *Quality and equity of schooling in Scotland.* Office of the Secretary General. OECD Publishing.

Owens, J. S., Y. Watabe, & K. D. Michael. 2013. Culturally responsive school mental health in rural communities. In *Handbook of culturally responsive school mental health: Advancing research, training, practice, and policy*, ed. C. S. Clauss-Ehlers, Z. Serpell, & M. D. Weist, 31–42. New York: Springer.

Pacheco, M., W. Powell, C. Cole, N. Kalishman, R. Benon, & A. Kaufman. 1991. School-based clinics: The politics of change. *Journal of School Health* 61 (2): 92–94.

Pappano, L. 2010. *Inside school turnarounds: Urgent hopes, unfolding stories.* Cambridge, MA: Harvard Education Press.

Parker, B. 2010. Community schools in Africa. A study of provision. http://www.icecsweb.org/media/file/Community_Schools_in_Africa.pdf.

Partnership for Children and Youth. 2013. Community schools. Aligning local resources with student success. http://partnerforchildren.org/storage/documents/csfinancinglayout.pdf.

Payne, C. M. 2008. *So much reform, so little change: The persistence of failure in urban schools.* Cambridge, MA: Harvard Education Press.

Peckover, C., M. Vasquez, S. Van Housen, J. Saunders, & L. Allen. 2012. Preparing school social work for the future: An update of school social workers' tasks in Iowa. *Children & Schools* 35 (1): 9–17.

Pencil. 2012. www.pencil.org.

Perfect, M. M., & R. J. Morris. 2011. Delivering school-based mental health services by school psychologists: Education, training, and ethical issues. *Psychology in the Schools* 48 (10): 1049–1063.

Phillippo, K. 2013. *Advisory in urban high schools: A study of expanded teacher roles.* New York: Palgrave Macmillan.

Plant, R. W., & P. A. King. 1995. The Family Resource Center: A community-based system of family support services. In *The family-school connection,* ed. B.A. Ryan, G. R. Adams, T. P. Gullotta, R. P. Weissberg, & R. L. Hampton, 288–314. Thousand Oaks, CA: Sage.

Poirier, J. M., & D. Osher. 2013. Understanding the current environment of public school funding: How student support services are funded. In *The school services sourcebook: A guide for school-based professionals,* 2nd ed., ed. C. Franklin, M. B. Harris, & P. Allen-Meares, 935–950. New York: Oxford University Press.

Province of British Columbia. 2010. Neighbourhood Learning Centres. http://www2.gov.bc.ca/gov/content/education-training/adminsitration/community-partnerships/neighbourhood-learning-centres.

Ramachandran, V., K. Jandhyala, & A. Saihjee. 2008. Through the life cycle of children: Factors that facilitate /impede primary school completion. In *School health services in India,* ed. R. V. Baru, 8–45. Los Angeles: Sage.

Ravitch, D. 2013. *Reign of error: The hoax of the privatization movement and the danger to America's public schools.* New York: Alfred A. Knopf.

Ravitch, D. 2014. Common Core, past, present, and future. Speech to the Modern Language Association, Chicago, January 11. http://dianeravitch.net/2014/01/18/my-speech-about-common-core-to-mla/.

Rebell, M. 2009. *Courts and kids: Pursuing educational equity through the state courts.* Chicago: University of Chicago Press.

Rebell, M. 2012. The right to comprehensive educational opportunity. *Harvard Civil Rights–Civil Liberties Law Review* 47: 47–117.

Rebell, M. 2013. *School-based health centers.* Washington, DC: Equity and Excellence Commission.

Rebell, M., & J. R. Wolff. 2012. Educational opportunity is achievable and affordable. *Phi Delta Kappan* 93 (6): 62–65.

Reeves, C. 2003. *Implementing the No Child Left Behind Act: Implications for rural schools and districts.* Naperville, IL: North Central Regional Educational

Laboratory. http://www.mc3edsupport.org/community/kb_files/NCLB_RuralPolicyBrief.pdf.

Resmovits, J. 2014. U.S. test scores remain stagnant while other countries see rapid rise. *Huffington Post*, January 23. http://www.huffingtonpost.com/2013/12/03/us-test-scores_n_4374075.html.

Reynolds, A. J., J. A. Temple, D. L. Robertson, & E. A. Mann. 2001. Long-term effects of an early childhood intervention on educational achievement and juvenile arrest: A 15-year follow-up of low-income children in public schools. *Journal of the American Medical Association* 285: 2339–2346.

Richardson, J. W., & T. D. Wright. 2012. Health and educational policy synergy. In *School-based health care: Advancing educational success and public health*, ed. T. D. Wright & J. W. Richardson, 163–176. Washington, DC: American Public Health Association.

Richman, J. 1910. A social need of the public school. *Forum* 43: 161–169.

Right to Education Fact Sheet. 2014. *India*. UNICEF. http://www.unicef.org/india/education_6145.htm.

Risher & Kabel. 2010. Child friendly schools. Case study: Bosnia and Herzegovina. UNESCO. http://www.unicef.org/education/files/BosniaandHerzegovina_CFSCaseStudty_June2010.pdf.

Rogers, J. S. 1998. *Community schools: Lessons from the past and present: A report to the Charles S. Mott Foundation.* Flint, MI: Charles S. Mott Foundation.

Rothstein, R. 2004. *Class and schools: Using social, economic and educational reform to close the black-white achievement gap.* Washington, DC: Economic Policy Institute.

Ruglis, J., & N. Freudenberg. 2012. Toward a healthy high schools movement: Strategies for mobilizing public health for educational reform. In *School-based health care: Advancing educational success and public health*, ed. T. D. Wright & J. W. Richardson, 371–386. Washington, DC: American Public Health Association.

Rural School and Community Trust. 2004. Good rural high schools: Principles and standards. Washington, D. C. http://www.ruraledu.org/articles.php?=2075.

Russ, S., N. Garro, & N. Halfon. 2010. Meeting children's basic health needs: From patchwork to tapestry. *Children and Youth Services Review* 32 (9): 1149–1164.

Russell, C. A., E. R. Reisner, L. M. Pearson, K. P. Afolabi, T. D. Miller, & M. B. Mielke. 2006. *Evaluation of DYCD's out-of-school time initiative: Report on the first year.* Washington, DC: Policy Studies Associates, Inc. http://www.policystudies.com/studies/youth/OST.html.

Russo, C., & J. Lindle 1993. On the cutting edge: Family resource/youth service centers in Kentucky. *Journal of Education Policy* (5–6): 179–188.

Sahlberg, P. 2007. Education policies for raising student learning: The Finnish approach. *Journal of Education Policy* 22 (2): 147–171.

Sanders, M. 2003. Community involvement in schools: From concept to practice. *Education and Urban Society* 35 (2): 161–180.

Saskatchewan Ministry of Education. 2012. *Nourishing minds.* http://www.education.gov.sk.ca/nourishing-minds/.

Schock, A. 2014. Congressman Aaron Schock. Press release. http://schock.house.gov/news/documentsingle.aspx?DocumentID=388863.

School-Based Health Center Alliance. *About the School-Based Health Center Alliance.* http://www.sbh4all.org/site/c.ckLQKbOVLkK6E/b.7505827/k.2960/About_SchoolBased_Health_Alliance.htm.

School-Based Health Center Alliance. *Adolescent health.* http://www.sbh4all.org/site/c.ckLQKbOVLkK6E/b.7697107/apps/s/content.asp?ct=11675171.

School-Based Health Center Alliance. *Rationale for youth engagement.* http://www.sbh4all.org/site/c.ckLQKbOVLkK6E/b.7796473/k.C203/Youth_ToolkitSec_1.htm.

School-Based Health Center Alliance. *School-based health centers and school nurses equal success.* http://www.nasbhc.org/atf/cf/{B241D183-DA6F-443F-9588-3230D027D8DB}/SBHCS%20AND%20NURSES%20FINAL.PDF.

Schools for All. 2014. *ICECS statement on community schools.* A Shared Workspace, Wiki-based Encyclopedia and Multi-partnership Knowledge Exchange Program. Promoting Health Learning, Social Development, Equity, Safety & Sustainability through Schools. http:*//schools-for-all.org.*

Sedlak, M., & R. Church. 1982. *A history of social services delivered to youth, 1880–1977.* Final report to the National Institute of Education. Contract No. 400-79-0017. Washington, DC: National Institute of Education.

Severns, M. 2012. *Reforming Head Start: What "re-competition" means for the federal government's pre-K program.* Issue brief. Washington, DC: New American Foundation.

Shah, S. C., K. Brink, R. London, S. Masur, & G. Quihuis. 2009. *Community schools evaluation toolkit.* Washington, DC: Institute for Educational Leadership.

Shin, S. H. 2004. Need for and actual use of mental health service by adolescents in the child welfare system. *Children and Youth Services Review*, 27 (10): 1071–1083. doi:10.1016/j.childyouth.2004.12.027.

Smink, J., & F. P. Schargel. 2004. *Helping students graduate: A strategic approach to dropout prevention*. Larchmont, NY: Eye on Education.

Smith, M. 2000, 2004. Full-service schooling. *The encyclopaedia of informal education*. http://www.infed.org/schooling/f-serv.htm. Snell, M. E., & R. Janney. 2000. *Collaborative teaming*. Baltimore: Paul H. Brookes.

Smith, M. 2012. Transforming social work identities: Toward a European model. In *The transformation of children's services: Examining and debating the complexities of interprofessional working*, ed. J. Forbes & C. Watson, 125–140. New York: Routledge.

Snell, M. E. & R. Janney. 2000. Teacher's guides to inclusive practices: Collaborative teaming. Baltimore, MD: Paul H. Brookes.

Soleimanpour, S., S. Geierstanger, S. Kaller, V. McCarter, & C. D. Brindis. 2012. The role of school health centers in health care access and client outcomes. In *School-based health care: Advancing educational success and public health*, ed. T. D. Wright & J. W. Richardson, 27–46. Washington, DC: American Public Health Association.

Soler, M., & C. M. Peters. 1993. *Who should know what? Confidentiality and information sharing in service integration*. New York: National Center for Service Integration.

Southern Education Foundation (SEF). 2013. *A new majority: Low-income students in the South and nation*. October. Atlanta, GA: SEF. http://www.southerneducation.org/getattachment/0bc70ce1-d375-4ff6-8340-f9b3452ee088/A-New-Majority-Low-Income-Students-in-the-South-an.aspx. Retrieved 7/20/14.

Splett, J., J. Fowler, M. Weist, H. McDaniel, & M. Dvorsky. 2013. The critical role of school psychologists in the school mental health movement. *Psychology in the Schools*, 50 (3): 245–258.

Starfield, B., J. Robertson, & A. W. Riley. 2002. Social class gradients and health in childhood. *Ambulatory Pediatrics* 2 (4): 238–246.

Steen, S., & P. Noguera. 2010. A broader and bolder approach to school reform: Expanded partnership roles for school counselors. *Professional School Counseling* 14 (1): 42–53.

Stetser, M., & R. Stillwell. 2014. *Public high school four-year on-time graduation rates and event dropout rates: School years 2010–11 and 2011–12*. First look (NCES 2014–391). Washington, DC: U.S. Department of Education, National Center for Education Statistics. http://nces.ed.gov/pubsearch.Stormshak, E. A., A. M. Connell, M.-H. Véronneau, M. W. Myers, T. J. Dishion, K. Kavanagh, & A. S.

Caruthers. 2011. An ecological approach to promoting early adolescent mental health and social adaptation: Family-centered intervention in public middle schools. *Child Development* 82 (1): 209–225.

Strahota, H. 2010. Dept. of Ed. Grantees form partnerships to coordinate, academic, social, and health services. http://www.americaspromise.org/news/dept-ed-grantees-form-partnerships-coordinate-academic-social-and-health-services.

Studulski, F., & J. Kloprogge. 2006. *Community development in the Netherlands.* Second version. Sardes Educational Services. http://www.sardes.eu/uploads/Sardes/sardes_EU/paper_community_development_in_the_netherlands.pdf.

Substance Abuse and Mental Health Services Administration. 2013. Safe Schools Healthy Students (SS/HS) initiative: A comprehensive approach to youth violence prevention. http://www.sshs.samhsa.gov/.

Substance Abuse and Mental Health Services Administration. 2014. *"Now is the Time." Project Aware; and, Healthy Transitions.* http://www.samhsa.gov/grants/grant-announcements/sm-14–019 and http://www.samhsa.gov/grants/grant-announcements/sm-14–017.

Tanner, A. 2004. *Finland's prosperity brings new migrants.* Finnish Directorate of Immigration, Migration Profile, Migration Information Source. http://www.migrationinformation.org/Profiles/display.cfm?ID=267.

Testa, D. 2012. Cross-disciplinary collaboration and health promotion in schools. *Australian Social Work* 65 (4): 535–551.

Thapa, A., J. Cohen, S. Guffey, & A, Higgins-D'Alessandro. 2013. A review of school climate research. *Review of Educational Research* (April 19). doi:10.3102/0034654313483907. http://rer.sagepub.com/content/early/2013/04/18/0034654313483907.

Theis, K. M., R. M. Krawczyk, & N. Gaspard. Issues in school health and expanding partnerships. In *Collaborative practice: School and human service partnerships*, ed. R. W. C. Tourse & J. F. Mooney, 155–179. Westport, CT: Praeger.

Thomson, L. 2008. *Community schools in Saskatchewan, a research project.* Report to Saskatchewan Ministry of Education and Regina Metis Sports and Culture, Inc. Regina, Saskatchewan: Loraine Thompson Information Services Limited. http://www.education.gov.sk.ca/community-schools-research.

Tourse, R. W. C., & J. Sulick. 1999. The collaborative alliance: Supporting vulnerable children in school. In *Collaborative practice: School and human service partnerships*, ed. R. W. C. Tourse & J. F. Mooney, 59–78. Westport, CT: Praeger.

Turnaround schools. 2014. *Education Week*, August 24. http://www.edweek.org/ew/collections/turnaround-schools/.

Tyack, D. 1992. Health and social services in public schools: Historical perspectives. *Future of Children* 2 (1): 19–31.

Tyre, A. D. 2012. Educational supports for middle-school youths in the foster care system. *Children and Schools* 34 (4): 231–238. doi:10.1093/cs/cds009.

Ukrainian Step by Step Foundation. 2004. Ukrainian Step by Step Foundation. http://www.issa.nl/network/ukraine/ukraine.html.

U.S. Census Bureau. 2013. *Educational attainment in the United States: 2013.* https://www.census.gov/hhes/socdemo/education/data/cps/2013/tables.htmlo.

U.S. Department of Agriculture (USDA). 2014. The White House and USDA announce school wellness standards. http://www.usda.gov/wps/portal/usda/usdahome?contentid=2014/02/0029.xml&navid=NEWS_RELEASE&navtype=RT&parentnav=LATEST_RELEASES&edeployment_action=retrievecontent.

U.S. Department of Education (DOE). 2002. *No Child Left Behind: A desktop reference.* Office of the Under Secretary. U.S. Department of Education, Washington DC. https://www2.ed.gov/admins/lead/account/nclbreference/reference.pdf.

U.S. Department of Education (DOE). 2012a. ESEA flexibility. Flexibility to improve student academic achievement and increase the quality of instruction. http://www2.ed.gov/policy/elsec/guid/esea-flexibility/index.html.

U.S. Department of Education (DOE). 2012b. *Race to the Top Fund.* http://www.ed.gov/category/program/race-top-fund.

U.S. Department of Education (DOE). 2013. *For each and every child: A strategy for education equity and excellence.* http://www2.ed.gov/about/bdscomm/list/eec/equity-excellence-commission-report.pdf.

U.S. Department of Education (DOE). 2014a. *Fast Facts. Charter Schools.* http://nces.ed.gov/fastfacts/display.asp?id=30.

U.S. Department of Education (DOE). 2014b. *Programs. Race to the Top.* http://www2.ed.gov/programs/racetothetop/index.html.

U.S. Department of Education (DOE). 2014c. Full service community schools program. http://www2.ed.gov/programs/communityschools/index.html.

U.S. Department of Education (DOE). 2014d. Project Prevent Grant program. http://www2.ed.gov/programs/projectprevent/index.html.

U.S. Department of Education (DOE). 2014e. *Programs. Promise Neighborhoods.* http://www2.ed.gov/programs/promiseneighborhoods/index.html.

U.S. Department of Education (DOE). 2015a. Fundamental change: Innovation in America's schools under Race to the Top. Office of State Support. Washington DC. http://www2.ed.gov/programs/racetothetop/rttfinalrpt1115.pdf.

U.S. Department of Education (DOE). 2015b. *Programs. Improving basic programs operated by local educational agencies (Title 1, Part A).* http://www2.ed.gov/programs/titleiparta/index.html.

U.S. Department of Education (DOE). 2015c. Programs. Full service community schools program. http://www2.ed.gov/programs/communityschools/index.html.

U.S. Department of Health and Human Services. 2003. *The role of educators in preventing and responding to child abuse and neglect.* Office of Child Abuse and Neglect, Child Welfare Information Gateway. https://www.childwelfare.gov/pubs/usermanuals/educator/educatorf.cfm.

U.S. Department of Health and Human Services. 2007. *Putting positive youth development into practice: A resource guide.* Washington, DC: DHHS.

U.S. Department of Health and Human Services. 2012. Administration for Children, Youth and Families. Information Memorandum. http://www.acf.hhs.gov/sites/default/files/cb/im1204.pdf.

U.S. Department of Labor. 2013. *College enrollment and work activity of 2013 high school graduates.* Economic News Release. Bureau of Labor Statistics. http://www.bls.gov/news.release/hsgec.nr0.htm.

U.S. Department of State. n.d. *Bosnia and Herzegovina.* http://www.state.gov/documents/organization/171686.pdf.

U.S. Department of State. 2012. *Croatia 2012. International religious freedom report. Executive summary.* http://www.state.gov/documents/organization/208512.pdf.

U.S. Environmental Protection Agency. 2014. Looking for homework resources or ideas for a school project? www.epa.gov/students/.

United Way of the Greater Lehigh Valley. 2014. *United Way Community Schools overview.* http://www.unitedwayglv.org/Community-Impact/Education/COMPASS/Overview-of-COMPASS.aspx.

Van Cura, M. 2010. The relationship between school-based health centers, rates of early dismissal from school, and loss of seat time. *Journal of School Health* 80 (8): 371–377.

Vandell, D., E. Reisner, & K. Pierce. 2007. *Outcomes linked to high-quality afterschool programs: Longitudinal findings from the study of promising practices.* Irvine: University of California, and Washington, DC: Policy Studies Associates. http://www.gse.uci.edu/docs/PASP%20Final%20Report.pdf.

Van Roekel, D. 2014. NEA president: We need a course correction on Common Core. *NEA Today.* National Education Association. http://neatoday.org/2014/02/19/nea-president-we-need-a-course-correction-on-common-core/.

Van Voorhis, F., & S. Sheldon. 2004. Principals' roles in the development of US programs of school, family, and community partnerships. *International Journal of Educational Research* 41 (1): 55–70.

Vinovskis, M. 2005. *Federal compensatory education policies from Ronald Reagan to George W. Bush.* Presentation at meeting of National History Center, Washington, DC. nationalhistorycenter.org/wp/wp-content/ . . . /10/vinovskislecture21 .pdf.

Waddock, S. A. 1999. Socioeconomic forces and educational reform. In *Collaborative practice: School and human service partnerships*, ed. R. W. C. Tourse & J. F. Mooney, 33–56. Westport, CT: Praeger.

Wade, T., M. E. Mansour, J. J. Guo, T. Huentelman, K. Line, & K. N. Keller. 2008. Access and utilization patterns of school-based health centers at urban and rural elementary and middle schools. *Public Health Reports* 123, no. 6. November–December: 739–750. www.ncbi.nim.nih.gov/pmc/articles/PMC2556719/#_ffn _sectitle.

Wagner, M. 1993. School-linked services. *Future of Children* 3 (3): 201–204.

Webber, M., K. Carpiniello, T. Oruwariye, Y. Lo, W. Burton, & D. Appel. 2003. Burden of asthma in inner-city elementary school children: Do school-based health centers make a difference? *Archive of Pediatric Adolescent Medicine* 157 (2): 125–129.

Weingarten, R. 2013. *Transforming the teaching profession.* Washington, DC: Equity and Excellence Commission.

Weiss, E. 2015. The elusive value in "value added." *School Administrator*, http://www.aasa.org/SchoolAdministratorArticle.aspx?id=20428.

Weiss, H., & R. Halpern. 1991. *Community-based family support and education programs: Something old or something new?* New York: Columbia University National Center for Children in Poverty.

Weist, M. 1997. Expanded school mental health services: A national movement in progress. *Advances in Clinical Child Psychology*, 19, 319–352.

Weist, M., E. Mellin, K. Chambers, N. Lever, D. Haber, & C. Blaber. 2012. Challenges to collaboration in school mental health and strategies for overcoming them. *Journal of School Health* 82 (2): 97–105.

Weist, M., M. G. Ambrose, & C. P. Lewis. 2006. Expanded school mental health: A collaborative community-school example. *Children & Schools* 28: 45–50.

Weist, M., S. W. Evans, & N. A. Lever. 2003. Advancing mental health research in schools. In *Handbook of school mental health: Advancing practice and research*, ed. M. D. Weist, S. W. Evans & N. A. Lever, 1–7. New York: Kluwer Academic/Plenum.

Wenger, E. C., McDermott, R., & Snyder, W. C., 2002. *Cultivating communities of practice: A guide to managing knowledge.* Harvard Business School Press: Cambridge, MA.

White, R., Jr., & B. Radin. 1969. *Youth and opportunity: The federal anti-delinquency program.* Washington, DC: University Research Corporation.

White, W. 1993. California's state partnership for school-linked services. *Journal of Education Policy* 8 (5–6): 171–178.

Williams, D. 2010. *The rural solution: How community schools can reinvigorate rural education.* Washington, DC: Rural School and Community Trust; Center for American Progress.

Williams, D. 2013. *Rural students and communities.* Washington, DC: Equity and Excellence Commission.

Williams, J. P. 2014. Who is fighting against Common Core? *U.S. News*, February 27. http://www.usnews.com/news/special-reports/a-guide-to-common-core/articles/2014/02/27/who-is-fighting-against-common-core.

The Williams case: An explanation. 2004. California Department of Education. http://www.cde.ca.gov/eo/ce/wc/wmslawsuit.asp.

Winerip, M. 2013. 2003 ex school chief in Atlanta is indicted in testing scandal. *New York Times*, March 29. http://www.nytimes.com/2013/03/30/us/former-school-chief-in-atlanta-indicted-in-cheating-scandal.html?pagewanted=all&_r=0.

World Health Organization (WHO). 1997. *Primary school physical environment and health: WHO global school health initiative.* Geneva, Switzerland: WHO.

Wright, T. D., & J. W. Richardson, eds. 2012. *School-based health care: Advancing educational success and public health.* Washington, DC: American Public Health Association.

Yang Su, E. 2012. Public schools relying more on private donors. *California Watch*, January 19. http://californiawatch.org/dailyreport/public-schools-relying-more-private-donors-14521.

Yeado, J. 2013. Intentionally successful improving minority student college graduation rates. College completion results on-line. Education Trust. http://www.edtrust.org/sites/edtrust.org/files/Intentionally_Successful.pdf.

Youth Development Institute. 2009. *Practices to keep in after-school and youth programs: Young people advocate for, plan, and provide services to their communities.* New York: Youth Development Institute.

Youth Engaged in Leadership and Learning. 2007. *YELL: A handbook for program staff, teachers, and community leaders.* Palo Alto, CA: YELL.

INDEX